Anonymous

Practical Politics

Anonymous

Practical Politics

ISBN/EAN: 9783337132590

Printed in Europe, USA, Canada, Australia, Japan

Cover: Foto ©ninafisch / pixelio.de

More available books at **www.hansebooks.com**

PRACTICAL POLITICS.

(ISSUED BY THE NATIONAL LIBERAL FEDERATION)

PRACTICAL POLITICS

I.
THE TENANT FARMER, by JAMES HOWARD.

II.
FOREIGN POLICY, by MOUNTSTUART E. GRANT DUFF, ESQ., M.P.

III.
FREEDOM OF LAND, by G. SHAW LEFEVRE, M.P.

IV.
BRITISH COLONIAL POLICY, by SIR DAVID WEDDERBURN, BART., M.P.

𝔏𝔬𝔫𝔡𝔬𝔫:
MACMILLAN AND CO.
1881.

The Right of Translation is Reserved.

THE TENANT FARMER:

LAND LAWS AND LANDLORDS.

BY

JAMES HOWARD.

B

THE TENANT FARMER:

LAND LAWS AND LANDLORDS.

INTRODUCTION.

SAGACIOUS men have long foreseen that the time would arrive when the land laws of Great Britain would have to undergo great changes in order to bring them into harmony with modern thought and the exigencies of the country. The signs of the times appear to indicate that, from sheer force of circumstances, the day is fast approaching when the legislature will be compelled to turn its attention to the amendment of the several laws which constitute what is popularly termed "the land question."

Changes indicated by the signs of the times.

Among the circumstances conspiring to bring about this result are—(1.) The depressed and declining condition of agriculture throughout the United Kingdom—a stern fact which has created in the minds of both landlords and tenants the greatest anxiety and alarm as to the future. (2.) The entire failure of the Agricultural Holdings Act to

The circumstances conspiring to bring changes about.

accomplish the avowed objects for which the present Government passed it, viz., the increased production of the soil. (3.) The enormous and ever-increasing sums paid for foreign supplies of food, amounting last year to no less a sum than one hundred millions sterling.

General scope of the Essay. In the following pages it is not my intention to discuss those complicated laws which relate to the inheritance, succession, and transfer of land, but to limit myself to that branch of the subject which embraces, more immediately, the relations of landlord and tenant, a branch of the general land question—as I shall attempt to show—by no means limited to the interests of these two sections of the community, but one to which the welfare and prosperity of the millions of our industrial population are intimately linked.

The writer's feeling toward the territorial class. If, in the following pages, I combat the opinions and prejudices of the territorial class, it springs from no feeling of animosity or hostility; on the contrary, I entertain, and have reason to entertain, a high regard for the nobility and aristocracy of the country; further, if, instead of farming my own land, I were a tenant farmer, long experience and observation would lead me to desire to live upon the estate of one of the old families of England.

BRITISH AGRICULTURE: ITS EXTENT AND NATURAL CAPABILITIES.

The general public, whilst fully alive to the importance of our manufacturing, mining, and commercial pursuits, and also fully aware of their gigantic proportions, are, to a great extent, ignorant of the importance of our agriculture, of the immense capital embarked in its pursuit, and the enormous annual value of our farm produce. *The general public ignorant of Agricultural affairs.*

In order, therefore, to show how vast are the interests at stake in this branch of industry, I would point to the fact that the annual value of the produce of our fields and homesteads is estimated at from two hundred and fifty to three hundred millions sterling (300,000,000*l.*), whilst the agricultural and pastoral value of the land of the United Kingdom is computed to be worth the prodigious sum of two thousand millions (2,000,000,000*l.*). *Immense value of farm produce and worth of land.*

Surely the mere announcement of these figures should be sufficient to arouse the attention of all classes to the imperative necessity of removing every impediment which stands in the way of the prosperity of this great branch of our national industry.

Hitherto the little band of land-law reformers, in their efforts to bring about needful changes, have received but little aid from popular support, whilst they have had to contend with the opposition of the most powerful, the most wealthy, and the most influential class of the community. The territorial class appears to regard with dread the least interference with what is termed "the sacred rights of property," and this notwithstanding that the very object of some of the proposed changes is to enhance the value of this property, and to ensure the permanent prosperity of both owner and occupier.

Land-law reformers have met with little support.

The British public has been repeatedly assured that the present produce of the land falls far short of that which it is susceptible of yielding. Notwithstanding the excellence of the farming to be seen in some parts of England and Scotland there can be no question that under more favourable conditions of tenure, the produce of both animal and human food could be immensely increased. The opinion expressed by a certain eminent Statesman that production might be doubled has often been quoted and as often denounced. Although the estimate formed by Lord Derby is, in my opinion, an excessive one, still in support of the Earl's views it would be easy to cite opinions expressed by well-known farmers. I prefer, however, to quote the opinions of another noble Earl, one who, by his own class and by the farmers of his own county—Norfolk—is acknowledged to possess as intimate and as practical a knowledge of the art of agriculture as any man in the

Farm productions susceptible of great increase. Lord Derby's opinion.

LAND LAWS AND LANDLORDS.

kingdom, be he farmer or landowner. The Earl of Leicester, in addressing a meeting of Norfolk farmers, remarked, "Since I last met you I have travelled through much of England and through parts of Scotland, and, taking into consideration the whole of the land I have seen under cultivation, I think I may safely state that the produce might be nearly doubled under a more perfect system of agriculture." *[The Earl of Leicester's opinion.]*

To Lord Leicester's I would add the recent testimony of a man of world-wide reputation. There is no higher authority upon agriculture than Mr. J. B. Lawes, of Rothamsted. In Mr. Caird's recent and valuable work, *British Agriculture*, this eminent author writes, "To Mr. J. B. Lawes the agriculture of this country is more indebted than to any other man living." Addressing the Berwickshire Agricultural Association in May of the present year, Mr. Lawes remarked:—"No one, I suppose, can doubt that the soils of this country are capable of producing very much more wheat as well as meat than they do at present, if not indeed *all that is required to support the population*."[1] *[Mr. Lawes' opinion.]*

If the increase be estimated at one-third—which, in my opinion, might profitably be raised—our fields and homesteads would yield more than they do by nearly one hundred millions a year. Surely, *[Estimate of increased yield and effect of such increased production.]*

[1] See Pamphlet—*Is Higher Farming a Remedy for Lower Prices?* Published by G. Macaskie, Berwick-on-Tweed.

then, this is a subject worthy of the gravest consideration of the people and of the Legislature, for what an enormous influence would be exerted by so much extra wealth raised from the soil, and this not only upon the interests of the farmers, labourers, and landlords, but upon the trade, the commerce, and the general prosperity of the whole nation.

In the following pages it will be the endeavour of the writer to show how a portion of this grand result may be brought about.

PAST AND PRESENT SYSTEMS OF AGRICULTURE COMPARED.

Modern farming compared with past methods.

It might prove interesting to many readers were the relations which have subsisted between landlord and tenant from feudal times to the present day recited, and the various changes which have taken place in these relations traced;[1] the immediate present, however, is that with which we are most concerned. One of the main objects of this essay is to explain to that large portion of the public, not practically acquainted with agricultural matters, how the existing relations between landlord and tenant tend to check production and limit the national wealth. In order to bring this part of the subject within the comprehension of such

---

[1] On this subject see W. E. Bear's Essay on *Relations of Landlord and Tenant.* Cobden Club Series.

readers it is necessary to become explanatory, and to go more fully into details than at first sight would appear desirable. I commence, therefore, by pointing out that until a comparatively recent period English farming was conducted upon an entirely different system to that of the present. The farmer of the past pursued what is termed an *exhaustive*, the modern farmer pursues what is known as the *restorative* system. The old practice required but little capital, the animals were fed entirely upon the food grown upon the farm, and the only manure used was that produced by the animals so kept. In order to prevent the exhaustion of the soil the old-fashioned farmer was compelled to have frequent recourse to fallows—*i.e.*, the land had to be rested—Nature's method of restoring fertility. Such a style of farming may be described as a penurious, routine, spend-nothing system, under which little capital was required, little produce raised, little labour employed, no enterprise required, and the small amount of produce sold was balanced only by the smallness of the outgoings. *Old method injurious to all concerned.*

The modern system of farming, properly carried out, requires considerable capital. The tenant must have a capital of from 10*l.* to 20*l.* per acre, according to the nature of the land occupied and the amount of live stock it is capable of carrying. Large purchases have annually to be made of oil-cake, corn, and other feeding stuffs, for producing *Capital required by the modern farmer and his outgoings.*

beef and mutton; costly manures have to be bought for raising roots and green crops to be consumed by the animals. The money expended on these substances often amounts to more than the rent of the farm. Then there is the purchase and maintenance of expensive machinery, and above all the labour bill, which again exceeds in amount the rent paid.

ORIGIN OF THE DEMAND FOR TENANT RIGHT AND EFFORTS TO OBTAIN IT.

The introduction of high farming led to the demand for tenant right. It is not surprising that soon after the introduction of the modern system of "high farming," under which, in addition to the outlay already mentioned, large sums were often expended in pipe-draining, removal of hedges, road-making, and other permanent improvements, greater security of tenure began to be demanded, and claims set up for an equitable tenant-right: that the occupier should, on quitting, be paid compensation for the unexhausted value of his outlay upon the farm was advocated as a simple act of justice, and the demand grew louder from year to year as the progress of high farming extended.

Mr. Pusey, M.P., introduces the subject into Parliament. Notwithstanding sustained efforts to stifle the cry, a formidable advocate arose in the person of the late Philip Pusey, M.P. for Berkshire, a landowner of rare sagacity, long recognised as the leading mind in English agriculture, and for many years the editor of the *Royal Agricul-*

tural Journal. As long ago as 1847, Mr. Pusey brought a bill into Parliament which recognised the tenant's right to his improvements. The preamble ran thus:—" Whereas it is expedient for the better security of farmers in the improvement of land, and for the consequent increase of produce therefrom, as well as employment for farm-labourers, to enlarge and extend the custom of agricultural tenant-right, in accordance with the modern advance of husbandry."

I believe that no more honest measure was ever proposed to the British House of Commons; it held the balance fairly between landlord and tenant, it gave the latter an absolute right to his improvements, whilst the interests of the owner were fairly and fully secured: moreover it contained a clause rendering null and void any agreement entered into contrary to the provisions of the Act. The Bill was referred to a Select Committee, which sent it down to the House with the compulsory clause struck out; notwithstanding this concession, owing to the opposition it met with, no further progress was made. The next session another Select Committee was appointed, "The Agricultural Customs Committee," of which Mr. Pusey was Chairman. Evidence was taken, which was clearly in favour of compulsory legislation; still, the measures recommended were permissive only. There was then, as of late, a strong prejudice against doing anything that threatened to restrict the "sacred rights" of

Fairness of Mr. Pusey's measure and its rejection.

"The Agricultural Customs Committee"; the importance of its report.

landowners. The Committee, however, after hearing many witnesses made the following important report :—" That this wider system of compensation to the outgoing tenant seems to be highly beneficial to agriculture, to the landlord, and to the farmer, to lead to a great increase in the productiveness of the soil, and to extended employment of the rural population." This declaration seemed encouraging, and being an expression of opinion by landowners forming the Committee, must never be forgotten by the advocates of tenant-right. After an opinion so deliberately expressed by a Committee of landowners, who had had the advantage of hearing the best witnesses the country could produce, it is idle for opponents to pooh-pooh the question and allege, as is so frequently the case, that nothing more is required than a good understanding between landlord and tenant—a very desirable thing unquestionably, but as precarious as it is desirable.

Mr. Pusey gives up the subject, which was allowed to slumber for twenty years: a lesson to farmers of the present day.

After persevering several sessions, Mr. Pusey dropped the Bill, finding the attempt to bring over his brother landowners to his enlightened views a hopeless task; and the subject was allowed to slumber for more than twenty years. Surely this fact alone should bring home to the minds of the present generation of farmers the necessity of having some representatives of their own class in the House of Commons, at all events, men who have a real sympathy with their interests. I would further remind them that when the subject

LAND LAWS AND LANDLORDS.

was revived in Parliament it was not by a county but by a borough member.

On April 18th, 1872, there appeared in the *Daily Telegraph* a communication headed "Evictions in Scotland" [*From our Special Correspondent*]. From this article the country learned the startling fact that the Hon. Nesbit Hamilton had suddenly terminated the tenancy of the foremost and most popular farmer in Scotland—the late Mr. George Hope of Fenton Barns, a man of world-wide reputation. To Fenton Barns, agriculturists from all parts of the world had been accustomed to resort to see one of the best examples of British farming. Mr. Hope's family had, moreover, been upon the estate for a century.

<small>Eviction of tenant farmers in Scotland.</small>

Mr. Hamilton, when in Parliament in 1849, was one of the most formidable opponents of Mr. Pusey's measure, and denounced in strong terms "all legislative interference between landlord and tenant," but in 1872, by the exercise of a right which an unjust law gave, he made the largest appropriation of a tenant's improvements hitherto made public. Mr. Sadler of Ferrygate, another tenant on the same estate, was also got rid of, solely, it was asserted, and generally believed, upon political grounds, as in Mr. Hope's case. Mr. Sadler informed the writer that his improvements were confiscated without the least compensation. I had known both Mr. Hope and Mr. Sadler for many years, and, without exception, they were the most enterprising farmers of my acquaintance.

Notice to introduce a Bill to amend the law of Landlord and Tenant.

Great consternation was created in the minds of farmers throughout England and Scotland by these high-handed proceedings, and much indignation was expressed by the press and the public. At the time these evictions were announced I sat in Parliament as member for the Borough of Bedford; at once, the same week, I gave notice of a motion " to call the attention of the House to the question of the insecurity of tenant farmers' capital, and to the injury sustained by the public thereby," and before the House broke up I announced that in the next session I would introduce "A Bill to amend the Law of Landlord and Tenant."

THE GOVERNMENT MODE OF DEALING WITH TENANT RIGHT.

The introduction of the Agricultural Holdings Act forced upon the Government.

The next year, in accordance with the notice mentioned, the "Landlord and Tenant Bill" was brought in, the aim of which was to give ample security to the tenant without trenching one jot upon the rights of the landlord. Parliament, however, broke up without any opportunity of carrying the Bill to a second reading, but it had been so much discussed out of doors, and public feeling among farmers had set in so strongly in its favour, that during the interregnum one of the present Secretaries of State informed me that this would be one of the first subjects the new Government would deal with.

Accordingly, soon after the meeting of the new Parliament, a modified edition of the Landlord and Tenant Bill was introduced, with a new name —" The Agricultural Holdings Bill." The fact was the Government felt that an inconvenient agitation had been raised among their own friends —the farmers—which it was desirable to quiet as speedily as possible, but in a manner which would not wound the sensibilities of their other and more powerful friends—the landowners—a difficult task, but no one doubted that the ingenuity of the Prime Minister would be equal to the occasion: whether, however, his party in the House were to be educated, or the farmers bamboozled could not be foreseen.

Upon the assembling of Parliament in 1875, a deputation from the Farmers' Club of England waited upon the Earl of Beaconsfield. On this occasion the writer was deputed to place the views of the Club before the Prime Minister. It being necessary at such interviews to put your case as concisely as possible, probably the following extract will contribute to as clear a comprehension of the subject as a more elaborate argument. After preliminary observations I spoke as follows :—" Their case was briefly this. The capital which a tenant embarked upon his holding consisted, for the one part, of his live and dead stock, which were removable, *Important deputation from the Farmer's Club of England to the Prime Minister.*

The Farmers' claim for compensation briefly stated.

and for the other part of labour, manure, and materials, sunk in or upon his holding which were irremovable. In respect of the live and dead stock the outgoing tenant had complete control, but over the irremovable portion, although paid for out of the same pocket, he had not only no control but, by the presumption of law, it belonged to the owner of the land. Their contention was that the tenant — whose moral right to improvements he had himself effected all acknowledged—should have a legal and absolute right to them, provided, of course, that an arbitrator should decide that the improvements made had added to the letting value of the land; whereas if they were held to be fanciful, or otherwise not valuable to the estate, then a tenant who had so foolishly expended his capital would have no claim in respect of them whatever. Again, they desired to point out that the principle of reciprocity was altogether wanting in the existing law, inasmuch as an owner had the power to sue a tenant for dilapidation or deterioration, and that independently of any question of breach of covenant or agreement; they maintained that such a law was one-sided and therefore unjust.

<small>The injustice of the existing law.</small>

"The next point to express an opinion upon was an extension of the notice to quit. I shall be followed by a gentleman who will show that this alone would not suffice to meet the case; for my own part I would say that the present system

<small>Longer notice to quit farms required.</small>

under which a man of capital and position was, on six short months' notice, called upon to quit his farm, to break up house and home, and to find another, was a system worthy only of a barbarous age.

"Of course the question arose, should legislation be permissive or compulsory? They were almost unanimously of opinion that if legislation took place at all it should be of a compulsory character. To their practical minds it seemed not to be of the slightest use to trouble Parliament to pass a measure to say in effect to landowners: 'You *may* give two years' notice to quit, or you *may* give security for unexhausted improvements.'"

Should legislation be permissive or compulsory?

The deputation was of course dismissed in the usual way, with assurances that the Government fully realized the importance of the subject and hoped when the measure, in course of preparation, was before the public the provisions would be satisfactory to both owners and occupiers.

I now propose to show, as briefly as possible, how the present Government proceeded to perform the promise. In the first place I would produce His Grace the Duke of Richmond as a witness to the need of Tenant Right legislation, and to the importance of the subject as affecting the food supply of the country.

The Duke of Richmond upon the value and effect of Tenant Right, and the Agricultural Holdings Act.

In his high position as Lord President of the Council in the present Ministry, the Duke of Richmond brought in the Agricultural Holdings

Bill. This Act came into force on April 14, 1876—if an Act can be said to come into force when no one is bound to come under its provisions. In introducing this Bill His Grace spoke as follows :—

"My Lords, I am sure I need not apologise for bringing this subject under your Lordships' consideration. It is in the highest degree important, because it has a very close connection with the production of food for the millions of the population of this country. It has a great importance and interest for your Lordships and all other landowners; it is obvious that it has not less importance and interest for those who cultivate the soil, and with whom all landowners are brought into intimate relations; and if it is important and interesting to those two classes, it is not of less moment to the community at large, who, as consumers, must be exceedingly desirous that the producing power of the agricultural districts of the country should be brought to such a pitch that it will go as close as it can possibly be made to go towards meeting the requirements of the country. My Lords, this is not a new subject, it is one which has long occupied attention out of doors; at almost every agricultural meeting held for some time past it has been the theme of discussion."

His Grace, after a passing reference to certain localised customs, and briefly reviewing the report of the Select Committee upon Mr. Pusey's motion —previously referred to—proceeded to comment upon the evidence given before the Committee as follows :—

"My Lords, I doubt whether any one would say that this is a condition of things which ought to be allowed to remain any longer. I think public opinion has been sufficiently roused, and that Parliament is now competent to deal with it. After twenty-five years of agitation this matter has been sufficiently digested, and the feeling is now in favour of legislation. No doubt the subject is a difficult one. According to the census returns in 1851, the population of England and Wales was then 18,054,170, in 1871 it was 22,712,266, showing an increase between the two periods of 4,658,096. At the former period there were 37,000,000 acres of land, of which 25,000,000 were cultivated. Of course the total acreage was about the same in 1871, but the cultivated portion was 26,000,000, showing an increase of only one million acres. My Lords, under these circumstances the Government have thought that a measure should be brought in *to secure to the tenant the capital he has invested in the soil.*"

Statistics, showing that Agriculture has not kept pace with population.

His Grace concluded this remarkable speech as follows :—" My Lords, I am not vain enough to think that this Bill will satisfy every one, but I think it ought to satisfy every moderate and reasonable man, for while, on the one hand, *it gives to the tenant that protection to which he is entitled,* on the other hand it does not invade those rights of the landlord which in this country have always been held *sacred.*"

Such was the testimony of a Conservative Minister to the necessity for a Tenant Right Bill, nor were the words of the Prime Minister, upon the same occasion, less explicit. The Earl of Beaconsfield characterised the measure as one "protecting the tenant's investments in the soil by placing him in a juster position," and "inducing him to apply capital to the soil, an application which it is in the interest of all classes to encourage." Mr. Samuelson, M.P., recently remarked in the House, that these "golden words" of the Prime Minister cannot be too often repeated, for they expressed his anticipation of what would be the effect of giving security to the tenant.

THE AGRICULTURAL HOLDINGS ACT; ITS FAILURE AND THE CAUSE.

Permissive character of the Act—the cause of failure. In the introductory remarks, allusion was made to the failure of the Agricultural Holdings Act to accomplish the avowed objects for which the present Government passed it. If the Act has failed, which is universally admitted, the reason is not far to seek.

Landlord and Tenant Bill compulsory. The Landlord and Tenant Bill contained the following clause: "Any contract made by a tenant after the passing of this Act, by virtue of which he is

LAND LAWS AND LANDLORDS.

deprived of his right to make any claim which he would otherwise be entitled to make under this Act, shall, so far as relates to such claim, be void both at law and in equity." This clause was violently denounced as an invasion of "the sacred rights of property."

Sacred rights of owners and sacred rights of tenants: how dealt with.

The Duke of Richmond, having fully acknowledged the justice of the tenant's demand for the security of his capital, and having made elaborate provisions in his Bill for the purpose, had the hardihood to insert a clause at the end giving landowners the power of declaring themselves out of the Act, and thus to retain full possession of what His Grace termed their "sacred rights."

That such a measure should be the outcome of such speeches as the Prime Minister's and the Duke of Richmond's, is not a little astounding. Can anything be more obvious than that in the opinion of their Lordships their own property was to be surrounded by "sacred rights," but no such "sacred rights" should be extended, by law, to the property of tenants? To the most casual observer it must be evident that the object of the Government was not to grapple with the tenant's claims, but to elude them.

At a later stage I propose to examine the general question of "Freedom of Contract"—the specious plea for the insertion of the clause in question. Whatever may be said in support of the general principle of Freedom of Contract, cannot avail the Govern-

The Government plea of freedom of contract examined.

ment in this case. It was open to the Ministry to refuse the tenant's demands for legal security, upon the ground that legislative interference would be contrary to the well-recognised principle of freedom of contract. Such a course would have been honest, intelligible, and defensible, but when the Government admitted the necessity for legislation, when the Duke of Richmond, as its mouthpiece, described in such glowing terms the national benefits which would flow from a measure giving the tenant security for his capital, the ground—freedom of contract—was surely cut from under them; nor does it require a trained logician to discover the inconsistency of such a plea; its indefensibility must surely be obvious to the most untutored.[1]

<small>Rush of landowners to contract themselves out of the Act.</small> That the permissive clause—so far as the compensation clauses are concerned—has rendered the Act worthless, is notorious, for when the time approached for its provisions to come into force,

---

[1] The Marquis of Huntly—a notable exception among the Peers—took throughout a broad view of the question, and after the Bill had passed gave expression to the following sentiments:—"I think," said the Marquis, "that when once the Legislature has been asked to interfere with the present law, to change the presumption of the law in favour of the tenant, to declare that, by the application of capital, increased industry and increased production resulted, to assume that it was of national advantage to promote that industry, and therefore to give security for that capital in order to maintain its application—I think, I say, that Parliament might have gone one step further, and made certain provisions in the new law *compulsory*."

something like a panic seemed to seize landlords, who, throughout the length and breadth of the land, rushed with inconsiderate haste to contract themselves out of the Act; even the tenants of the Crown Lands were served with the necessary notice; indeed, the farmers of England soon came to the conclusion that, so far as their interests were concerned, the Act was not worth the paper upon which it was printed, and it is universally regarded as the greatest sham in modern legislation.

TENANT RIGHT A NATIONAL QUESTION. FOREIGN IMPORTS CONSIDERED.

Having shown, in the preceding pages, how the question of Tenant Right has grown with the growth of modern farming; how its importance has been fully recognised and acknowledged, even by Conservative Ministers; how the efforts to secure a comprehensive measure, giving security to invested capital, has been defeated; I would express the conviction that until the great town constituencies come to the rescue and take up the subject as one affecting themselves as well as the farmer; until the general public see that the crippling of agriculture is one fruitful cause of depression in trade, a full measure of justice to the food-producing section of the community stands but a poor chance of recognition; and the delusive Act, which undoes by one clause

Subject should be taken up by the large constituencies as a national question.

all the good set forth in the other clauses, will remain unrepealed.

<small>Drain upon the national purse in the purchase of foreign food.</small>

In the opening pages, brief allusion was made to the interests of the whole community being intimately connected with those of agriculture, and evidence has been adduced that from causes which ought not to exist the food produced at home is utterly inadequate to support the population. In addition to the great drain upon the national purse in the purchase of foreign supplies, there is the terrible, if remote, possibility of a time arriving when, owing to adverse seasons abroad, or to wars or famines, we may find these sources fail us at the critical hour of our need.

<small>Tables of Food Imports.</small>

The Board of Trade has issued a complete set of Returns, showing the value annually, since 1858, of the imports of food per head of the population, and also in the gross. Complicated statistics, however, would not be attractive to the reader. I therefore give the following abridgment:—

Years.	Population of United Kingdom.	IMPORTS.			Total.
		Live Cattle, Sheep, and Pigs.	Corn, Grain, and Flour.	Dead Meat and Provisions.	
		£	£	£	£
1877	33,444,419	6,012,564	63,536,322	30,144,013	99,692,899
1872	31,835,757	4,394,850	51,228,816	18,604,273	74,227,939
1867	30,334,999	4,148,382	41,368,349	12,489,331	58,006,062
1862	29,255,015	1,888,236	37,774,148	10,630,734	50,293,118
1858	28,339,770	1,390,068	20,164,811	4,343,592	25,898,471

That these imports have grown much faster

than the population is more clearly seen by the following table :—

Years.	Value per head of imported food.		
	£	s.	d.
1858	0	18	3
1862	1	14	5
1867	1	18	3
1872	2	6	8
1877	2	19	7

These official returns—coupled with the state- *The growth of foreign imports of food imperils the future.* ments and figures given in the speech of the Duke of Richmond, showing the area of cultivatable land still uncultivated—as well as the steady decrease in the number of those who live by agriculture, are so startling as to require no effort of mine to magnify the gravity of the national peril to which we are exposed. Should the supply of food continue to decline in proportion to the population at this increasing ratio, a great calamity awaits our country, and this at no remote future; a calamity which wise measures, promptly adopted, may avert, but if postponed will be powerless to check.

In the face of these facts, and in spite of the *Six months' notice to quit the general rule.* long agitation for greater security of tenure, three-fourths of the land of England—as pointed out by Mr. C. S. Read, M.P., at a recent meeting of The Farmers' Club—is held subject to a six months' notice to quit. The phrase "farm as a lodger," common in some parts of the West of England, expresses most forcibly the result of this insecurity.

A Scotch friend of mine, Mr. M'Neel Caird,

Opinions of Mr. M'Neel Caird, late Chairman of the Scottish Chamber of Agriculture.

has put the case in the following words:—" When France had paid her heavy indemnity to the Germans—three hundred millions sterling—she had done with it. But our tribute to the foreigner for food is perennial, and it is equal to a capital of three thousand millions bound on the neck of the industrious people of this country for ever, if no remedy can be found."

In vacating the chairmanship of the Scottish Chamber of Agriculture, Mr. Caird also spoke as follows:—"The improvements created by a tenant's skill, capital, and industry, are in substance and in justice, though not in law, the property of the tenant who makes them. No doubt they are attached to or combined—in the case of drains and manures inextricably combined—with land which belongs to another. But the just solution of that state of things is not that the one should swallow up the other without compensation, but that the owner of the land who takes such improvements should pay for them, according to the benefit which he appropriates—and that the tenant-farmer should thus cease to be oppressed by an exceptional law. That law robs the tenant of his property when he is evicted without compensation. And this species of injustice is probably productive of much greater injury to the community than even a robbery by violence, because it operates on a much wider scale; and by the fear of subjecting tenants' property to confiscation, spreads distrust everywhere, and deters great numbers of tenants from making the expenditure which is necessary for the due cultivation and for the unrestricted growth of food. It also warns off much free capital which would naturally seek profitable investment in agriculture, if the law did not make it artificially insecure. Thus the injustice operates with great severity on the occupier, while the loss to the country from restricted production is incalculable. But if by making the municipal law just, and allowing natural laws to act, capital were made safe to come freely to the enrichment of the soil, and the development of agriculture, a country peopled and wealthy as this is—so many mouths to be supplied, and such abundant means to supply them, if you took away hindrances—this country, I say, would rapidly exhibit such a change, and such an expansion of growth, as is almost inconceivable to those who have not attended to the results which may be attained by the application of capital to land, with freedom and judgment. And who would lose by it? No doubt, under the present system, a landlord may, now and then, snatch an advantage by unexpectedly appropriating an occupier's improvements without compensating him. But that, though it rankles deep when it occurs, is necessarily exceptional. Most men beware of subjecting themselves to it. Every flagrant instance of it makes them more wary. Still, cultivation would be worse, and tenants' improvements more rare than they are, if landowners generally were to use, to the full, the advantage which the law gives them. The main action of the law is really as a deterrent. Land owners as a body are thus, in truth, great sufferers by this and by everything that hinders the enrichment of the soil that belongs to them. Their rents are just a share of the profit derived from the land. The greater the production and profits, the greater in the long run will inevitably be the share going to the landlord."

At a previous discussion, Mr. Caird conclusively showed that the much-extolled Scotch system of leases signally failed through the absence of tenant-right. He remarked :—" On a seven-course farm, held on a nineteen years' lease, you may reckon that the last five years will be a period of reduced expenditure by the outgoing tenant, and of exhaustive cropping. Then the first seven years of the new lease will be a period of liberal expenditure and gradual restoration of productive power. For the next seven years you may expect the farm (unless it had been greatly reduced), to be in full fertility ; and then begins again the evil cycle of exhaustion. You will have on the individual farm seven years of Egyptian fatness, alternating with periods of comparative leanness ; *but the lean years will be in the proportion of twelve to seven.*" The shortcomings of the system of leases without tenant-right was also forcibly exposed by the late Mr. C. Wren Hoskyns, M.P.

From his valuable work, *The Land Laws of England*, I extract the following :—" A lease, even for twenty-one years, underlain by a law which confiscates to the owner whatever is left unremoved or *unexhausted* by the tenant, is deceptive in operation, because it includes those years near its termination, during which productive outlay has to be withdrawn, and '*the mill works half time*'; and of necessity restricts all investment to that which can be withdrawn within the term."

FEUDAL LAWS AND USAGES, IMPEDIMENTS TO AGRICULTURE.

Nothing is more astounding than the fact that whilst England abounds in wealth, and is in a position to find millions on millions of money for all sorts of foreign enterprises, our own fields are left to languish for want of the capital so freely lavished in other lands. We may well inquire into the causes of such an anomaly. Were I to maintain that the root of the evil lay in the relics of feudalism, the statement might be objected to as merely the emanation of a prejudiced mind or a disordered imagination. I prefer, therefore, to give the views of one of the most sagacious and candid among the younger members of our nobility—one whose opinions already carry with them no little weight. The Marquis of Huntly, in his opening address to the Social Science Congress at Liverpool

England' wealth lavished on foreign enterprises.

The Marquis of Huntly on feudal laws and their bearing on Agriculture.

—of which he was President—remarked as follows:—" The application of capital to the soil by both landlord and tenant, so as to increase its productive powers and consequent value, is the great necessity of these times, and requires *many changes in usage and laws that had a feudal origin.* In ancient times the great ambition of the Baron was to maintain his power by maintaining his connection with the land; and so the laws he made were intended to secure its continued and unbroken descent to his descendants. But as his land now represents so much capital—by wise expenditure and adequate care capable of indefinite increase—the old laws have lost their *raison d'être*, and become, in many ways, either useless or mischievous. They so tie up the landlord's hands as to prevent an adequate outlay on his part, and so deny security to the tenant as to hinder a sufficient expenditure of means and labour on his, and thus prevent the growth of our real and agricultural wealth."

The Laws of Distress and Hypothec; their influence in impeding agriculture and injuring the farmers' credit.

The "usage and laws," referred to by the Marquis, have both a social and an economic bearing; for instance, the Baron-made English Law of Distress, and the Sister (Scotch) Law of Hypothec, lower the credit of the farmer with the banker, the merchant, and the trader, and thereby erect an artificial dam against the flow of capital into the land. At the same time, these laws have the effect of extracting from the tenant more of his own capital in the shape of increased rent; for dependence upon these laws for the recovery of their rents often acts as an inducement to landlords to accept tenants with inadequate means—sometimes with little or nothing to lose—such tenants being generally ready to agree to higher rents than men, with capital to risk, consent to give. The preference given by these laws to the landlord over every other creditor is unjust, impolitic, and unquestionably injurious to the public interest. Their injustice would at once be realised if, instead of giving priority to the landlord, they gave security to the banker for any advances made to a tenant to carry on his farm. I would ask, if a proposal were made to secure the banker, would it not receive universal condemnation? Undoubtedly it would. Further, if put forward for the first time on behalf of the landlord, would not the proposal be unanimously rejected? Why this feudal privilege of the landlord should be retained I have yet to hear any valid reason advanced to show.

The Game Laws and the usages which flow from them have had no little share in repelling capital from the land, and also of hindering successful farming where it is applied. It would be easy to dwell upon the manifold evils, moral, social, and economic, which result from the undue preservation of game, but I will confine myself to one feature. Men of capital and spirit are repelled from the pursuit of agriculture by the fact that being called upon to hand

Game Laws and the preservation of game: their evil results in repelling capital from the land.

over game, reared at their expense, is felt to be lowering to their social standing, if not a sore degradation.

<small>An example given.</small> Take the following instance :—Not long ago I was requested by a friend to go into a distant county to look over a farm of more than a thousand acres, which had been offered to him by a nobleman. This farm required a tenant's capital of about 20,000*l*., of which sum my friend was possessed, and which he was ready to embark; but upon an intimation being given that the game was reserved by the landlord, my friend immediately dropped the negotiation, bluntly remarking that he had once held a farm, belonging to another noble owner, on this condition and never intended again to put himself in such a hazardous position or submit to such serfdom.

<small>Rent not the only consideration in taking a game farm.</small> The taking of a game farm is not altogether a question of rent, as many allege. No tenant can make a safe bargain for such a farm, inasmuch as it is impossible that he can foresee the extent to which preservation will be carried, and thus to form an estimate of the stock of game which the farm will have to carry; moreover, and this is what a respectable man feels most, he is often exposed to the petty tyranny of a gamekeeper, who, upon many an estate, is regarded as a more important personage than the chief tenant. Having been a keen sportsman for many years, I write with no bitter animosity upon the topic; but, being a sportsman, I have had the greater opportunities

of observing the evils of over-preservation. A highly respectable farmer, whom I have known many years, wrote to me in the spring of the present year, as follows:—"I have just threshed the produce of a field of twenty acres, situated near the wood, and have got barely twelve quarters of saleable wheat [100 quarters might have been expected]. This loss, on one field only, will indicate to you what I have had to suffer from this wretched practice of game preservation." My readers will not be surprised to learn that this tenant has given the noble owner of the farm notice to quit. Farmers do not object to winged game; in moderate number, they are thought to be useful, but ground game, hares and rabbits, are their abomination. These animals, from their habits, destroy or spoil ten- or twenty-fold more food than they consume; these are the creatures which repel men of capital from the soil, but around which the law throws the mantle of its protection.

Probably there has been no more potent influence at work in repressing the embarkation of capital upon the land than that emanation of the feudal system, the scheme of "settlements," a plan which has enabled owners to burden their estates with permanent charges, and to reduce their successors to the position of life-owners. On this subject, the late Joseph Kay, Q.C., justly remarked:—"It is difficult to conceive a system more certain to repress any efforts for improvement, or to discourage

The legal system of "Settlements" discourage outlay in improvements by both owners and occupiers.

any outlay of capital upon the land." The life-owner is often compelled, in justice to his younger children, to abstain from outlay upon the improvement of an estate which he has no power to dispose of or to will. I should not, however, have touched this branch of the subject, but from a desire to supplement Mr. Kay's statement by pointing out that tenants are just as much discouraged by the system as owners. It can easily be conceived how the enterprise of a tenant must be damped when he finds that his landlord is not in a position to make the permanent improvements in buildings, roads, draining, cottages, or other works,[1] necessary to the successful farming of the occupation. The Agricultural Holdings Act, it is true, has, by the powers conferred on Limited Owners, done something for the abatement of the evil, but a far more comprehensive measure is needed before the root of the evil will be reached.

Feudal dependence of tenants upon landlords checked enterprise.

The most apparent, as well as the most potent of all the repelling influences, has been that legacy of the feudal system under which the tenant was placed completely in the hands of his landlord, who could eject him from his house and farm on the shortest notice; could, up to the passing of the Ballot Act, claim his vote at Parliamentary Elections; and can confiscate any irremovable

[1] Since this has been in type, the Marquis of Hartington, speaking on Mr. Chaplin's motion, expressed a strong opinion upon the evils of our system of entail and settlement of estates.

property he has, in or upon the land, at quitting. The marvel is that so many men of spirit have submitted to such conditions, and that any progress at all has been made under such a system of dependence and uncertainty.[1]

To some extent the charms of country life have counteracted these adverse influences. Remove those repelling causes from this attractive pursuit, which carry with them loss of independence and social status; let the social standard of the class be thereby raised, and men of capital and intelligence will flock into its ranks. The more independent the position of the tenant, the more the latent energy and locked-up capital of the class will be called forth. Unless these are forthcoming we shall never be able to hold our own against the foreign producer.

Desirability of raising social status of tenants.

Whether the relics of feudal laws, or the usages which have come down with them, have exerted the greater influence in checking the flow of capital toward the land is difficult to determine; but there can be no question that the antiquated system, so general throughout the kingdom, of tying the hands of the farmer by covenants as to the crops he shall

Restrictions upon the growth and sale of crops injurious.

---

[1] "It is obvious, almost to a truism, that the occupation which most resembles ownership itself must, by the imperative laws equally of the soil and of human instinct, be the most profitable to both parties by the *uninterrupted* progress of improvement and addition to the land."—*The Land Laws of England*, by C. Wren Hoskyns, M.P.

grow, or the rotation in which he shall grow them, and further restricting his liberty as to what of the produce he is to be allowed to sell, or what to consume upon the farm, has had a most mischievous and paralysing effect. I propose to enter more fully upon this topic before concluding.

COMMERCIAL PRINCIPLES AND FREEDOM OF CONTRACT IN RELATION TO FARM TENANCIES.

Landowners by contracting out of the Act have proved the uselessness of permissive legislation. I have already attempted to show that by the admissions of the Ministry and the course pursued, the question of freedom of contract, so far as the Government is concerned, has been removed from the controversy. So again, the action of the landowners of the kingdom in contracting themselves out of an Act which a house of landowners had passed with great unanimity, has placed them out of court on the same point; for by such a course they have conclusively proved that permissive legislation has failed, and that if those beneficent changes in British agriculture—so graphically and eloquently portrayed by the Duke of Richmond—are to be brought about the Agricultural Holdings Act must be made compulsory.

Long before the Act was introduced, Mr. C. S. Read, M.P.—who, as a tenant farmer of wide experience, was likely to know whether freedom of contract existed or not—stated to the Farmer's Club " that he would not take the trouble to walk across the floor of the House to pass a Bill without a compulsory clause." The result has justified his anticipations as to the uselessness of such a measure as that passed by the Government.

On the grounds above stated, I should not have entered upon this point in the controversy, but I am aware that "freedom of contract" is regarded by some legal and economic minds as a thing not to be meddled with on any consideration; indeed it is looked upon by many educated people as something almost as sacred as the rights of property. Maintenance of freedom of contract.

Whilst prepared to enter upon an examination of the subject, I do not for a moment admit that the principle of freedom of contract is an element in the discussion of the question in hand. The fact is that the law leaves a portion of the property of an important class of the community dependent upon the will of another and a stronger class; whilst at the same time it not only protects the property of this stronger class in respect of its capital, but it also secures the interest which such capital bears, viz., the rent. The Law of Distraint secures the latter, and the right to sue for dilapidations protects the former. When, therefore, the weaker class comes forward and appeals to the legislature to protect its capital against appropriation by the stronger, to raise the cry, "Freedom of contract!" is simply raising a side issue and diverting attention from the main argument. Outside the scope of the discussion, but nevertheless examined.

Such opponents, when unable to sustain their

Plea for the application of commercial principles examined. objections to a compulsory tenant-right upon the ground of freedom of contract, are in the habit of falling back upon a plea for the application of commercial principles to the hiring of land. Such reasoners appear to lose sight of the fact that in our sea-girt isle the landowners are in possession of a monopoly—*i.e.*, land is a fixed and limited quantity—and further, that if commercial principles are to be applied to the tenant or lessee, it is equally necessary that they should be applied to the owner or lessor. Until, therefore, the privileges secured to landowners by law are swept away the discussion of the question is premature.

If the question of the application of commercial principles be raised at all, it must take a far wider range than that proposed. The policy of the State preparing the way for their application would have to be fully considered, and this would involve not only the abolition of all privileges, but the more important question of the overhauling of the whole system which tends to keep the monopoly of the land in few hands.

The main point, freedom of Contract, resumed: moral right of the tenant to improvements universally acknowledged. To return to the main point under discussion—freedom of contract—I would observe, that I have never yet met with a man who would not acknowledge that a tenant has a moral right to any property he may be called upon to leave behind him; but go a step further, and urge that as a matter of abstract justice, that in the interests of the community the right ought to be secured to him by

LAND LAWS AND LANDLORDS.

law, at once the objection is raised by the class of persons alluded to: "Surely you would not interfere with the great principle of freedom of contract?" It is not wise to be frightened by a phrase, the expression is simply a comprehensive brevity, and like many other such convenient brevities, which although they may embody a valuable principle, often lead to confusion of ideas and to error.

Freedom, to be real, must be both just and rational, and not confounded with licence; it means liberty—not, however, the liberty to oppress or extort unfair conditions, but a liberty which, like the freedom enjoyed by a subject of a free country, is controlled by rules, founded on right, on reason, and the welfare of the State. Lord Bacon said: "True liberty exists only where there is a cheerful obedience to wise and just laws." If, therefore, it can be shown that any law which affects the tenant is unwise or unjust, what becomes of the plea for freedom? *Legal definition of freedom.*

Without stopping to inquire whether in relation to farm tenancies this boasted freedom of contract really exists—a freedom, I would remark, seldom paraded except by one side, and this the stronger—let us inquire what, in other matters, the State has thought it right to do in the way of control. *The plea for freedom advanced by one side only.*

I gather from legal sources that the theory of Government proceeds upon the assumption that all

Theory of Government in respect of bargains or contracts. bargains must be subordinate to the general interest; that contracts conflicting with the common welfare cannot be permitted. That if it can be shown that the making of any class of bargains is irreconcilable with the public good then, although the agreement be not unreasonable as between the actual parties, a broad and solid ground exists for legal intervention. Further, that if from any reason the parties to a certain class of agreements cannot meet on equal terms, and those who hold a stronger position can obtain advantages at the cost of those who are in any degree dependent, if the arrangement be one of public importance and frequent occurrence, then controlling influence is both necessary and salutary.

So clear is the doctrine that contracts must not contravene the common good, that, unaided by enactments, the rigid Courts of Common Law, as well as the elastic Courts of Equity, have not scrupled at pronouncing the most diverse agreements illegal, on the simple ground that they were opposed to public policy.

Public policy, the foundation of action by Government and rules the courts. The late Lord Chief Baron Pollock said, "Public policy being the foundation of law, is supported by decisions of every branch of the law, and an unlimited number of cases may be cited as directly and distinctly deciding upon contracts and covenants on the avowed broad ground of the public good, and on that alone."

If we turn to Parliamentary enactments, we find

also the same broad principle asserted. In the Merchant Shipping Act, an act designed for the protection alike of seamen and the public, any stipulation in an agreement inconsistent with the provisions of the Act is rendered void; and Mr. Plimsoll, in his praiseworthy efforts, sought further to control freedom of contract between shipowners and owners of cargo, on the ground of the present waste of property and loss of life. *[Parliamentary enactments limiting freedom of contract.]*

Does freedom of contract exist between railway companies and their customers—the public? Has not Parliament in the matter of fares, of rates, and in a variety of ways in the interests of the community, stepped in and controlled the freedom of the companies? An important principle is contained in Mr. Cardwell's well-known Act; by this Act special contracts entered into by consignors, by which the companies' legal liabilities would be evaded, are declared void.

The Truck Act, again, is a direct interference with freedom of contract; so was the abolition of Purchase in the Army; so are all the statutes that govern the time and conditions of labour, such as the Factories and Mines Acts.

Then again if "*musty precedents*" are wanted, there are the famous statutes of frauds, and the statutes of limitation; by the latter, the remedy for breach of contract, after defined periods, was swept away. Numerous other examples of Parliamentary restraint of free contract could be adduced, *[Ancient precedents.]*

such as the Licensing Acts, the laws relating to Usury, Wager Policies, Gaming, and Simony. For instances in recent legislation, I would refer to the well-known provisions rendering contracts subversive of the Irish Land Act void, both at law and in equity, also to the Cattle Plague Rating Act, by which the landlord was bound to pay half the rate, notwithstanding any agreement to the contrary.

The Property Tax an example of interference with freedom of contract.

Perhaps, for the present purpose, there is no better example than the Property Tax. In support of the principle of this tax, and in the interests of the revenue, Parliament enacted that any contract, covenant, or agreement under which the tenant is made liable for the property tax, shall be void both at law and in equity. Not long since a tenant upon the estate of a sharp owner, submitted to me a farm lease he was about to sign, in which he was bound to pay all rates and taxes now chargeable, or which should be hereafter imposed, "property tax excepted."[1] It was a very arbitrary document, and I remarked, "You may thank Parliament for the property tax not being included. If, when the

[1] Although rates fall ultimately upon the owner, there can be no question that when fiscal charges—local or imperial—fall on the occupier in the first instance, and no legal provisions exist for deducting them from the rent, they have a tendency to remain upon the occupier, and often do so remain for a longer or shorter period. If the interests of the farmer had been well looked after in Parliament the Education rate, the rates for sanitary purposes, and similar local charges, would never have been placed upon the shoulders of the tenant.—(J. H.)

Property Tax Act was passed, a tenant had been left in the enjoyment of freedom of contract, the tax would have had to come out of your pocket." I maintain that, in passing the Property Tax Act, the two Houses of Parliament virtually declared that in making contracts the tenant did not meet his landlord on equal terms, and surely a parliament of landowners must be considered competent and impartial judges of the point.

Perhaps enough has now been said to show that interference with freedom of contract, or the right to control it, is neither so revolutionary nor so unconstitutional a doctrine as is often alleged ; that our laws, written and unwritten, can and do control contracts. I would, however, before dismissing this branch of the subject, call attention to the doctrine of "restraint of trade." If it can be shown—and to me the fact has always appeared self-evident—that the present insecurity of the tenant's capital acts in restraint of trade, and therefore the interests of the community would be subserved by further legislative interference between landlord and tenant; then I hold that Parliament would be proceeding upon the ancient lines of the constitution in giving the legal security demanded. If parliamentary action is justifiable in respect of any trade, surely it is justifiable when dealing with the most important and the most essential of all trades,—the one upon which the food of the community depends. *Control of contracts constitutional.*

CONCLUSION.

The value of our tenant-farmer class.

Gathering up the conclusions arrived at by a general review of the subject, the result would appear to be that the future of agriculture depends very largely upon prompt means being employed for raising it from its present prostrate condition, and for invoking a spirit of enterprise which has been all but stamped out by adverse influences.

I have had more opportunities than fall to the lot of most men, of seeing the agriculture of other countries as well as my own. In Hungary, and other parts of Eastern Europe, are estates of immense size, which the owners are compelled to keep in their own hands in consequence of there being two classes only, owners and labourers. Some of these foreign proprietors farm estates of 100,000 to 300,000 acres each, and rumour says that the majority of them are gradually becoming more and more impoverished. The value of our own tenant-farmer class, to my mind, can scarcely be over-estimated. No other nation possesses anything comparable to it, either as to numbers, wealth, or intelligence; their property is estimated by Mr. Caird as "equal to one-fifth of the whole capital value of the land." That so important a section of the community should be permanently crippled would be nothing less than a national calamity. I have been taught that the ultimate object of government should be to find out the wants of the community, and to supply them; here, then, is a subject worthy of the gravest consideration.

The question naturally arises, What remedies are within reach which will enable the present and future race of farmers to cultivate the land of Great Britain to a profit, and to withstand the foreign competition which has set in? *Remedies within reach.*

A return to protection, whether in its own name or under a counterfeit, may be at once dismissed as beyond the range of possibilities. The unexampled prosperity of the past thirty years, and the progress made in the condition of the working classes, are too fresh in the memories of people to admit of a doubt upon the point. Were, however, the question raised, say on behalf of the tenantry, the people would not be slow to discern that the British farmer had been handicapped in the race with the foreign producer—both by the landowner and the State; with one voice the public would demand, before protection was even considered, that the farmer should be freed from the restrictions imposed upon him, and a fair chance be given him of competing with his foreign rivals. If raised in the interests of owners, it requires no prophet to foretell the fate of an appeal for protection on behalf of the most opulent and the most powerful class in the country—the rents of whose lands, moreover, have in less than *Protection impossible.*

twenty years advanced upwards of ten millions a year.¹

It is idle for any section of the community to attempt to disguise the fact that the population of the United Kingdom will never again submit to have its food taxed for the advantage of a class. Any Government, which should forget that one of its chief functions is to see that the people are able to provide themselves with the first necessaries of life —food and clothing—without artificial restrictions, and should venture to propose import duties, would, assuredly, be driven from power, or very soon be brought face to face with civil commotion.

Obstacles to progress which a landlord can remove.

In addition to any power which the legislature can exercise in the removal of the impediments to the advance of agriculture much remains for the landowner. On previous pages some of the obstacles to progress which an owner can remove or lessen have been indicated. I now proceed, very briefly, to allude to some others.

Effect of frequent re-valuations of farms.

To induce a tenant to farm with spirit, it is obvious that the first element must be security—security not only that he shall reap what he sows, but that his own improvement of a farm shall not, for a specified time, lead to the raising of his rent. The plan of re-valuations at unexpected periods—so commonly resorted to, of late years, upon many estates—has a most paralysing effect upon even the most enterprising tenant. Leases are often objected to both by

¹ See Caird's *British Agriculture*, page 49.

landlord and tenant; the former does not like to part with the control of his land, and the latter does not care to bind himself to a particular farm and to be bound to pay a fixed rent for the same for so lengthened a period ; but where this is the case, with a view to encourage a tenant freely to embark his capital in the improvement of his holding, an undertaking should be given that no advance of rent would be asked for a prescribed period, and a long notice to quit agreed to.

In this respect Lord Tollemache has taken a step which is quite a new departure in farm agreements. In a letter addressed to his Suffolk tenantry, in May of the present year, his Lordship remarked: —"If my farm agreements can be improved so as to benefit the tenants without injury to the land I shall be very glad to give my best attention to any suggestion that can be offered. Many writers strongly advocate the granting of long leases, but I doubt the prudence of any man of capital who would accept, in these times, the offer of a lease which would bind him to the payment, for fourteen or twenty-one years, of such a rent as a landlord could agree to. Indeed, I have tenants in another county to whom I had agreed, on their application, to grant long leases, and who have since begged to be released from their engagements. In substitution for a lease, I have, in Cheshire, given to the tenants a lease-note, that is, a written promise which secures to him, upon certain conditions,

Lord Tollemache and stability of tenure.

undisputed possession of his farm for twenty-one years without any increase of rent. Under such a promise, although the landlord is bound, so long as these conditions are fulfilled, to retain the tenant at his present rent, the tenant is at liberty at any time to give up his farm. I should not at all object to extend this promise to my Suffolk tenantry upon such conditions as would ensure the land, with our united action,[1] being brought into a high state of cultivation."

I have no hesitation in stating that, although the agreement will be regarded by landowners as one-sided, Lord Tollemache has taken a most effectual step towards attracting capital to his estate. The stipulation would not satisfy the Irish demand for "fixity of tenure," but it assures that stability of tenure so much desired by English farmers, and which is so essential to calling into play the energy and the means of the occupier.

Four years' notice to quit.

This radical change, although it will doubtless prove beneficial to both parties, will, judging by the past, be an example rarely followed. The tenacity with which " the rules of the estate " are adhered to, is too well known to justify hopes of the example being adopted. Parliament alone can

---

[1] The increased energy and activity of the tenant demand the outlay of capital by the landlord before his own can be safely thrown into the partnership; for such the relation in England must become. *The Land Laws of England*, by C. Wren Hoskyns, M.P.

make general that stability of tenure recognised by Lord Tollemache as essential to success. The term for the ordinary rotation of crops upon a farm is four years, and I do not think this an unreasonably long notice for Parliament to sanction; it would probably satisfy the notions of the present race of English farmers if the shorter period of two years were made the legal term; the longer period however, is the time adopted by that practical agriculturist, Lord Leicester, who, four years before the expiration of a lease, gives his tenant notice whether or not the lease is to be renewed.

One very general and formidable impediment to a farmer's success is the want of efficient and sufficient homestead accommodation. The production of meat has become as important a branch as corn-growing, often of greater importance. To carry on this branch suitable homesteads are indispensable; it is now known that warmth and comfort to the animals are equivalent to a certain amount of food, and no man can produce meat to a profit in the cold, comfortless homesteads so common throughout the country.

Necessity for homestead accommodation. Renewal of fences, water supply, cottages, &c.

Again, small inclosures, crooked fences, and insufficient water-supply are serious obstacles to success, especially in the use of steam-power in tillage. These drawbacks lower the value of an estate, and very materially increase the farmer's difficulties and expenses.

Upon these topics I would again quote Lord

Lord Tollemache on the removal of impediments.

Tollemache. From the very sensible letter to his Suffolk tenantry I give the following extract:—
"From information I have received from various quarters I am led to believe that really energetic and skilful farmers of sufficient capital can contend successfully with the existing low prices provided; that they are supplied with good and convenient houses and homesteads and an ample number of labourers, who, with good cottages and half-acre allotments attached to their cottages, have every inducement to behave well to their employers; that their fields are well arranged and sufficiently free from hedgerow timber, and that they sustain no injury whatever from the preservation of game. It is most necessary in these times, for the sake of the tenant as well as of the landlord, that the land should be thoroughly well farmed, otherwise heavy losses must accrue to both."

Cost of labour and means of keeping up a supply.

The cost of labour upon a modern farm is, as already shown, one of the main outgoings; an adequate supply is, therefore, of the utmost consequence to the tenant, and little less so to the owner; for the value of an estate, to a great extent, depends upon the labour supply. Owners who would maintain the value of their estates, and at the same time aid their tenants, will have to look well to cottage accommodation. To keep a full supply of labour in the rural districts, sufficient cottage accommodation must exist, and this of a superior kind to be found in most of our villages; for as the people become better educated they will demand better homes, and if not forthcoming the more enterprising and best men will go where they are to be obtained. Experience leads me to the conclusion that nothing is more attractive to a labourer than a good cottage with large garden or an allotment ground; an orchard is also much appreciated, and it is of great advantage to the labourer, for whilst often bringing in a good portion of the rent, little or no extra labour is entailed.

Desirable as are the matters already dwelt upon, there is no more important step which an owner can take than conceding to the occupier freedom in cultivation and the sale of his crops. *Freedom in cultivation and sale of crops. Restrictions unnecessary.*

How many of the difficulties which hamper the farmer would at once be swept away if freedom in the growth and the sale of crops were conceded! That owners might grant greater freedom to their tenants without damaging or risking their own interests, accumulated knowledge abundantly proves. The important discovery of Mr. Lawes, known to every intelligent agriculturist, ought to assure owners how little they have to fear. To the lasting honour of this gentleman, after many years of persistent labour and exhaustive experiments, he has demonstrated that no amount of bad farming can destroy the natural fertility of the soil. Through his long and well-conducted experiments, we now know that the power to inflict permanent injury upon Mother-Earth has been withheld. Nature herself has to a certain extent protected the landowner, for when a grasping farmer has exhausted, what is well known as the "condition," the land simply refuses to yield up her increase — Nature steps in and says, "Hitherto shalt thou go, but no further."

<small>Continuous corn cropping possible.</small>

Again, Mr. Lawes, by experiments carried on at Rothamsted for nearly thirty years past, has shown that land managed in accordance with the teachings of science may be cropped continuously without injury. To quote his own words, "I have taken the liberty of growing twenty-seven crops of barley in succession on my own land, and I am not aware that it is any the worse for it." Further, "Not only does the quantity keep up where it is continuously grown and manured with the proper manure, but the quality in weight per bushel is increased, so that the average weight of the last thirteen years is higher than that of the first thirteen years." Again, the notion that it is indispensable to retain the straw grown upon the farm, has been exploded by Mr. Lawes—a conclusion confirmed by the experience of others of his followers; indeed, the manurial effect of straw has been shown to be all but *nil*.

No reasons, scientific or practical, remain why the farmer of the future should be tied down to the antiquated routine of the past. Let all such restrictions, begotten of suspicion and distrust, be swept away, and let the British farmer be as free as those with whom he has to compete. I have faith that under these circumstances the energies of the race would triumph over all difficulties. Examples are not wanting to prove that the interests of the owner can be secured without crowding agreements with covenants which hamper the liberty of the tenant, and which, if persisted in, will prove the most effectual means of checking the development of the vast industrial pursuit that ruin is staring in the face.

Inquiry and research, however protracted, into the condition of agriculture, or speculation as to the future, must culminate in the broad conclusion that if a large increase in our food productions is to take place, there must of necessity be a corresponding increase of capital attracted to the land and embarked in its cultivation. Without such increase the result is simply impossible. A farm is, in this respect, precisely similar to a factory; a larger output involves a larger investment of capital. How more capital is to be attracted toward the cultivation of the soil is the great problem to be solved. *[margin: Increased production involves increased capital.]*

It has been shown how our ancient laws, under which land is inherited and held, check the flow of capital; how insecurity of tenure, and insecurity of money embarked in cultivation, aggravate the evil. Capital, as every mercantile man, every member of the Stock Exchange, knows, is proverbially shy, and the first element in attracting it is, and always will be, security. *[margin: How capital is to be attracted.]*

In 1873, a Committee of the House of Lords

was appointed to inquire into and take evidence upon "The Improvement of Land," of which Committee the Marquis of Salisbury was Chairman. The main question to be considered, as put by these owners of property themselves, was, in effect, "How can the owners of landed property more easily obtain the capital needed for its further development and improvement?" The end the Committee had in view was clearly not their own private interest but the public weal. Their Lordships' question does not appear a difficult one to answer. Let the landowners, who have not the capital needed for the improvement of their estates, consent that legal security shall be given for the capital of tenants, and, ere many years have passed, it will be forthcoming to an extent that may astonish the most sanguine. Land, in this case, would be regarded in the light of a bank of deposit without the attendant risks incident thereto.

Opinions of noble proprietors. In the foregoing pages it will have been noticed that in support of the arguments I have advanced, the opinions and example of noble landed proprietors have been quoted. My object, in this course, has been to show that the changes I have advocated are not so visionary or revolutionary as many, in the absence of such aristocratic support, would regard them.

Concluding observations. In conclusion, I would observe that we have a limited area on which to raise the food of the people. We have a population fast growing in numbers. The production of our fields and homesteads is crippled. The chief impediment to increased production—in this nation teeming with wealth—is want of capital. The farmer, alone of all tradesmen, is the only one whose stock-in-trade is liable to confiscation. To attract the necessary capital security is indispensable. Judging by the experience of the past and by the present stagnant condition of agriculture, the first step for the legislature to take is to give the tenant a legal claim to the property he may have put into or upon the land of another.

If the feeding of thirty millions of people strains to the utmost the resources of the country, does it not behove us to look ahead and inquire how the wants of fifty millions are to be met?—a population which we may expect at no remote period will have to be provided for.

JAMES HOWARD.

CLAPHAM PARK, BEDFORDSHIRE,
    July 1, 1879.

FOREIGN POLICY.

BY

MOUNTSTUART E. GRANT DUFF, M.P.

FOREIGN POLICY.

INTRODUCTION.

"THE Gods have appointed it so; no Pitt nor body of Pitts, or mortal creatures, can appoint it otherwise. Democracy, sure enough, is here: the tramp of its million feet is on all streets and thoroughfares, the sound of its bewildered thousandfold voice is heard in all meetings and speakings, in all thinkings and modes and activities of men."

These words of Mr. Carlyle's, published about a generation ago, were recognised as true by many at that time, and will now find few gainsayers. There are still, as all may see, powerful monarchical and powerful aristocratic influences in our society, which may continue to work for long ages, but to a very great extent the United Kingdom has become a crowned democracy. *The United Kingdom has become to a very great extent, a crowned Democracy.*

To some political philosophers this forms a subject of rejoicing, to others of regret. The politician, as such, neither regrets it nor rejoices at it. His business is to use the facts and forces *Attitude of politicians in relation to this fact.*

around him, as best he can, to promote the happiness, first of the community of which he finds himself a member, and secondly of the world.

Two charges made against democracies. There are persons who say that a democracy crowned, or not crowned, however successful it may be in the management of internal affairs, is incapable of governing distant dependencies or of carrying on international relations without disaster.

Only one of them relevant to the present subject. To discuss the first of these allegations lies beside my present purpose, but to the second I will endeavour to reply.

How the relevant charge is to be met. It is certainly true that if international affairs are to be successfully managed by a democracy, care must be taken to adapt new means to old ends; the methods which were perfectly appropriate to a pure monarchy or a crowned oligarchy will not be *necessarily* the methods which are most appropriate to the altered circumstances.

The defects which are supposed to incapacitate a democracy for the management of international affairs are its fickleness, its ignorance, its liability to be carried away by gusts of passion. Now the whole of these defects have frequently been found, and found together, in the management of international affairs by a pure despotism; and if the first and last have been less often observed under an oligarchic government, the second has assuredly not been wanting. We must meet the accusation brought against democracy with a frank admission of its truth in the past.

Democracies, putting aside the case of the United States, the circumstances of which are too unlike ours to make the example of much consequence in the present connection, *have* usually been fickle in the management of international affairs, *have* been ignorant, and *have* been liable to be carried away by gusts of passion.

The remedy lies not in ignoring the fact, but in guarding against a manifest danger. <small>The remedy threefold.</small>

In order to do this successfully, three things are requisite.

1. The democracy must be led by chiefs in whom it confides.

2. These chiefs must act upon a thoroughly well considered system of policy.

3. They must not only be fully informed themselves, but must have the art of making the people see that they are so and of taking it with them.

CONSIDERATION OF THESE THREE REQUISITES.

The first of these propositions will not be disputed, but some will say that the chiefs, in whom one portion of the public confides, will be necessarily distrusted by another. <small>I. The democracy must be led by chiefs in whom it confides.</small>

This is far from true in relation to international affairs. There ought to be no division of parties with reference to them, and as a matter of fact there have, for a long time back, till quite recently, been no such divisions in this country.

Lord Aberdeen was perfectly right when in

December, 1852, he said in the House of Lords, "The truth is, that, though there may have been differences in the execution according to the different hands entrusted with the direction of affairs, the principles of the foreign policy of the country have for the last thirty years been the same."

There are divisions about international affairs now, not at all because the Liberals distrust the Conservatives *quâ* Conservatives, but because they, and not they alone, have come to the conclusion that those at present in power have no clear ideas and very little knowledge as to international affairs. The great majority alike of Liberals and Conservatives belong in international affairs to the same party, and that is the party of Great Britain and Ireland; but most Liberals and the best Conservatives have felt for the last two years in the position of men who find themselves passengers in a vessel, the crew of which is obviously unacquainted with the simplest duties of seamanship, which has touched ground once or twice already, and may at any moment be run on a rock-bound coast.

We need not then linger over the first of the three requisites which I have indicated. A man, who is fitted by natural disposition and by acquirement to be at the head of the Foreign Office, will if he understands how to make his policy intelligible to his countrymen, be, except on the rarest occasions supported by both sides, whatever be his political sympathies in our internal disputes, for the broad outlines of British foreign policy are commanded by circumstances, and there is no dispute about them amongst reasonable men.

That brings me to my second requisite, that the chiefs of our crowned democracy, whether Liberal or Conservative, must act upon a thoroughly well considered system of policy.

II. These chiefs must act on a thoroughly well considered system of policy.

What then should that system of policy be?

It should be a policy which abhors aggression, which tries to promote peace everywhere, which, while always letting it be clearly seen that we possess sufficient force to make it highly imprudent for any one to assail us, behaves in the society of nations as men of the world behave in ordinary society, with as little inclination to take as to give offence—a policy which recognises the truth that nations become great, not by squandering their resources in Quixotic enterprises, but by husbanding them; and that true glory depends, not upon military success, which is at best splendid misfortune, but upon brilliant achievements in the arts of peace, upon wealth wisely and nobly used for public and private purposes; upon long lists of great statesmen, great poets, great historians, great artists, great orators, great men of science; upon thinking first the thoughts which other nations adopt, and building up first the institutions which other nations imitate; upon deserving to obtain from the future the praise

What should that system of policy be?

of having been wise and just. That and that alone entitles any people to claim for itself the first place amongst the nations.

Mr. Gladstone's six principles. It would be difficult to set forth the principles upon which British foreign policy should be based more clearly than Mr. Gladstone did in his speech at West Calder in November last. He said, as reported in the *Times*:—

1. That we should *foster* the strength of the Empire by just legislation and by economy at home, thereby producing two great elements of national power, viz., wealth which is the physical element, and union and contentment which are moral elements, and that we should *reserve* the strength of the Empire for great and worthy occasions.

2. That we should do our utmost to preserve the peace of the world.

3. That we should use every endeavour to maintain the concert of Europe, remembering that common action for a common object is the only way in which we can unite the Great Powers in obtaining objects connected with the common good of all.

4. That we should avoid needless and entangling engagements.

5. That we should acknowledge the equal rights of all nations.

6. That we should have a sympathy with freedom, and a desire to give it a scope founded not

upon visionary ideas, but upon the long experience of many generations within the shores of this happy isle.

But it may be objected "*dolus versatur in generalibus;*" all this is too vague, let us enter a little more into detail. *Examination of details.*

What should be the national attitude with regard to our Empire as it exists? *Our national attitude to the Empire as it exists.*

To that I reply that we should defend every portion of our Empire from foreign attack with the whole strength of the Empire, and that we should maintain that Empire pretty much as it is now—a general rule which would not of course prevent us giving up from time to time any portion which we deliberately considered a "*damnosa hæreditas,*"—such as the Ionian islands certainly were, such as, there is every reason to suppose, Cyprus will ere long prove itself to be—or from acquiring additional territory, if really convenient, in a proper and honourable way, as has, for example, often been done in India.

What should be our national attitude with regard to our treaty engagements? *Treaty engagements*

I reply, that we should construe our treaty engagements exactly as honourable men construe their private engagements, always fulfilling them to the utmost of our ability, but remembering, in public as in private, the sound maxim "*Nemo tenetur ad impossibilia.*" But just because we should be very careful to keep our treaty engagements, our tendency should be to enter into as few onerous engagements, and above all treaties of guarantee, as possible. There are occasions when to enter into a treaty of guarantee is the lesser of two evils, but such occasions are very rare.

<small>Intervention and non-intervention.</small> Are we then, in matters which are not provided for by any actual treaty, to be partisans of intervention or of non-intervention?

I reply, that we should be partisans of neither the one nor the other. We should lean to non-intervention, just as well-conditioned people in ordinary society make it a rule to intervene as little as possible in the disputes of their neighbours; but to assume an attitude of absolute non-intervention, to try to be to Europe what Corcyra tried to be to Greece, is to engage in a vain labour, unless we can tow these islands into the middle of the Atlantic and give up India. But there is surely some mean between what a great jurist has called the "bloody meddlesomeness" of the half-educated Chauvinist or Jingo and that absolute non-intervention to which our geographical position says "No."

<small>"Peace at any price"—what that phrase means.</small> Attempts are often made by unscrupulous writers to attribute to the Liberal party an opinion in favour of "peace at any price." I need hardly say that there is not the slightest foundation for such an attribution. The phrase "peace at any price" not indeed a very happy one, even when used in

relation to the very small section of politicians with whose name alone it is brought into connection by any one who cares to use correctly the ordinary terminology of politics. There is no such thing as an advocate of "peace at any price." The most pacific of politicians are in favour of meeting force by force if these islands, or any of the world-wide possessions of England, are attacked, and they are further in favour of standing by any treaty engagements to which the honour of this nation is decisively and unequivocally committed.

The advocates of "Peace at any price" would object however to extending the treaty obligations of this country, and would get out of all existing treaty obligations which bind us to go to war under any circumstances, as quickly as good faith would allow; nor would they, I apprehend, under any circumstances whatever, go to war for an idea, or for any national interest about which there could be the slightest difference of opinion.

The *peace almost at any price* party, which comprises the vast majority of sensible men both in the Conservative and Liberal camps, only in so far disagrees with the "peace at any price" politicians, that it would by no means bind itself not to go to war for an idea, nor to get, as soon as good faith would permit, out of all treaty engagements which oblige us to go to war. With the members of this great party these questions resolve themselves

Peace almost at any price.

into questions of "relative duties." It would be easy to imagine a case which in no way touched the interests of this country, in which it would be distinctly right for us to make war. But then it would have to be a case in which it was clear that our intervention would produce far more good than harm, and in which it would be morally certain that the misery which results from war would not be misery in waste. Happily such cases are very uncommon in actual affairs. The case of the support given in 1826 to the Constitutional party in Portugal is not really in point, for we were bound by treaty to defend Portugal against Spanish or any other external aggression. If Pesth had been a town on the Atlantic seaboard a strong case might possibly have been made out for interference in 1848. The Hungarians had in the earlier stages of their struggle with Austria a perfectly good cause, and it would have been much to the advantage of Europe that they should have succeeded then, instead of nearly twenty years later. Hungary, however, was not a country in which we could have effected anything at all without turning Europe upside down, and in which it was more than doubtful, under the circumstances of the time, whether we could have effected anything if we *had* turned Europe upside down.

Wars for an idea.
Every case in which we are asked to interfere for the general good of mankind, or in other words to fight for an idea, must be examined on its own

merits. We must take infinite care that we really understand what we are asked to fight about. We must be on our guard against the generous error, that because a power is weak and appears to be bullied by a stronger power, it is necessarily in the right; and whenever there is a doubt we must remember that our first duty is to our own people, and above all, to that large class which, although it is the most apt to ring the bells at the commencement of a war which appears to be generous in its objects, is always the first to be obliged to wring its hands, if the war becomes a serious or long-continued one.

We shall rarely go wrong if we remember that hardly any occasion can arise on which it can be wise for us to adopt in European affairs an isolated position. Our *rôle* should be that of a cementing force which holds together the great Continental Powers, all of whom have more or less conflicting interests. Except at one point, which is hardly a portion of the continent, namely, the rock of Gibraltar, we have absolutely no separate interest on the continent of Europe. Whatever is conceived by any school of British politicians to be our interest on the continent of Europe is either a chimera, or it is the common interest of nearly the whole of Europe. If in European affairs we find ourselves isolated, the chances are ten to one that we are mistaken in our aims, or in the way in which we try to carry them into effect. This may

We can rarely be right in European affairs if we are alone.

not always be so. It has certainly not been so always.

Yet sometimes, as just before February, 1848.

It was not so, for example, in the end of the year 1847, when it is but too possible that we were on the verge of being attacked by a coalition of France and the despotic powers leagued together to crush the one state which represented the principle of freedom in this part of the world. At that period, however, although we were isolated with respect to the governments, we had allies in the people from one end of Europe to the other, and if we had been attacked, we might have lit up a war of opinion from the Bay of Biscay to far beyond the Vistula.

But such a state of circumstances not likely to recur.

It is hardly possible to conceive such a state of circumstances again arising. The whole course of events since the outbreak of the Sicilian revolution in the winter of 1847–8 has been playing the game of England, if only England is wise, and does not throw herself, as her insane rulers nearly led her to do in the spring of 1878, across the path of necessary and inevitable progress. If ever again there comes a time when the state of things which existed in Europe before 1847, or during the reaction which followed the year of revolutions, is reproduced, then we may again find ourselves isolated; for it is to be hoped that the love of being free ourselves and of seeing others as free as circumstances will permit, has got so into our blood, that not even a long continuance of

Beaconsfieldian rule could make a majority of the British people sympathize with anything analogous to the Congress policy—the policy with which we broke even before the Reform Act of 1832.

But what is the likelihood of anything of the kind coming to pass?

The stream of tendency is the other way, and we have nothing to do but to let well alone; not to attempt to prevent chemical processes by mechanical means; not to try either to galvanize dead nations or to prevent new ones from rising into life.

If we remember that it is only under the most peculiar circumstances that we can act wisely in European affairs without being on the same side as an overwhelming majority of the Great Powers, it is seldom, indeed, that we shall have to interfere by force of arms. Our wars for an idea will be few and far between.

A fussy anxiety to be interfering in the concerns of other people is as undignified as it is foolish, and proceeds not seldom from a secret doubt of our own strength. When foreign newspapers, trading upon the weakness of a section of our countrymen, try by taunts to engage Great Britain to do the work which ought to be done by other members of the European State system who are more immediately concerned, it would show more confidence in the greatness of the Empire if we were to remember two passages in the speeches of a Minister who was

A desire to interfere abroad often arises from a secret doubt of our own strength.

certainly not prone to distrust the powers either of himself or of his country.

<small>Two quotations from Mr. Canning.</small> "What," said Mr. Canning, "is it to become a maxim with this country that she is ever to be a belligerent? Is she never, under any possible state of circumstances, to remain neutral? If this proposition be good for anything, it must run to this extent—that our position, insulated as it is from all the rest of the world, moves us so far from the scene of Continental warfare, that we ought always to be belligerent—that we are bound to counteract the designs of Providence, to reject the advantages of nature, and to render futile and erroneous the description of the poet, who has said to our honour, that we were less prone to war and tumult, on account of our happy situation, than the neighbouring nations that lie conterminous with one another." And again at Plymouth, "Our present repose is no more a proof of inability to act, than the state of inertness and inactivity in which I have seen those mighty masses that float in the waters above your town is a proof that they are devoid of strength, and incapable of being fitted out for action. You well know, gentlemen, how soon one of those stupendous masses, now reposing on their shadows in perfect stillness—how soon, upon any call of patriotism, or of necessity, it would assume the likeness of an animated thing, instinct with life and motion—how soon it would ruffle, as it were, its swelling plumage—how quickly it would put forth all its

beauty and its bravery, collect its scattered elements of strength, and awaken its dormant thunder. Such as is one of these magnificent machines when springing from inaction into a display of its might—such is England herself, while, apparently passive and motionless, she silently concentrates the power to be put forth on an adequate occasion."

What then should our attitude be as to wars for British interests? <small>Wars for menaced interests</small>

In the case of wars which are recommended on the ground of their being in defence of our legitimate and undoubted interests, we must inquire most carefully, first, whether the menaced interests cannot be secured without a war; secondly, whether they are worth a war; and thirdly, we must remember that we have always in the midst of us large classes who have a personal interest in war, which they quite naturally confound with a national interest.

We all recollect the story of the man who said in the spring of 1878, "D——n it, is there to be no fighting? Why, I've two sons in the army!"

We ought also to be certain that we know at least the broad facts on which a judgment must be formed.

"What I most fear," a person of position said to a friend of mine, when the Russians were advancing in Armenia, "is that they should reach Lake Van. If they once do that, they will descend the Amoor and attack India!"

This is hardly a caricature of the kind of considerations which rallied a great many supporters to the views of the present Government, but all things are not British interests which ill-informed partisans fancy to be so.

When the causes of error which I have noticed, and others, such as the love of excitement, natural to all men, have been weighed and allowed for, if it is still found necessary to fight in defence of our undoubted and legitimate interests, by all means let us do so.

<small>Seldom indeed shall we have to fight for our interests if we take proper precautions.</small>

But the occasions in which any Power will be mad enough to interfere with the undoubted and legitimate interests of this country will be few indeed, if we take reasonable and obvious precautions.

<small>What should these be?</small>

Now, what should these precautions be?

We should, I answer, have a supreme Navy, an adequate Army, a first-rate Diplomatic Corps, Foreign Office, and Consular Service.

<small>A supreme Navy.</small>

By a supreme Navy is meant a navy which (1) is strong enough to meet and overcome any combination of fleets which it is reasonable to imagine could be brought against it; (2) is sufficient to make a landing on our shores perfectly out of the question; (3) is able to clear the seas of the armed vessels of an enemy at the very commencement of a war, and to keep them clear.

As to the first of these points there will probably be no difference of opinion. The navy was in a position to cope with any possible combination of fleets under the late Administration, and is, it may be hoped, able to do so now.

The importance of the second can hardly be overrated. No victory, however decisive, won over a force which had landed on our coast, could re-establish the position of this country as the one place in Europe which is perfectly safe from invasion. The fabric of British credit would be disastrously shaken by a successful landing, even if the army which had landed was hopelessly beaten within a day or two.

It will be observed that under the third head nothing is said of damaging the commerce of an enemy. That is omitted advisedly, for our commerce is now so enormous that our navy will often, especially at the beginning of hostilities, find that it has enough to do in sweeping the enemy's armed ships from the seas and in sealing up his war harbours, while it will frequently be evident that any attempt to stop an enemy's commerce or to blockade his commercial ports will do to us as much or more harm than it will do to him.

By an adequate Army is meant an army sufficiently strong to co-operate with the navy in rendering a landing impossible, to take its share in holding India, to garrison and defend the various fortresses and harbours which we have scattered about the world, and to take, when occasion arises, under our treaty engagements, along with our allies, a part in <small>An adequate Army.</small>

operations on the European continent—regard being had to the fact that it is *mainly* for pecuniary and naval assistance that our allies have a right to look to a country situated like the United Kingdom.

The army should be relatively small, but every exertion should be used to make it superior to any equal number of troops that could be brought against it, and while the system of short service introduced by Lord Cardwell should be carried further, the question should be carefully investigated, whether it is quite impossible to work that system in a manner which is not too disastrous to the finances of India.

While endeavouring in every way to make the army efficient, the Liberal party and the sounder part of their opponents should never so far forget their traditions as to cease to be jealous of militarism, the most dangerous at this moment of all the diseases which afflict the European body politic. I say the sounder part of their opponents, for the real Conservatives, the conservatives who still exist in some rectories and country houses, have just as little sympathy with the bastard Imperialism of the Prime Minister and his immediate following, as had the French Legitimists with the system of Napoleon III. which it attempts to reproduce in miniature.

A first-rate Diplomatic Corps,   By a first-rate Diplomatic Corps, Foreign Office, and Consular Service, is meant such an organization of our means of obtaining information with regard to foreign countries and of influencing their Governments, as was sketched some years ago before the Diplomatic Committee by our present ambassador at Berlin, Lord Odo Russell, who, true to the ancient spirit of his house, and speaking with all the authority which belongs to his knowledge and experience, said, "I am of opinion that diplomacy will become one of the most powerful engines for the promotion of peace and good relations. At the present moment we look to armies to establish peace and goodwill among Christians; but I am sure diplomacy will be a better engine when properly developed and organized. The more feelers you have all over the civilized world, the better informed you are, and the more influence you can exercise; and I think that through an organization of that kind you are more likely to establish peace and goodwill among Christians than you are through armies, Armstrong guns, breechloaders, Minié bullets, and so on."

Foreign Office, and Consular Service.

And this brings me to the third requisite, that the chiefs of the democracy must be fully informed about international affairs themselves, must have the art of making the people see that they are so, and of taking it with them.

III. The chiefs of the democracy must be informed themselves, and must make the people see that they are informed.

It is under this head that there is most room for improvement in the method of conducting our affairs which has prevailed even under normal Administrations, for it is impossible to deny that neither party has taken enough pains to see that it has had at its disposal a sufficient number of men who have aptitude for and acquaintance with international affairs.

The second order of statesmen in some countries of the Continent are far better informed about what is going on in Europe than are many statesmen amongst us who in all other respects have the advantage of them.

This is not only true, but it is an open secret. Everybody knows it, and the fact that it is known weakens all Governments. That was not so important when the mass of the people took no great interest in international affairs, except during great crises; nor had any means, if they had a view on foreign policy, of making that view prevail. Now, however, when international affairs are discussed in every newspaper and at every public meeting, is it not high time that we should take care that the natural leaders of the people should have some right to say, "You know that these things want anxious study, and you know we have given them anxious study"?

Never again shall we have international affairs managed on a firm and consecutive system until successive Cabinets become sufficiently strong, in the number of persons accustomed to consider international affairs which they contain, to give a reasonable guarantee to the mass of the people that their rulers really know more about foreign policy than they do themselves.

Improvement in this respect can, it is to be feared, only be brought about gradually by the conviction of its urgent necessity forcing itself upon the minds of men who engage in public business. When it has done so, I cannot doubt that there will once again grow up a general agreement about the part we should take in Europe, and that we shall once more be able to quote the words of Lord Aberdeen, which I have cited above, as correctly describing the actual state of things.

The late Government acted in all respects in accordance with the traditions of English foreign policy since the final abandonment of the ideas of Castlereagh, but it made one very great mistake; it did not remember that in dealing with a democracy you must not only *be* right, but *seem* right.[1] {A mistake of the late Government.}

If it had occurred to Mr. Gladstone to take the same pains to put his foreign policy before the country as he did to put before it the question of the Irish Church, that policy would undoubtedly have been enthusiastically supported; but the amount of mental vigour which was used in expounding the views of his Government upon internal affairs was so enormously greater than that used in expounding its views upon international affairs, that numbers of people here and abroad jumped to the conclusion that it neglected the latter.

Nothing could be better, as I have said, than the *résumé* of the principles on which English foreign {The Periclean dictum.}

---

[1] The present Government takes as its motto in *all* affairs, *Videri non esse.* The late Government took as its motto in *foreign* affairs, *Esse non videri.* The right motto for *all* Governments in *all* affairs is *Esse et videri.*

policy should be conducted which was given by Mr. Gladstone at West Calder, but the phrase which he used immediately before, and in which he recalled the Periclean *dictum* about women, that the less they were heard of the better, was of course taken hold of by his critics. Doubtless the less foreign affairs are heard of the better, but that they should not be heard of is, as the Germans say, "a pious wish," and it is of the last importance that the Liberals should make the country feel, that though they are occupied chiefly with domestic matters, they know more about foreign affairs than their opponents; that during the last twenty years more correct forecasts as to what was likely to happen on the continent of Europe have been made by Liberal than by Conservative politicians; that it would be just as easy to prove that some of Lord Salisbury's critics have been habitually right as that Lord Salisbury, the only man now in the Conservative Cabinet whom decently informed Conservatives believe to know anything whatever about foreign affairs, has been habitually, hopelessly, and even ludicrously wrong.

The mistake of the late Government will hardly be repeated. The error on the part of the late Cabinet, of appearing, though only appearing, to neglect international affairs, has led to such grave consequences that we may be pretty sure no English Government will ever fall into it again; and it may be hoped that the amending of this error will draw attention to the deeper and more persistent evil to which I have directed attention above—the evil, namely, that few English politicians find it worth their while to make a specialty of the study of foreign questions.

As soon as the leaders of party see that it will be to their advantage that their countrymen should consider that they have a better acquaintance than their opponents with international affairs, a wholesome rivalry will be introduced, and both parties will begin to give an amount of attention to the organization of their means of acquiring information which they have never done before. The strengthening both in quantity and quality of the Foreign Office and of the Diplomatic Service, to which I alluded above, will be seen to be absolutely necessary, and I trust it may fall to the Liberal party to initiate a reform which is so much wanted.

The two parties in the State may, it is hoped, learn to vie with each other in acquaintance with foreign affairs and in perfecting our means of information.

That party, or at least an important section of it, has always taken up a rather critical and not too friendly attitude with reference to the services which are directed by the Secretary for Foreign Affairs. This is intelligible enough, for there is unhappily no doubt that in the good old times appointments in these services were often scandalously jobbed. Useless posts were kept up and filled by useless or worse than useless people. Persons passed into the service and even rose high in it who were emphatically hard bargains, merely in virtue of their having powerful patrons. Now however all that is very much changed. The diplomatic service is not over-manned, but under-manned. It would be difficult to propose any wiser economy than that which would add a good many thousands a year to the diplomatic estimates, provided at the same time further security were taken for the money being well spent.

New securities wanted. One of these securities should undoubtedly be throwing access to the service open to merit irrespective of party. Whether a Liberal or Conservative Government is in power, the sons of Liberal or Conservative fathers should, if their attainments and merits justify it, be able to come forward for the diplomatic as well as for the military service, not as a matter of favour but as a matter of right.

A modified system of competitive examination. The Foreign Secretary must in the last resort be the person to appoint his own agents; and if he has to choose between the son of a political friend and of a political enemy, both young men having been stamped with the same stamp by competent examiners, he will naturally choose the son of the friend. Such cases however would rarely arise if entrance to the service always involved taking a good place in a competitive examination of a very high order, such as has been frequently suggested.

Supreme power over his department still to be left to Secretary of State. Competitive examination is, as we all know, liable to many drawbacks, but if the object of the examination is not to place men in order as first, second, third, and so on, but to select a class of men out of which the Secretary of State may choose, almost all its evils are avoided.

What is true of the Diplomatic Service is equally true of the Foreign Office. It greatly wants strengthening. Nowadays it is virtually entered by competition, but by a competition which, unlike that which has been suggested for the Diplomatic Service, begins at the wrong end, all candidates who have to compete requiring to be nominated, an arrangement which, to say nothing of its other bad consequences, does not give the Secretary of State the opportunity of having good men brought to his notice if their connections belong to the opposite party in the State. *The Foreign Office.*

Not until our public men take more seriously the duty of being students of foreign affairs before they can claim with any right to lead public opinion about them ; not until, by making the Foreign Office, the Diplomatic and Consular Services, as good as they can be made, we have provided Government with proper eyes and ears all over the world, are we authorized to say that our crowned democracy cannot manage international affairs. The truth is, it has never had a fair chance of doing so, it has never possessed proper organs for their management. *Till the suggested changes have been made, our crowned democracy will not have a fair chance of managing its international affairs.*

It has been sometimes imagined that the gradual democratizing of Europe would be fatal to diplomacy, the most exclusive and aristocratic of professions. No one will continue to hold that opinion who looks below the surface at the realities of things. A great deal of the glitter and frippery that were once associated with diplomacy and made it the laughing- *Great future of diplomacy* stock of serious men, has already fallen off it, and something more has still to fall, but the real importance of diplomacy is only beginning. More and more the diplomatist will think of himself, not merely as the representative of his Sovereign, out of whose personal income the English diplomatist used till recent times to be paid, but as the representative of the whole nation, from the Sovereign downwards. More and more will he recognize himself to be the expression of what ought to be, and, in spite of occasional Jingo outbreaks, *is* with every decade becoming more and more the prevailing feeling of this country in its relations at least with civilized States, " Peace on earth, goodwill towards men." More and more will he recognize that his is indeed the highest of all the services, that the army and navy are merely the necessary and honoured instruments which the nation keeps in reserve, with which to meet unreason, if he who is the representative of reason shall unfortunately fail.

But the Diplomatic Service must be improved to enable it to fulfil its destiny.

In order, however, that diplomacy should hold this position, we must take care to make the Diplomatic Service and all that is connected with it what it ought to be, and good though it is in many respects now, it is susceptible of very great improvements.

The objects that we should set before us by those improvements are fourfold:—

1. That in every spot of political importance in the world there should be a thoroughly competent

person, whose business it is to collect and to transmit to the British Foreign Office the most correct and early information about all matters of importance.

2. That the Foreign Office should be so organized as not only to store and arrange all this information for the use of the Foreign Secretary for the time being, but to make public as much of it as can with advantage be made public.

3. That in every place of political importance this country should be represented by a man to whom his countrymen can point as a thoroughly creditable representative of what is best in these islands, that every British embassy and mission should be a centre of the best kind of British influence, and that no trouble or expense should be spared to make all their members fit to take, and capable of taking from the first, a distinguished place, not only in Court society, to which our diplomatists sometimes too much confine themselves, but amongst the men of letters and politicians of the countries in which they reside.

4. That diplomatists should not be quite so much "up in a balloon" as they often are. They will pardon the expression to one who has the sincerest admiration for their craft; and indeed all the best of them will admit, that it is a real misfortune that they are not oftener enabled, without too great sacrifices, to come into contact with our home political life. They greatly need "*se retremper*" from time to time in its boisterous but

health-bestowing currents. Leave should be more freely given and on easier terms for this purpose to those in the regular line; and there should be, if possible, more frequent exchanges from parliamentary to diplomatic, and from diplomatic to parliamentary activity. That a man should be at once a member of the House of Commons and a representative of his Sovereign abroad, as was the case, for example, with Philip Stanhope, was no doubt an anomaly, but it was an anomaly which had its advantages.[1]

The evil which I would propose to meet is by no means one confined to our own diplomatists. Other free nations suffer just as much or more from it, but it would be worthy of the mother of free nations to devise a remedy.

Some increase of expenditure would be required, but not very much.

I do not deny, I have indeed already admitted, that in order to effect the necessary improvements some increased expenditure would be required, but it would not be very much; and for every thousand a year judiciously added to the diplomatic estimates, we might safely withdraw five from the naval and military estimates as framed, not by Ministers who are thinking more of by-ends than of either economy or efficiency, but from the estimates of really honest Ministers, Ministers who do not mind harassing interests if they serve the public.

"Si vis pacem para bellum."

"*Si vis pacem para bellum*" is a sensible motto enough, if it means "do not trust too much to

See Chesterfield's *Letters*.

reason in a world in which there is a great deal of unreason;" but "*Si vis pacem para pacem*" is a *Si vis pacem para pacem.* still better one, if it is understood to mean, "take care to have all your agencies for seeking peace and ensuing it in the foreground and in thoroughly good order, so as to give reason the best chance you can."

Much of the good, however, that might result from the increased knowledge of statesmen about foreign affairs will be lost, if they do not take more pains to spread their own knowledge and ideas amongst their countrymen. If they do not do so, their hands may be forced at any moment, and they may be driven into courses which will be equally disagreeable to sane Liberals and sane Conservatives, by some sudden enthusiasm, which would never have taken hold on the popular mind if men in the front rank of politics had been wise in time, and had kept their countrymen a little more *au courant* of their thoughts. The Russophobic nonsense which is in a fair way to ruin India, would never have got the influence it has, if statesmen had not blinked the Central Asian question a dozen years ago.

<small>Know and diffuse knowledge.</small>

THE ABSENCE OF THE THREE REQUISITES IN THE MANAGEMENT OF FOREIGN AFFAIRS BY THE PRESENT GOVERNMENT BRIEFLY ILLUSTRATED.

Having then laid down and explained what appear to me the requisites for the management of international affairs by a democracy, I will take the two great questions which have been before the public of late years, and point out, by way of illustration, one or two of the errors that have been committed from want of attention to these requisites.

The first requisite not fulfilled.

The first requisite, that a democracy, if it is to manage internationa affairs successfully, must be under the guidance of leaders in whom it confides, has never been fulfilled since Lord Salisbury succeeded in tripping up Lord Derby and installing himself in the Foreign Office.

Lord Derby's policy

It is from that event that the distinctive foreign policy of the present Government dates, for the policy of Lord Derby was in the main the policy of which Lord Aberdeen spoke—the foreign policy which belongs to no party or to both. Up to the rejection of the Berlin Memorandum, Lord Derby was supported by his Liberal predecessors in office. From that event to his resignation, the fault which most Liberals attributed to his action was, not that it departed from the old lines, but that it had not been equal to the "occasion sudden" which was brought about by the Bulgarian massacres and the effect produced by them in this country.

While respecting the spirit we should have broken with the letter of the old tradition, that the maintenance of the Turkish power on the Bosphorus was an European necessity. Letter of traditional policy in the East.

The spirit of that tradition was that Constantinople and the narrow seas between Europe and Asia must not fall into the hands of Russia or of any other Great Power. Its letter only required the Crescent to remain on St. Sophia. It was the moment for a great decision, a decision as great and more wise than that which Canning announced when he said, "I resolved that if France had Spain it should not be Spain with the Indies. I called the New World into existence to redress the balance of the Old." Spirit of traditional policy in the East.

Surely it was not beyond the resources of statesmanship to find some combination by which the legitimate aspirations of Russia might be satisfied, Greece, Italy, France and the Western Church might be left unalarmed, while England remained just as she was, with no necessity for undertaking new responsibilities in the present, and freed from the apprehensions about Constantinople which so often trouble the repose of her statesmen.

Surely it was not beyond the resources of statesmanship to find some combination by which all these good things could be accomplished, with great advantage to the populations of the Eastern

Peninsula—Bulgarians, Turks, Servians, Albanians, Greeks, and all the rest of them of every creed and every degree of civilization?

I can only say as I have said before, *Scribantur hæc in generatione alterá;* but at least no such decision *was* taken, and our Foreign Office entered with the unhappy Conference of Constantinople into the region of half measures and resolute irresolutions. "England wills strongly in the East," said a sagacious looker-on, "but she knows not what she wills."

<small>Lord Salisbury's policy.</small> In the spring of 1878, however, the scene changed. A new Foreign Minister seized the helm, and with a courage and an intelligent appreciation of what ought to be done, which his previous career had led all careful observers to expect, put the ship about and ran straight for the nearest reef.

<small>No evidence that it has received the support of the nation at large.</small> There is, however, no evidence that this wild helmsman, or the foreign policy which he represents, ever had the slightest support from the nation at large. His being helmsman is the result of a mere accident.

<small>The last election.</small> Nothing was further from the thoughts of the nation when it returned the Parliament of 1874, than that that Parliament would be mainly occupied with foreign affairs. The history of what occurred was given to perfection by the man who said, "The parsons and the publicans have let in the sinners." Petty questions and little spites possessed the minds of the men who were the active agents of the change, but it was caused much more

by Liberal inaction in some places and electioneering blunders in others, than by those agents. The most superstitious incumbent, the most assiduous frequenter of the public-house, might well have thought twice about his vote, the most crotchet-mongering or apathetic Liberal might have raised his voice for united and vigorous action, if he could have foreseen that events of the greatest magnitude were preparing, and that the question before him was whether England was to be given up in dark and difficult times to the guidance of "audacity and pugnacity untempered by sagacity."

No one however foresaw this, and the majority voted under the joint influence of beer and fear as intelligently as the man who did his best to ostracise Aristides simply because he was bored by hearing him called "the Just," while too many Liberals pressed their crotchets to the bitter end.

It is well known too that the majority of votes cast at the last election were cast in favour of the Liberals. Their defeat was owing to numerous small defeats, the result in more than twenty cases of running too many candidates, and which, while showing clearly that a trifling majority was against them in a variety of electoral colleges, said little or nothing as to the opinion of the country.

Even if this had been otherwise, to accuse the democracy of having sanctioned the foreign policy of the Anglo-Turkish Convention, the appropriation of Cyprus, and the Afghan war, would have been {No inference as to the power of a democracy to manage foreign} *affairs can be drawn from it.* grossly unjust. It has never been consulted about any one of these things, which have been the result of the perverse folly of a very small number of persons. No argument whatever, either for or against the power of a democratic society to manage well its international relations, can be drawn from the proceedings of the present Parliament.

The second requisite not fulfilled. Our second requisite was that the chiefs who had the confidence of the democracy should act on a thoroughly well-considered system of policy.

Lord Derby's policy not that of Lord Salisbury. It will hardly be maintained by the most enthusiastic supporter of the present Government that this has been the case with our rulers during the recent foreign complications. No one would for a moment maintain that the policy of Lord Derby was that of Lord Salisbury. If it had been so, Lord Derby would still be in the Government, and the admission that the policies are different is sufficient to enable us to say that our second requisite has not been fulfilled—that the men who have directed our foreign affairs since the beginning of 1874 have not acted on a well-considered system, but at the best upon two quite opposite systems.

Lord Salisbury's policy of 1876 not his policy of 1878. Putting that however on one side, let us examine very briefly whether Lord Salisbury's own policy on the Eastern Question has been consistent with itself. And for this purpose, with a view to give every possible advantage to an opponent that the severest advocate of deciding all moot points against ourselves could require, let us forget the line which he took at the time of the Constantinople Conference, and speak only of what he has done since the 1st of April, 1878.

The policy on which the present Foreign Secretary purposed to act was solemnly explained to the world in a despatch whose periods recalled the good teaching of the *Saturday Review* upon its promotion, in the years which immediately followed the Crimean war. Lord Salisbury's policy of 1878 not consistent with itself.

In that despatch Lord Salisbury, amidst the applause of all those Continental politicians who, loathing both England and Russia, ardently desired that we should shed each other's blood and waste each other's resources, placed himself between the Czar and the advantages which he and his people thought they had a fair right to claim in return for the sacrifices and sufferings of a terrible and exhausting struggle. The despatch of April 1st, 1878.

That policy might have been right or wrong, but at least it was intelligible. It might have been the commencement of a series of acts which showed that the Foreign Secretary knew what he was about, and was acting on a well-considered system. The events of the next few weeks made it clear, that unless Lord Salisbury had composed his Circular for the express purpose of deceiving his partizans and the world, he was acting upon no well-considered system; for if it was right to stand between Russia and her ends, it was clearly not right to make a secret agreement with her in The Salisbury-Schouvaloff agreement.

virtue of which she obtained all the most important of those ends. In the forcible words of the Duke of Argyll when discussing the notorious Salisbury-Schouvaloff Agreement, "The whole scope and purport of the transaction was to represent England as bent on setting up again, as far as she could, some semblance of a real Turkish Empire in Europe; and yet at the same time as yielding up almost everything which was really substantial in the fatal demands which the military success of Russia had enabled her to enforce upon the Sultan. Let us take, for example, one sentence from the 'Salisbury Circular' of two months before—the sentence which perhaps, as much as any other, had inspirited the friends of Turkey—'The compulsory alienation of Bessarabia from Roumania, the extension of Bulgaria to the shores of the Black Sea, which are principally inhabited by Mussulmans and Greeks, and the acquisition of the important harbour of Batoum, will make the will of the Russian Government dominant over all the vicinity of the Black Sea. The acquisition of the strongholds of Armenia will place the population of that province under the immediate influence of the Power which holds them; whilst the extensive European trade which now passes from Trebizond to Persia will, in consequence of the cessions in Kurdistan, be liable to be arrested at the pleasure of the Russian Government by the prohibitory barriers of their commercial system.'

Now to every one of these formidable results of the Treaty of San Stefano, except the very last, England virtually gave her assent in this secret Agreement. It made it all the worse and not the better that she reserved her right to keep up a show of remonstrance and of resistance in the Congress. She was not to push her objections to any decisive issue. The restoration to Russia of her old Bessarabian frontier was expressly acquiesced in. The Armenian fortresses were not to be rescued from the Muscovite. Batoum, although not taken by Russia, was to be surrendered to her demand. Well might those who had cheered the Circular be ashamed of their own credulity when they found themselves duped by the Agreement."

It would be a useless as well as a disagreeable task to go in detail through the policy of the Government in Eastern Europe, pointing out its inconsistencies. The instance which I have cited is quite sufficient for my purpose. It would be as easy to prove that two and two make four and also make five, as to prove a policy to be homogeneous in which the Circular and the Salisbury-Schouvaloff Agreement were nearly-related incidents. *If the Circular and the Agreement can be reconciled, two and two make four and also make five.*

I pass on to show that the same inconsistency, the same utter want of any consecutive and thought-out system, which made futile the efforts of the Government on the Bosphorus, was present with even more disastrous results in their action upon the north-west frontier of India. *The same inconsistency on the north-west frontier of India.*

The despatch of January 22nd, 1875.

There is no reason to suppose that when in January, 1875, Lord Salisbury first pressed upon Lord Northbrook the establishment of a British agent within the territories of the Ameer, he had any intention of re-commencing what had been called forty years before " the great game of Central Asia."

If he had, I should still have called him a rash and dangerous politician, but should not have been so much frightened as I am when I see the Foreign Office in charge of a man who has the haziest notions as to the direction in which his own acts are leading him.

The answer to Lord De Mauley of June 11th, 1877.

On June 11, 1877, in reply to Lord de Mauley, Lord Salisbury spoke as follows:—" The noble Lord appears to have left out of his calculation that there are deserts to be traversed, and that perhaps a fortnight or three weeks, but certainly not less than ten days, across these deserts, would be required for the journey between the nearest accessible points of the two territories. I can assure the noble Lord that any danger of a Russian inroad on the frontier of British India is not quite so far advanced as he seems to imagine. The nearest point on the Caspian at which supplies could be gathered by Russia is over a thousand miles from our Indian frontier. The consideration of the danger to which the noble Lord refers may possibly interest a future generation of statesmen, but that calamity is not of such imminence as to render necessary the motion by which the noble Lord seeks to avert it. I will not dwell longer on the geographical circumstances, except to protest against the statement of the noble Lord that the Empire of British India knows no bounds. My Lords, the bounds of that Empire are very minutely marked out, especially on the north-western side. Whatever the Empire of Russia may be, there is no doubt whatever as to what the frontier of British India is. It is perfectly well known, I cannot help thinking, that in discussions of this kind a great deal of misapprehension arises from the popular use of maps on a small scale. As with such maps you are able to put a thumb on India and a finger on Russia, some persons at once think that the political situation is alarming, and that India must be looked to. If the noble Lord would use a larger map—say one on the scale of the Ordnance Map of England—he would find that the distance between Russia and British India is not to be measured by the finger and thumb, but by a rule. There are between them deserts and mountainous chains measured by thousands of miles, and these are serious obstacles to any advance by Russia, however well planned such an advance might be."

Now is it humanly possible that the man who spoke these words knew that he was lending himself, and had been lending himself for more than two years, that is since January, 1875, to carrying into effect the most extravagant views of the school of which Lord de Mauley had made himself the spokesman—knew that in less than eighteen months he would have to rely on the Russophobic mania, and on that alone, for honest political support?

What Lord Salisbury had been doing from Jan. 1875, to June 11th, 1877.

Why, what had happened since the 21st January, 1875? The day after that Lord Salisbury had addressed his despatch to the Government of India, pressing Lord Northbrook to procure the assent of the Ameer to the establishment of a British agency at Herat. Lord Northbrook and his Council, thoroughly alarmed, had telegraphed to ask whether the orders were peremptory or whether a discretion would be allowed to the Government of India, pointing out at the same time that the despatch was based upon some quite erroneous assumptions as to the feelings of the Ameer. Lord Salisbury had replied, the Government of India had set forth their views as to the extreme danger of the course proposed, in their despatch of the 7th June, 1875. To that Lord Salisbury had sent as a rejoinder upon the 19th November, 1875, the despatch in which occurs the too famous passage which led straight to the murder of Sir Louis Cavagnari: "The first step, therefore, in establishing our relations with the Ameer upon a more satisfactory footing, will be to induce him to receive a temporary Embassy in his capital. It need not be publicly connected with the establishment of a permanent Mission within his dominions. There would be many advantages in ostensibly directing it to some object of smaller political interest, which it will not be difficult for your Excellency to find, or, if need be, to *create.*"

To this ill-omened despatch Lord Northbrook and his Council had again replied. Lord Northbrook had resigned, and Lord Lytton had been appointed and instructed to do what Lord Northbrook had never been instructed to do, that is, to offer something to the Ameer in return for the sacrifice that was being demanded—every care being taken to ensure that we should give with one hand and take with the other, in the spirit of the remarkable paragraph which has just been quoted. In return for mere deceptive guarantees the largest demands had been made upon the Ameer in violation of treaties and of the pledges given by Lord Mayo. That these instructions were given we know, because they have been laid before Parliament; but they have been laid before Parliament only in extract, and we are left to fill up the outline of the unrevealed instructions from the ordinary sources of information and from the acts of the person instructed.

Armed with these instructions, Lord Lytton had gone to India, had selected Sir Lewis Pelly, of all men in the world—the one whose name was likely just at that moment to be most terrible to the Ameer—as a special envoy—had found an "opportunity and pretext" for sending a complimentary and special mission to Cabul, such as Lord Salisbury had desired Lord Northbrook to find or make—had been shown by the Ameer that the pretext was seen through, and that the assigned objects of the mission were merely ostensible. Coaxing having failed, threats had been resorted to. The letter of the 8th July, 1876, had been written, and the Ameer warned that the responsibility of refusing to receive the envoy would rest entirely upon his Government. The Ameer had replied in September. Lord Lytton had intimated to the Ameer that we could break him as a reed, that he was an earthen pipkin between two iron pots, that if he did not desire to come to a speedy understanding with us, Russia did, and desired it at his expense. Large bodies of men had been collected at Rawul Pindee ; a bridge of boats—the same of which Lord Salisbury, astounding to relate, declared in June, 1877, that he had never heard—had been thrown, or prepared to be thrown, over the Indus ; officers had been sent forward to inspect the ground at a point on the Afghan border; the Peshawur Conference had taken place, and Sir Lewis Pelly had threatened the Ameer, that if he did not accept the offers made, we would " continue to strengthen the frontier of British India without further reference to him, in order to provide against probable contingencies." Our native agent had been withdrawn from Cabul, and the Peshawur Conference had come to an end without anything satisfactory having been arranged, while proceedings had been going on at Quetta which were quite enough to have forced on a war with Afghanistan, even if they had stood alone.

We were drifting into war when Lord Salisbury replied to Lord de Mauley, not in the sense in which Lord Clarendon used on a celebrated occasion that, as originally used, most accurate and picturesque expression, but in the sense in which it is ordinarily employed. We were drifting because neither Lord Beaconsfield nor Lord Salisbury, who have been the authors of the whole mischief, had taken the trouble seriously to reflect what they were about. The second had begun by wishing to have his own way about a dangerous crotchet, the establishment of a British agent at Herat; the first thought that a manifestation of "pluck" would have a good effect on the constituencies, and from one blunder to another they were being led on to the invasion of Afghanistan. We were drifting into war when Lord Salisbury made his reassuring speech of June 11th, 1877.

The far more notorious words which Lord Salisbury used in replying to the Duke of Argyll a few days later, may be defended by his friends, as they were in effect defended by Sir Stafford Northcote, on the ground that his policy, alas! required him to make statements inconsistent with accuracy; but the reply to Lord de Mauley is couched in language which is quite irreconcilable with the theory that he so far understood that policy as to know that in the years 1878-9, the only argument of any The statements made by Lord Salisbury four days afterwards not incompatible with the theory that he understood his own policy, but the reply to Lord De Mauley incompatible with it.

weight, even with his own party, in favour of his policy, would be the alleged necessity for improving our old frontier in case of a Russian invasion.

<small>The speeches of Lord G. Hamilton, and Sir S. Northcote in August, 1877, incompatible with the theory that they understood what was being done.</small>
A perusal of the debate of August 9th, 1877, on the subject of Quetta, and of August 14th, 1879, on the subject of the Treaty of Gandamak, will, I am convinced, leave on the mind of any conscientious man of either party who reads them through, an indelible impression that the Ministers who replied on both those occasions to the speeches of the Opposition, were absolutely blind to the consequences of what their colleagues were doing. They made statements which on that theory alone can be reconciled with what is permissible, and happily they were, unlike Lord Salisbury on June 15th, 1877, not necessarily acquainted with the exact state of facts about which they made startling statements.

On these, however, I will not dwell, for one illustration is quite enough to make clear what I mean, when I say, that the person mainly responsible for the recent disastrous policy on the northwestern frontier had no consecutive well-thought-out system in his head when he took the initial steps of that policy. The natural result followed. "Everything may be left, in part, to the hazard of adventure, everything except the fate of nations."

<small>The third requisite not fulfilled.</small>
The third requisite, that the chiefs of the democracy must be fully informed themselves, must have the art of making the people see that they

are so, and of taking it with them, has not been fulfilled, and could not by any possibility have been fulfilled, by the present Government, "*Ex nihilo nihil fit.*" These gentlemen were not in possession of sufficient information, and had not taken the trouble necessary to enable them to manage properly our Foreign affairs, and they could not in the nature of things give to the people a confidence in their possessing what they manifestly did not and could not possess.

The office of Foreign Secretary is by no means, in the opinion of some, the place in the Cabinet which requires the greatest amount of ability. Far more brain power is required, it is said, to enable a man to contrive and carry through Parliament such a measure as the Disestablishment of the Irish Church than would suffice to conduct well and wisely our international affairs for a long time. That may or may not be so, but pre-eminent amongst things indispensable for the successful conduct of these affairs are knowledge of facts, knowledge of men, the critical faculty, caution, and common sense.

Qualities essential to a Foreign Secretary.

You could never make a good manager of foreign affairs out of a man in whose brain the craziest fancies were always running races; you could not for example have made a good foreign secretary out of the Emir Fakredeen.[1] "There is a combination," said that individual, "which would entirely change the whole face of the world, and bring back Empire to the East. .... Nobody ever opened my mind

Defects fatal to a Foreign Secretary—the Emir Fakredeen.

---

[1] For the history of this personage see *Tancred*.

like you; you will magnetise the Queen as you have magnetised me. Go back to England and arrange this. You see, gloss it over as they may, one thing is clear—it is finished with England. Now, see a *coup d'état* that saves all. You must perform the Portuguese scheme on a great scale, quit a petty and exhausted position for a great and prolific Empire. Let the Queen transfer the seat of her Empire from London to Delhi. There she will find an immense Empire ready made, a first-rate army, and a large revenue. I will take care of Syria and Asia Minor. The only way to manage the Afghans is by Persia and the Arabs. We will acknowledge the Empress of India as our Sovereign, and secure for her the Levantine coast. If she like, she shall have Alexandria as she now has Malta—it could be managed. Your Queen is young; she has an *avenir*. Aberdeen and Sir Peel will never give her this advice; their habits are formed. They are too old, too *rusés*. But, you see! the greatest Empire that ever existed; besides which she gets rid of the embarrassment of her chambers! And quite practicable, for the only difficult part, the conquest of India, which baffled Alexander, is all done."

The Emir Fakredeen Prime Minister.

But some one may say " *Quid ad rem?* " What has the Emir Fakredeen got to do with our Foreign Office? What has he got to do with it? Why, for the last two years the Emir Fakredeen has been Prime Minister and Director-general of all our affairs at home and abroad. Do we not see in the passage I have just quoted, at once Lord Beaconsfield's astounding influence at Court? the disproportionate importance which India—in the hands of men, most of whom know nothing about India—has lately obtained? the Delhi pageant, the Imperial title, the design on Syria which was frustrated by Lord Derby's resignation? the protectorate of Asia Minor? the distrust and dislike of Parliament and of hum-drum statesmen like the late Sir Robert Peel? to say nothing of the war on the north-western frontier of India, and perhaps some further development of insanity which may be concealed under the phrase, "the only way to manage the Afghans is by Persia and the Arabs."

No; you certainly could not make a good Foreign Secretary out of the Emir Fakredeen; but I do not know that he would not have made quite as good a one as you could make out of a man like Lord Salisbury, with whom the fates seem to have a *vendetta*, and who has hardly ever espoused a cause during all his parliamentary life without the mocking voice of Destiny being immediately heard from behind the scenes of the political stage, crying, Lost! Lost! Lost! *The Emir Fakredeen as compared with Lord Salisbury.*

Well, but Lords Beaconsfield and Salisbury, although the most powerful, are not the only members of the Cabinet. Good and well, we know the names of its other members, and all of us, who care to do so, can with great ease find out their antecedents and judge for ourselves how far they are likely to mend matters. No fair critic would deny to some of them very considerable merit. *The other members of the Cabinet in their relations to Foreign affairs.*

Every one admits that Lord Cairns is a great English lawyer; that Mr. Cross has managed, to the general satisfaction, the administrative as distinguished from the legislative duties of his office, and that he made one good speech about Foreign affairs; we all know that Sir Stafford Northcote is a sufficiently good financier to shudder in secret at the statements which he makes in public—but all that has nothing to do with the matter in hand, and I maintain that no Conservative who knows what he is talking about and has the slightest self-respect can venture to say that these men, or any of them, have made a sufficient study of foreign affairs to be able to direct this country wisely and well in its international relations, for no one, I presume, will assert that the kind of knowledge necessary for that purpose comes by inspiration, or is transmitted on taking office through some magical power latent in the Sovereign, like that which was supposed to make the Royal touch effective for the cure of the King's Evil.

But even if the present Cabinet had knowledge, would its members have tried to make their policy intelligible?

But even if the members of the present Cabinet had possessed the requisite knowledge to frame a consecutive foreign policy, there is no evidence that they have at all realized the importance of enlightening the country as to what they were doing, or making their foreign policy intelligible. It has been throughout a policy of startling effects and surprises, arranged to dazzle the unthinking—not to convince the judgment of the thinking part of the community. I should like to know when in modern times a critic so kindly and so responsible as Lord Aberdare has ever brought against his opponents, with the approval of all well-informed and honest men, such a charge as the following: "Certain Ministers have not treated Parliament and the country with openness, candour, and sincerity; because they have concealed many things they ought to have revealed and have used language studiously calculated to mislead the people of England."

Years ago the Prime Minister boasted of his consistency; and consistent he has been in one thing, in that view of his surroundings which was the key-note of his first work, "The world is mine oyster, which I with sword will open." *The Prime Minister consistent in one thing.*

"*Populus vult decipi et decipiatur*" has been the motto of his Administration ever since Lord Derby left him, and will be its motto to the end. *"Populus vult decipi et decipiatur."*

HOW FOREIGN AFFAIRS SHOULD BE CONDUCTED.

The proper way to conduct foreign affairs is, it appears to us, diametrically opposite to that which we have recently witnessed. Details as distinguished from broad principles must of course be kept secret while negotiations are proceeding; there may be and should be infinite reserve and caution in the means adopted abroad; but there must be no surprises, the country must understand thoroughly whither it is being led and why it is being led, in a particular direction. There must be reticence, and a good deal of it, but the less reticence the better. The Foreign Secretary must recognise that it is distinctly his business not only to conduct foreign affairs but to lead the opinion of his countrymen about them, and in this he must be aided by his colleagues. If this be true it follows for the proper management of foreign affairs that a great deal more speaking will be required of the Ministers of the future and of their supporters. The fusillade of oratory which we have had this autumn will be not an exceptional but a normal occurrence. It will no longer be possible for Ministers, of however secretive a turn, to reserve their explanations to the month of February. This increased openness of speech will lead to many inconveniences; but although the government of a free people by itself (when as in this country it has the inestimable advantage of having the highest prize of all withdrawn from the contention of party, thanks to our monarchical institutions, and when a very large number of offices are also withdrawn from being a subject of contention, thanks to competitive examination) is unquestionably the best in the world, no sensible man ever denied that it has its evils, and the atmosphere of constant discussion, in which we and our sons are destined to live, is one of these. Still it is an evil which has its good side. An atmosphere of constant discussion is necessarily an atmosphere of intellectual life, and many minds will be strengthened by political discussion to do good work in fields far removed from politics.

CONCLUSION—RESULTS RECAPITULATED.

I may recapitulate in conclusion the results to which I have wished to bring my readers.

1. That there is no reason to fear that this country, which is now so largely democratic, and which will, like all other European communities become in the next two or three generations more decisively democratic than it is now, should find itself at all hampered thereby in carrying on its international affairs.

2. That the methods which have hitherto been approved for the carrying on of our international affairs are not in all respects appropriate to our altered circumstances, but require some revision and improvement.

3. That the improvements chiefly wanted are these :—

(*a*) That our statesmen should try to become more and more international in the sense in which M. Drouyn de Lhuys called Mr. Cobden an international man.

(*b*) That they should not only know more than they do of foreign countries, foreign modes of thought, and foreigners generally, but be known by their countrymen, to have a real knowledge of these things.

(*c*) That they should act upon clear, well-understood principles, never laying themselves open to the charge, as the present Government has done, of involving the nation in new and tremendous liabilities, not only behind the back of Parliament and without having given any opportunity for their schemes being discussed, but under circumstances which involved a complete abandonment of principles which have hitherto been considered sacred by both parties in the state.

(*d*) That the good-ordering of the Diplomatic Service should be recognised as a matter of supreme national importance—of as great importance as the good-ordering of the army or the navy; that no expense and no trouble should be spared for the attainment of this object; and that we should set before ourselves no lower ideal than that suggested by Lord Odo Russell when he said, in 1871, to the Diplomatic Committee, " Our Diplomatic Service ought to be as well organized for its purposes as the ' Prussian army or the Society of Jesus ' are for theirs."

(*e*) That our statesmen should remember that they have now to deal with a far more mobile constituency than that which existed before 1868, and that they should take much greater trouble than formerly to be thoroughly intelligible; that alike by their own speeches and by all other legitimate agencies they should keep their views upon our foreign relations clearly before the people, not trusting merely to being right, but remembering the words of a wise man: "*Reality and Appearance.* Things do not pass for what they are, but for what they seem. Few be those who look at the inside, and many be those who are contented with what is on the surface."

CHRISTMAS, 1879.

FREEDOM OF LAND.

BY

G. SHAW LEFEVRE, M.P.

FREEDOM OF LAND.

THE NEW DOMESDAY BOOK.

THE modern Domesday Book, as the Parliamentary Return, giving the list and acreage of the Landowners of the United Kingdom, has been happily termed, enabled the country for the first time since the Domesday of the Conqueror, to form an estimate of the ownership and distribution of its landed property.

Compared indeed with the original, it is very deficient in details. It is so framed as to give very little local information as to the ownership of land in particular parishes or districts, or the number of tenants of the various owners, or as to the nature of the ownerships. It does not distinguish between leaseholders, copyholders, and owners in fee; it omits all reference to the owners of land let on long lease; it does not distinguish what is mere house property from landed property; it does not

The New Domesday Book.

The New Domesday Book. enable us to estimate how many members still exist of the class formerly so numerous, the yeomen of England, cultivating their own lands, or how many can be considered as forming a class of peasant proprietors; it is admittedly inaccurate in many of its details.

These inaccuracies, however, do not, it is believed, disturb the general results; and faulty though it may be in many respects, it is still most valuable; it enables us to compare the numbers of landowners of different classes in the three kingdoms with the number of owners in other countries. At first sight indeed the aggregate is apt to mislead. It appears to indicate a much larger number of proprietors than was supposed to exist. A gross total of 1,153,816 landowners is given for the United Kingdom: of these, however, no less than 852,438 are entered as owners or lessees of less than one acre of land, with an aggregate of 188,000 acres only, valued at 36,300,000*l*. per annum. It is obvious that with rare exceptions these must be owners, and most of them leaseholders, of mere house properties. From the 301,378 entries of owners of above one acre, further reductions must be made in respect of duplicate entries, holders of glebes, corporations, and charities. A careful examination of the Return has shown that, after making these deductions, there are certainly not more than 166,000 owners of land, as distinguished from houses, in England and Wales; 21,000 in Ireland;[1] and 8,000 in Scotland.

<small>The New Domesday Book.</small>

It may be safely stated then that the number of landowners of the United Kingdom is under 200,000. How then is the land divided among these owners?

A careful analysis has shown that 955 persons own between them 29,743,000 acres out of the 72,000,000 acres accounted for, exclusive of manors, woods, forests, property let on long lease, property within the metropolis, and house property generally; giving an average to each of nearly 30,000 acres, consisting of estates situate generally in two or more counties. A further analysis has shown that about 4,000 persons, in the next rank of landowners own between them about 20,000,000 acres, with an average of 5,000 acres each; that 10,000 persons own between 500 and 2000 acres, with an aggregate of 10,000,000 acres; that 50,000 persons own between 50 and 500 acres with an aggregate of 9,000,000 acres; and that 130,000 own between one acre and fifty acres with an aggregate of 1,750,000 acres. These figures however rather

---

[1] Including about 5,000 holdings bought by their tenants under the Bright clauses of the Church Disestablishment Act (1869) and the Irish Land Act (1870).

The New Domesday Book.

understate than overstate the proportion of land held by large owners as compared with small owners. An addition should be made to the acreage of the former, in respect of woods and manors which are not accounted for in the return, and which probably amount to nearly 4,000,000 acres. Making an addition on this account, it may be safely said that 15,000 persons own between them 64,000,000 acres out of a total $76\frac{1}{3}$ millions; of the remainder about 1,500,000 acres are held in mortmain, by the Crown, the Ecclesiastical Commissioners and other Church Corporations, the Universities, Public Schools, Hospitals and Charities.

It will be seen, however, from the above figures, that the distribution of land is very different in the three countries. In Scotland more than half the country consists of mountain and moor, of little agricultural value, and held in immense blocks. The remaining half is owned by a very small number of persons; peasant proprietors do not exist there. One person only out of every 400 owns land; and one in twenty-eight owns a house.

In Ireland the proportion of landowners would have been about the same as in Scotland, but for recent legislation promoting the purchase of land by tenants, which has added about 5,000 to the number of small owners, or nearly 30 per cent. of the previous number; with this addition, one

FREEDOM OF LAND. 117

person in 257 owns land, and one in 120 owns a house. <small>The New Domesday Book.</small>

In England and Wales the number of owners of land is proportionally larger than in the other countries. There are parts of the country, such as Cumberland and Westmoreland, where the class of yeomen has not altogether died out. There are considerable numbers of owners of small properties in the neighbourhood of towns, which would be more properly classed as owners of villas. In Lincolnshire and Cambridgeshire there are a certain number of owners of small holdings. With these exceptions there cannot be said to exist a class of yeomen farmers or of peasant proprietors. One person out of 130 is probably an owner of land, and, omitting London, one person in twenty-six is probably the owner of a house.

LANDOWNERS IN OTHER STATES.

If we compare the state of landowning, as thus disclosed, with that existing in others of the civilized countries of the world, whether in Europe or in the New World, we cannot fail to be struck by the extraordinary difference. Nowhere is there anything at all comparable to the state of this country, except in parts of Spain, in Bohemia, and in Southern Italy and Sicily. Throughout the <small>Landowners in other States.</small>

Landowners in other States. whole of Western, Central, and Northern Europe the greater part of the soil is everywhere owned by a large body of persons, including large numbers of what we should call the yeomen class, or small farming proprietors, and still more of the class of smaller owners, more properly called peasant proprietors.

France is said to be owned in respect of two-thirds of its total cultivated area by small farmers and peasant proprietors, and one-third of it only is owned by larger proprietors, who let their lands on farming leases to tenants. M. de Laverne, the highest authority on this subject, stated a few years ago, before the separation of Alsace and Lorraine, that the owners and occupiers of land in France might be divided into three classes, as follows :—

France (Ownerships).

	Total Acres.
5,000,000 owners averaging 3 hectares (7½ acres)	37,000,000
500,000 medium sized owners averaging 30 hectares (75 acres)	37,000,000
50,000 large proprietors averaging 300 hectares (750 acres).	37,000,000
5,550,000	111,000,000
State domains and Communal property	10,600,000
	121,600,000

FREEDOM OF LAND.

FRANCE (AGRICULTURAL HOLDINGS).

Landowners in other States.

	Total Acres.
1,815,000 occupiers of less than 5 hectares (7½ acres) . . .	12,540,000
1,256,000 occupiers of between 5 hectares and 40 hectares (100 acres)	43,800,000
154,000 occupiers of over 40 hectares (100 acres)	27,142,000
3,221,000	83,482,000
Woods and forests	19,980,000
Moors and uncultivated land . . .	18,200,000
	121,662,000 [1]

---

[1] It is of interest to compare this table with a similar one for the United Kingdom :—

OWNERS.

	Total Acres.
130,000 small owners averaging 13 acres	1,750,000
50,000 medium sized owners with an average of 180 acres . .	9,000,000
15,000 large owners averaging 4,260 acres	64,000,000
195,000	74,750,000
Crown lands and lands in mortmain . .	1,600,000
	76,350,000

AGRICULTURAL HOLDINGS.

	Total Acres.
750,000 occupiers of less than 10 acres	4,500,000
316,000 occupiers of from 10 acres to 100 acres	14,700,000
92,000 occupiers of above 100 acres .	28,000,000
1,148,000	47,400,000
Mountains, moors, and woods	29,000,000
	76,400,000

Land-owners in other States.

From these figures it appears that France is neither owned nor cultivated to the extent that is generally believed by peasant proprietors; one-third only of its area is owned, and one-tenth of it only is cultivated by this class. Another third part is owned by half a million of persons we should more properly class as yeomen, and one-third of it is cultivated in farms of about the same size. The remaining one-third is owned by what are called large proprietors, 50,000 in number, and one-third of the cultivated part of France is held in large farms, most of them on tenancy. One half the area of cultivated France is held on tenancy; and the farms of over 100 acres very much outnumber those in the United Kingdom. Compared with this, five-sixths of the area of the United Kingdom are owned by 15,000 persons, and not one fiftieth part of it by small owners. The number of small cultivators however is considerable; they number three-quarters of a million and hold one-tenth of the cultivated land; the large farms are under 100,000 in number, but they contain about two-thirds of the cultivated land of the United Kingdom.

Switzerland, Baden, the Rhine provinces of Prussia, Bavaria, and Hesse are almost wholly owned and farmed by their cultivators, varying only between the moderate-sized farmers and peasants. The same may be said of Sweden and Norway. Belgium, in respect of one-half of its area, is cultivated by its owners, and in respect of the other half by a very numerous class of small tenants farming the lands of others. Throughout the remaining parts of Germany, whether Austria or Prussia, the land is owned by large proprietors and small proprietors in about equal proportions: large properties are not unfrequent, but among them are dispersed an immense number of small owners, for the most part cultivating their land themselves. The same may be said of Piedmont, North Italy, and of the northern parts of Portugal and Spain. *Landowners in other States.*

In none of these countries does there exist the entire and absolute separation between the three classes of landowners, farmers, and day labourers, which is the distinguishing feature of the English system; in many of them there are numerous large properties cultivated by tenants and labourers; but the tenant-farmers are members of a class of whom many are themselves owners; and a great proportion of the labourers are also owners of land. Throughout all the countries named at least 50 per cent., and in France probably 75 per cent. of the labouring population in the rural districts are owners of small properties, which they either cultivate themselves, or let out to their neighbours or relations to cultivate, while working for wages themselves.

In the United States also the separation of the rural community into landowners, farmers, and labourers has not begun to show itself.

The land is everywhere owned by its cultivators.

Land-owners in other States. There are more than three millions of landowners cultivating their own lands. Even in the oldest settled States, in the neighbourhood of large cities, where wealth has accumulated to an extent quite as great as the great manufacturing towns of this country can show, and where land has attained a very high value, the same features exist. Ownership everywhere prevails as opposed to tenancy. The State of New York may be compared in extent with Ireland. It contains 22,190,000 acres of land held in farms. Of these there were, by the last census, in 1870, 216,000 owners as compared with the 21,000 owners of land in Ireland. These owners have increased since 1860 by 20,000, or 10 per cent.; and this increase has been mainly in the class of persons owning between three acres and twenty acres. Of these there were 17,800 in 1860, and 31,000 in 1870.

CAUSES OF DIFFERENCE.

Causes of Difference. What then is the cause of this extraordinary difference? Why is it that land in England is in the possession of so few, and in every other part of the world of so many? Is it the result of economic laws only, working freely, without any artificial aid or encouragement by the State, or is it the result of legislation, and of political or social causes? Has it resulted in the full development of the resources of the land? Has it tended to the well-being of all classes, and Causes of Difference. stimulated the industry and promoted the thrift of the lowest, as well as subserved the enjoyment of the highest?

Where a very marked difference is observed in the conditions of one and more countries, the political inquirer instinctively looks about for other differences, and on finding them concurrent in all cases, connects them together as cause and effect. In the case therefore of landownership, it is not strange that we should at once have our attention called to the fact, that this country differs not only in its condition but in its laws; while in every other country above referred to, the laws either give no sanction to the accumulation of landed property upon eldest sons, or, as in the case of France and some others, compel its distribution equally among all the children on the death of their parent, and generally offer no facilities for the maintenance of property in particular families by means of entails, in this country the law gives prominent sanction to the one practice and facilities for the other.

There are, however, economists, and by no means an unimportant class, who believe that the present distribution of land in England has no reference whatever to these laws, and that it is due solely to economic causes, which they conceive tend in a wealthy country to the inevitable aggregation of land in a few hands, and to a complete separa-

Causes of Difference. tion of the functions of landowners, farmers, and labourers. In the view of such persons, the existing condition is defensible on the ground that it leads to the best development of the resources of the land, and is inevitable, as with the growth of wealth and luxury, land itself must become a luxury of the highest quality, the ownership of which can be indulged in only by the rich.

According to this school the existing tendency will be carried much further, and we may look forward, as wealth increases in this country, to the gradual but certain extinction of those few small ownerships of land which still exist in rural districts, and to the absorption of all small estates in larger properties; and they preach the doctrine that the further this monopoly of land, as they frankly admit it to be, is carried, the better will it be for the country, as the better prospect there will be of the duties of landlords being carried out. Land is, and should be, in this view, an article of luxury which only the rich can afford to hold; and it is only to be expected, and is certainly to be desired, that the smaller proprietors should convert their capital as landowners into tenants' capital, by selling their land and becoming the tenants of five times as much land as they could hold as owners.

It may be replied to this, that in other parts of Europe, where there is great accumulation of wealth, there is no such tendency. Belgium is

one of the wealthiest parts of Europe. It com- *Causes of Difference.*
pares with the manufacturing districts of England.
In proportion to its size and population, there is
certainly as much of capital invested in manu-
factories and railways; and yet so far from the
tendency being to a reduced number of owners,
the reverse is the case, and the movement of
property is towards a gradually increasing number
of landowners. Small capitalists outbid the larger
capitalists for landed property; and not only is
a great part of Belgium cultivated by its owners,
but of the remaining half a large portion is owned
in very small portions, and is let out to farming
tenants at very high rents. Land is there the
luxury of all classes, although there are many very
large proprietors.

The same may be said of Normandy, the
wealthiest, happiest, and most populous part of
France. It is a rich manufacturing district.
There would be the same motive there, as is
alleged to exist in England, for small proprietors
to sell their lands, become tenants of what they
previously owned, and to invest their money either
in industrial enterprises returning a much higher
rate of interest, or in tenants' capital, enabling
them to hire more land than they could own.
Yet such is not the fact. Small proprietors give
higher prices than large proprietors, prices that
would appear to be excessive in the agricultural
parts of England, yet there is no tendency for land

Causes of Difference. to fall into few hands. There is great variety of ownership in that part of France; large owners and small owners intermix; large farms and small farms are found side by side; but the large owners are not prone like pike in a pond to swallow up the smaller fry of their kind.

The price of land in rural districts of France is generally forty years' purchase of the annual value, and often more. The peasants are not without appreciation of other investments giving higher returns; it is well known that the great loans raised of late years to meet the war expenses and the German indemnity, have been mainly raised from the savings of the peasants; they are not the less ready however to purchase land returning one-half less interest. M. de Laverne has shown that the common statement about the indebtedness of the small proprietors in France is not true; the mortgages on their properties average no more than ten per cent. of the value of the land.

The same may be said of Holland, a country where there is more accumulation of savings than in any other part of Europe; whose inhabitants are accustomed to lend out money to every borrowing power in Europe, and often in loans of the most risky nature. They appear none the less able to understand the value of safe investments in land at a very low return. Land is even more valued by the small capitalist than by the wealthy.

So again in the United States. In many of its

States the general condition of society is much the same as in England. Land in some of the older States has attained a value approaching closely to its agricultural value in England and Ireland, but there is not the smallest tendency to its passing from the hands of the occupiers to a class of proprietary landlords. The land is universally owned by its occupiers. *Causes of Difference.*

So far then from being able to draw any conclusions from other countries in favour of the proposition that with advancing civilisation and with increasing wealth and luxury, land tends to fall into fewer hands and to become more exclusively the luxury of a particular class, the very reverse is the case; and everywhere we find other classes competing for land with the wealthy, and giving for it prices, which would be considered very high even in this country.

We are not, however, left to the resource only of comparing existing things and tendencies in other countries with what we experience in this country; we are also able to point to the changes which have been made in those countries, with the very object of bringing about their present state, and of avoiding the condition which this country presents.

It is important to recollect that the condition which exists in England was that exhibited not many years ago throughout the greater part of Europe, that the laws such as we now have in

Causes of Difference. England were the laws of the whole of Europe, and that Europe has within the last hundred years almost universally abandoned them; and further, that our colonists took these laws with them to the New World, but there speedily got rid of them, finding them opposed to the principles on which their communities were founded, and intolerable in their results upon the free commerce of land.

LAND LAWS OF FRANCE.

Land Laws of France. In France, before the Revolution of 1789, large properties prevailed throughout a great part of the country. They were held and preserved in families by laws very similar to those which still prevail in England. Primogeniture and entail were almost universally in practice among the upper classes. These laws, however, were the exclusive privilege of the nobility. The law was different for inferior classes. There existed even in those days a large number of small owners. This class had existed from time immemorial, and were either descendants of small freeholders, or of Roman coloni, holding on payment of small and hereditary rents, and who had been brought within the range of the feudal system, or were emancipated serfs who held by certain tenure, but subject to most arbitrary and galling services and dues, under feudal lords. These people had inherited from the Roman law the principle of equal and com-

pulsory division of property on death. The prin- *Land Laws of France.*
ciples of feudal law had never been extended to
them. Primogeniture was not their privilege;
entail was expressly prohibited to them.

Even before the Revolution great complaints were made of the effect of entails, in causing multiplicity of suits, in creating uncertainty as to title, in depriving creditors of their just rights, in promoting clandestine arrangements of property, in withdrawing from the freedom of commerce so large a portion of the land, and in tending to the accumulation of property in few hands; many attempts were made by the executive government to restrict and curtail this process, and to make it as little noxious as possible.

The celebrated chancellor, D'Aguesseau, wrote of entails, in the year 1750, in language which might be used of England in the present day. The president of Aix, another distinguished lawyer, had written to him as follows:—

"One may doubt whether it would not be advantageous to the interest of the State wholly to abolish entails (substitutions); they help to preserve family property, but it is only by sacrificing the creditors of the family, who have lent their money in good faith. Nothing is more unjust than this; and as it is a matter of indifference to the State that the property of such families should be preserved, it seems that no general reason exists for permitting the maintenance of entails, which

Land Laws of France.

were invented by people possessed of a foolish obstinacy to prolong their names, but who forget that a bankruptcy, occurring in every second generation, dishonours them."

D'Aguesseau, in reply, wrote as follows:—

"The complete abolition of entails would probably, as you say, be the best of all laws; and there might be found more simple means of preserving a sufficiency of property in great families to sustain their position. But I fear that in order to arrive at this, we should have to commence by reforming men's brains, and this would be the enterprise of one whose own head might be in danger of being reformed away. It is in truth a great misfortune that the vanity of mankind is the predominating influence of legislation."[1]

It was by the inspiration of D'Aguesseau that a law was passed in 1747 greatly limiting the power of entail, and compelling publicity of them. In the preamble of this law, it is stated that among other evils of entails, they provided an order of succession different from that of the State; that what had been intended for the benefit of the family often ended in its ruin; and that entails interfered with the freedom of commerce in land. The statute, however, effected little; it left untouched all the existing entails, which still continued to spread their noxious influence throughout France.

---

[1] See letters of D'Aguesseau, quoted in treatise on Substitutions by Cossé.

One of the earliest efforts of the Revolution of 1789 was to deal with the land question. In the celebrated meeting of the National Assembly of the 4th of August, it was at the instance of Vicomte de Noailles and the Duc d'Aiguillon, the foremost and wealthiest members of the nobility, that all feudal rights and privileges were abolished, and among these were the privilege of primogeniture and the power of making entails. Of the spirit which animated the Assembly on these subjects we can best judge from the well-known speech of Mirabeau on the law of succession. "Is it not sufficient," he said, "for society, that it has to bear the caprices and passions of the living? must it also suffer from those of the dead? Is it not enough that society should be charged with all the evil consequences resulting from testamentary despotism from time immemorial to the present? must we also subject it to all that future testators may add to this evil by their last wishes, so often whimsical and unnatural? Have we not seen a multitude of wills which breathed of pride or vengeance; in some an unjust, in others a blind preference? The law cancels those wills which are termed *ab irato*, but does not and cannot quash those which we may call *à decepto, à moroso, ab imbecilli, à delirante, à superbo*? How many are there of these acts of the dead towards the living, where folly seems to dispute with passion, and where the testator makes a disposition of his

<small>Land Laws of France.</small> property which he dared not confide to any one when alive; a disposition in respect of which he must have detached himself from all regard to his memory, and have thought that the tomb would protect him against ridicule and reproach? . . . . There are no longer eldest sons or privileges in the great family of the nation; there should be none in the smaller families of which each State is composed. How many are there who, born without fortune, succeed by some means or other in enriching themselves. Puffed up by this accident, they often conceive a respect for their name, and they will not let it pass to their descendants, except under escort of a fortune which may recommend it to consideration; they choose an heir among their children; they decorate him by will with all that can sustain the new existence which they prepare for him, and their ambitious pride paints for itself by anticipation, even beyond the tomb, a line of descendants who will do honour to their blood. Let us then stifle this germ of useless distinctions, let us break these instruments of injustice and folly!"

Under the influence of this passionate oration, the Assembly not only voted the repeal of the laws of primogeniture and entail, but would not even permit primogeniture; it made universal and applied to the nobility that which had been previously the law of the lower classes, namely, the compulsory division of the greater part of the paternal property, of whatever nature, equally among the children, leaving only a small proportion to the discretion of the testator.

In 1792 the Assembly carried the same principles further; it abolished all existing entails; the expectant heirs under entails were all irrevocably deprived of their expectations; and property subject to these settlements was, in the interest of the public, freed from all limitations and placed at the absolute disposal of existing holders.

It is worthy of notice, that so speedily did these great changes commend themselves to the habits, customs, and opinions of all classes, even of the upper classes and of the nobility, and so rapidly did the principle of equal division of property on death gain acceptance, that when after the restoration of the Bourbon monarchy, the reactionary government of 1826 endeavoured to restore, to a very limited degree, the principle of primogeniture and the power of entail, so great was the force of public opinion against the project, so strong was the family feeling even of what remained of the old nobility opposed to a restoration of such privileges, that the Chamber of Peers rejected the proposals; the leading members of the old nobility voted against them, and hundreds of eldest sons petitioned against them on the ground that they would introduce disagreement and discord into their families. This shows how strongly the principle of equal distribution of property had commended

Land Laws of France.

Land Laws of France. itself, even to the families of the old nobility ; and it is not too much to say that there is no institution in France so popular and so immutable, as that which requires equal division of property among children. The law permits a father to dispose of a certain portion of his property, and to accumulate this upon any favoured child, but the universal custom of France is to disregard this power, and to distribute equally among the children.

The French Revolution did more than merely alter the law. It took further measures to promote the wider distribution and ownership of property. The vast possessions belonging to the Church were appropriated by the State, and sold; 600,000 tenants became purchasers of their holdings, paying for them probably in depreciated "assignats." A portion of the property of the Emigrés, though less than is generally supposed, was dealt with in the same way. A portion of the communal property was also sold. Not less than a million tenants were thus enabled to become owners. Long after the Revolution, speculators, known under the name of *bandes noires*, bought up large properties and sold them to the tenants. The result of all these operations was vastly to increase the number of landowners, and to produce the state of ownership which we now see there. Has the condition of the peasants improved ? Who can doubt it who reads the description given of them before the Revolution and compares it with their present condition? Has France gained or lost in a political, social, or economic view, by this great accession to the number of her landowners? There is only one answer possible for those who look back at her history of the last few years. It is universally admitted that she has been able to emerge from her difficulties of foreign invasion, of a crushing war indemnity, of the gravest political convulsion, and of struggles with the Commune of Paris, only by the conservative force of her great mass of property owners, and the vast accumulations of wealth created by their industry and thrift. *Land Laws of France.*

The principles of the Revolution, especially as regards the land laws, were carried by the triumphant arms of the new Republic, and yet more by the spirit which had created this force to many other countries, to Belgium and Holland, to the Palatinate, to Baden, to Switzerland, and to a great part of Italy. Everywhere the old laws of primogeniture and entail were abolished, and the principles of the French Code were adopted.

LAND LAWS OF GERMANY.

Even Prussia, and others of the German states, felt something of this impulse. The first sign they showed was by secularising, as it was gently called, the vast possessions of the Church; and later, when Prussia was at its lowest ebb, the legislation of Stein and Hardenburg did much to renovate *Land Laws of Germany.*

Land Laws of Germany. her and reanimate her people, by modernizing her land laws, favouring the creation of absolute owners, and substituting full ownership for feudal dependency.

It may be worth while to dwell shortly upon the changes which occurred in Prussia,[1] as they were the model on which many other states have subsequently acted. Indeed it may be said that two methods have been followed by Europe, in getting rid of the feudal land system—the French method of the Revolution, where little regard was paid to private interests, where feudal services and dues were abolished without compensation, and feudal tenures were converted into absolute ownerships; and the Prussian method, or the legal method, by which the values of feudal rights were commuted, or a partition was made of the land occupied by the tenants, a portion being awarded to their feudal superiors in compensation for the loss of rights.

In Germany, as in France, the feudal system had not extinguished altogether the anterior existing class of small proprietors. They were indeed brought within the feudal system, and were considered as serfs; but they continued in possession of their small holdings, and exercised the rights of property and of bequest in respect of them.

---

[1] This account of the Reform of the Land Laws in Prussia is taken mainly from Mr. Harriss Gastrel's able report in the papers laid before Parliament in 1870.

The subjection of the peasant to their lords Land Laws of Germany. was so great that "the air makes us serfs" became a common expression. The oppression of the serfs was carried to the utmost, and they were not unfrequently sold to foreign governments as soldiers; but notwithstanding this, the class continued in possession of their small holdings of land. The power of the lord did not extend to the appropriation of the peasant's lands. The lord cultivated his own demesnes, either personally or by his bailiffs, with the aid of the services of his feudal dependents, and by the labour of the serfs due in respect of their separate holdings.

It appears, however, that there was from an early date a disposition on the part of the nobility and feudal lords to encroach upon the lands of their peasants, and gradually to convert the latter more completely into labourers without land of their own. We find, for instance, that in the fifteenth and sixteenth centuries the small country towns petitioned the King of Prussia to protect and maintain the yeomanry and peasantry, on commercial and political grounds; on the former, because the nobles traded with the large commercial towns, while the yeomanry traded with the small country towns; and on the latter, because it was good for the state that the yeomanry and peasantry should not disappear and leave nothing but nobles and labourers. The Hohenzollern princes took this view of the case, and directed their policy

<small>Land Laws of Germany.</small> to the maintenance of the peasantry. They prohibited the nobles from annexing the peasants' lands; and later they even forbad the eviction of a peasant, except upon well-founded grounds, and upon the lord of the manor replacing him by another peasant. Frederick the Great, actuated probably by military motives, issued severe edicts on this subject, prohibiting the absorption of peasants' lands.

At the beginning of this century Prussia had retained the feudal system in some of its most objectionable features. Her subjects were divided into three classes—Nobles, Townsmen, and Peasants. Each class was carefully restricted by law from mingling with the others in any way. The lands of each class were compulsorily maintained in its possession. The nobles' lands were for the most part the subject of unlimited entails. Freedom of commerce in land did not exist. Though the peasants were sustained and protected in their holdings, they were subject to the most arbitrary, capricious, and galling services and dues to their lords.

The French Revolution and the humiliating defeat of the Prussian armies by the French, brought on a crisis in this political and social system. After the treaty of Tilsit, the Prussian statesmen set to work to remodel her system, to modernize her land laws, and to abolish the remains of the feudal system. This great work was mainly

accomplished by the legislation of Stein and Harden- Land Laws
burg. It was temporarily arrested in 1816 by the Germany.
reaction which set in after the close of the French
war, and was not finally accomplished till 1850,
after the revolutionary rising of 1848. The effect
of this legislation was to convert the feudally
subjected peasant, with more or less imperfect
rights of property in land, into a perfectly free
peasant with absolute ownership, subject only to
a temporary rent-charge for commutation of the
feudal services; to convert the feudally restricted
lord, with more or less perfect rights of property
in his land, into a perfectly independent landowner; to relax the system of entails; to abolish
all restrictions on the sale of land as between the
different classes; and to establish the great principle
of freedom of sale of land. The operation was
assisted by the creation of Land Credit Banks, supported by loans from the State, and which in their
turn lent money to the tenants, repayable by
instalments spread over a term of years, for the
redemption of their rents.

The result of this legislation is that the land in
Prussia is now the absolute property of a large
number of owners, and that each owner is quite
independent of any other owner. The law recognizes
no distinction between land and other property in
respect of succession, and both are equally divided
among the children on the death of the owner.
Comparatively little land is now withdrawn from

Land Laws of Germany. free exchange by entail. Entails are not absolutely prohibited by law; though the prohibition of them was promised by the Constitution. The law of obligatory heritage (as it is called), by which a proportion of every man's property must descend to his children (in Prussia one-third of the property must go to the children equally if there be two children, and one-half if there be more than two), tends to prevent the accumulation of very large landed properties, and the equal division of real as well as personal property on intestacy, runs counter to any existing custom of primogeniture. Title to land has been made clear and almost indefeasible. The law of mortgages has been simplified; foreclosure and public sale are facilitated. By all these measures, and above all by the prevalence of absolute ownership of numerous owners, the free exchange of land has been fully attained.

The present state of Prussia as regards her land ownership is this: exclusive of the Rhine provinces and Westphalia, it consists of 70,000,000 acres, of which about 50,000,000 acres are cultivated and 17,000,000 are forest. The land is owned by 1,300,000 proprietors, of whom about 16,000 are large proprietors with properties of over 400 acres; 350,000 are medium-sized proprietors and 925,000 are small proprietors. About half of the latter are wholly employed on their small holdings, and the remainder are occupied mainly as day labourers or have other industries. The large proprietors, who own between them about 45 per cent. of the country, of which however a large part is forest, either farm themselves or through their bailiffs, and the relation of landlord and tenant is comparatively rare; there are not more than 30,000 farm tenants. Of the total area not more than $\frac{1}{16}$th is withdrawn from free exchange by reason of entails; new entails are very seldom created, and old entails are dying out.

<small>Land Laws of Germany.</small>

In the Rhine provinces and Westphalia, owing to the fact that they were subjected to the French laws at the beginning of the century, the land is even more distributed; with an area of about 11,000,000 of acres, there are said to be 1,157,000 proprietors, giving an average of 10 acres to each.

Of the beneficent results of this legislation with respect to land in Prussia, extending over a period of nearly fifty years, and but recently completed, there cannot be a doubt. The universal testimony of the country is in its favour. It promotes ownership *versus* tenancy; it aims at free exchange; the discouragement of entail and the withdrawal of sanction to primogeniture prevent accumulation of land; and the concurrence of all economists and statesmen is in favour of the yeomanry class as the main support of the empire. There are nearly a million owners of land living wholly upon the results of their own labour; they are said to form the most valuable section of

Land Laws of Germany. Prussia's population, although not the most wealthy. Many of them have raised themselves from the rank of day labourers. A well-known economist says of them :—"The inclination of the German to establish his family upon its own plot is a blessed trait of the greatest moral advantage. It has been sufficiently shown that the possibility of acquiring land fosters hope, encourages energy, and never allows useful activity to flag."

It has been thought well to dwell upon this Prussian legislation, because it formed the model which many other States have subsequently taken for their legislation with respect to land. Austria, Saxony, Hanover, Hungary, and Denmark, followed in the wake of Prussia; and the general principles under-lying the more recent changes in Russia and the abolition of serfdom in that great empire, have been to a great extent borrowed from the same source. Generally it may be said that the French Revolution gave the first impulse to these changes: a reaction occurred at the close of the war in 1814, which stopped further advance, and in some cases, caused a return to the old system; the revolution of 1848, as a rule, compelled a final change.

It is not too much, then, to say that for the last ninety years a large part of the Continent, and for the last thirty years nearly the whole of the Continent, has been moving in the direction of more absolute and more distributed ownership of land. Its legislators have not been content with merely abolishing primogeniture and entail; they have more actively thrown the weight of their laws and their institutions in favour of individualism, and in favour of ownership as distinguished from tenancy. The sale of Church property and State domains has largely assisted in this process. In some countries, as in Sweden, old entails are permitted to wear themselves out, but new entails cannot be created. In Denmark the constitution of 1849 forbade the creation of new entails, and promised that entailed estates should be converted into free property. This last promise, however, has not yet been fulfilled.

Land Laws of Germany.

In Portugal, it is reported to our Government, "that every opportunity is seized to necessitate the transfer of land. The extinction and dispersion of old estates ensuing from the laws now in force have been sought for rather than prevented; there is a direct movement towards democratic institutions, to which all measures of the legislature have for some years tended. Another blow dealt against the agglomeration of landed property is the abolition of *Prasos de Vita*, a sort of right of primogeniture which allowed property of a certain kind to be left as an undivided inheritance for three generations."

Portugal.

Of Gallicia, it is said, the local tribunals greatly facilitate dispersion and division of land. The Austrian civil code of 1869 accords no preference to eldest sons; exception is made in favour of

Gallicia.

Land Laws. *majorats*, or family entails, but these cannot be constituted without the consent of the legislature.

Sicily. Even in Sicily, one of the most backward parts of Europe, changes have been made in the same direction. Since 1812, when the feudal tenures which had their origin in the Norman Conquest, were abolished, the tendency of legislation has been to favour the alienation and division of landed property. In 1819 entails were put an end to, and the testamentary power of a father was limited to one-half of his property. In 1862 a law was proposed for the disposal of the Church lands, which amounted to one-sixth of the landed property in the island; by 1869 about 20,000 lots of 451,000 acres were disposed of, averaging 23 acres; yet we are told that, in spite of these legislative changes, the greater part of the soil of the island is still in possession of the few. It has not been found possible as yet to extirpate brigandage.

RESULTS OF CHANGES OF LAND LAWS.

Results of Changes of Land Laws. The methods and results of all these changes in Europe are described at length in the series of Reports from the representatives of this country at foreign courts, which were laid before Parliament in 1870. They are unanimous as to the benefits which have resulted from the changes they report. Everywhere the production of the soil has been increased. Industry and thrift have been stimulated. Pauperism has been greatly reduced, in many districts almost extinguished. Content has taken the place of chronic discontent. The rights of property have been greatly strengthened and are now everywhere secure. *Results of Changes of Land Laws.*

In the case of France, it is interesting to compare the account given of its present condition by Mr. Sackville West, with the description given of it by the well-known writer, Arthur Young, immediately before the Revolution of 1789. The state of France as described by Arthur Young was most wretched; everywhere he found, on the one hand, proprietors owning immense tracts of country heavily encumbered with debt, and which they were unable or unwilling to improve, and on the other, a vast body of poverty-stricken tenants overburthened with unjust taxation. In parts of France, however, there were even in those days, a considerable number of small peasant owners, cultivating their own land; and Young, with his usual discrimination, pointed out the difference in the condition of these as compared with the mass of the small tenants. He said of them, "their unremitting industry is so conspicuous and meritorious that no commendation would be too great for it. It is sufficient to prove that property in land is of all others the most active instigator to severe and incessant labour." In another passage he said, "The property in land is of all others the most active instigator to severe and incessant labour; and this

<small>Results of Changes of Land Laws.</small> truth is of such force and extent that I know of no way so sure to carry tillage to the mountain top as by permitting the adjoining villagers to acquire it in property;" and he added the words which have become a proverb, "Give a man the secure possession of a bleak rock, and he will turn it into a garden; give him a nine years' lease of a garden, and he will turn it into a desert. The magic of property turns sand into gold."

This opinion of Arthur Young, of the influence of ownership upon production and industry, is the more important, as, while admitting the merit of small properties, he feared they would result in indefinite sub-division of the land, and in the increase of population to an extent which the soil of France could not support. "The population flowing from this division, he said, would be the multiplication of wretchedness;" and "properties much divided would prove the greatest source of misery that could be conceived." In this opinion he was followed by many English economists. Of these the ablest exponent was the late Mr. McCulloch, who, writing in 1823, thirty years after the French Revolution, prophesied of France "that in half a century it would certainly be the greatest pauper warren in Europe, and along with Ireland have the honour of furnishing hewers of wood and drawers of water for all other countries in the world."

So far from these prophecies proving true, the very reverse has been the case, and the extension of ownership, the bringing within the reach of all classes the opportunity of becoming owners, the efforts made by the Government to facilitate the connexion between ownership and cultivation, and the enormous increase in the number of small ownerships of land consequent upon the measures of the Revolution, have not led to a great increase of the population and to a consequent multiplication of a pauper class. They have had the very opposite result. Production has been greatly stimulated by the sense and security of ownership; but the population has not increased relatively in the same proportion; the average condition of the people therefore is vastly improved; pauperism is almost unknown in rural districts; the habits of industry and thrift are universal. The complaint now made by many economists is the reverse of that which was predicted by Arthur Young and McCulloch; they contend that the system of small ownerships is to be condemned because it tends to check the increase of population.

Results of Changes of Land Laws.

It is true that the population of France increases so slowly that it may almost be said to be stationary. It is not by any means certain however that this can be attributed wholly to the prevalence of peasant proprietors. In Belgium and Switzerland, countries differing widely in their commercial conditions, but agreeing in this that they have a very large number of peasant owners, the population is by no means stationary, and the

Results of Changes of Land Laws.

births exceed the deaths in a proportion not far different from that of England. Let us, however, assume for the purposes of argument that the prevalence of peasant proprietors, and the wide distribution of property in land, act as a restraint upon individuals in such a manner as to reduce greatly the rate of increase of population; is it a great disadvantage and a matter to be deplored? France is not a nation which has a genius for emigration; her sons love her soil too much, and care not to face the unknown in other climes. Without emigration, and with the rate of progress of population that prevails in England, France would not long supply a sufficiency for her population. The increase of the *prolétariat* without corresponding increase of subsistence, would not be considered a matter for satisfaction. The prophecies of Arthur Young and M'Culloch, that her system of small cultivators would lead to her becoming the pauper warren of Europe, and her sons the hewers of wood and drawers of water for the rest of Europe, have not been fulfilled; but they make us feel what might have been the destinies of France under a different system. Both objections to her system of widely distributed property— namely, that it may lead to her becoming a pauper warren, or that it may tend to a very slow rate of increase of population—cannot be sound; which of them would be the most serious?

If the institutions of France have resulted in a

self-acting process of adapting the growth of her population to the means of subsistence, it would seem to be not the least merit of a system which is based upon the wide distribution of property, bringing home to the lowest, as well as to the highest, the motives of restraint.

<small>Results of Changes of Land Laws.</small>

Of the general condition of the small owners in France and of the influence which the sense of property has on agriculture, there can be no better account than that of Mr. Sackville West, who in 1870 was Secretary of the British Embassy at Paris, and who thus reported to the Foreign Office.

"The small proprietor is seen under more advantageous circumstances in France than in any other country in Europe, for he has in fact been the creature of a system which, whatever may be urged against it, has reconstituted the rural economy of the nation and more than doubled the produce of the soil. His mode of life presents a striking contrast and instruction illustrative of the system, for it is based upon the proceeds of the land in which he has a direct personal interest, and he lives, therefore, as an independent member of society according to his means in the social scale. . . .

"The condition of the small proprietors varies very much in different Departments, as also does the mode of cultivation; but they will generally be found in easy circumstances and living always in the hope of bettering themselves; and it is this hope which absolute possession engenders tha:

Results of Changes of Land Laws.

stimulates them to fresh exertions, beneficial not only to themselves but to the community in general."

This testimony in favour of the effects of a widely distributed ownership of land is not to be displaced by shewing that the average produce of wheat in France is considerably below that of England. It has already been shown by statistics that France is not a country wholly of small owners; nearly half her cultivated area is farmed by tenants; and there are 154,000 farmers who cultivate upwards of 100 acres as compared with 92,000 tenants of the same size in the United Kingdom. The wheat crops in France are mainly produced by the tenant farmers on these larger farms. The small owners as a rule do not produce wheat. The low average production of wheat in France is due to the soil and climate of her middle and southern provinces. In the north, the average production is as high as in England. No argument therefore can be drawn from this difference as against small ownerships.

Even Monsieur de Lavergne, who fully appreciates the system of large farms, and who is not in favour of an universal system of small proprietors, says on this point, " Is it right to extol the large property system to the disparagement of others, as has been done—to wish to extend it everywhere and to proscribe the small ? Evidently not; for viewing the question merely from an agricultural point of view, the only one now under considera- *Results of Changes of Land Laws.* tion, general results argue more in favour of small properties than of large."

The same testimony meets us from almost every part of Europe. Of Baden, where landed property is very much divided, Mr. Bailie reports to the Foreign Office.

"The prevalent public opinion is that the system of small freeholds tends to promote the greater economical and moral prosperity of the people, to raise the average standard of education, and to increase the national standard of defence and taxation. It seems to be a generally established fact that the small farmers realize larger returns than the larger farmers do from the same number of acres, and the result is that the large properties and large farms are disappearing, and being parcelled out among a number of small farmers. In fact, the price of landed properties is determined less by their intrinsic value than by the possibility of selling or letting them in small holdings."

He adds that, "the small peasant proprietors do not differ from the larger proprietors in respect of dwellings, clothing, mode of living, or education. There is no doubt that since the revolution of 1848 there has been a great improvement in the houses of the peasants and their mode of living, and in the cultivation of the soil; and their present condition must on the whole be regarded as favourable in respect of their means and general well-being."

Results of Changes of Land Laws.

Of Hesse Mr. Morier says : "An able-bodied pauper is a being altogether unknown. I even found a difficulty in describing the sort of person respecting whom I endeavoured to obtain information.

"The most vivid impression which I carried away from Viernheim was the equable manner in which the wealth of the place appeared to be distributed amongst its inhabitants. The whole population seemed to be on the same level of material comfort and well-being. I could not bring back to my recollection any sight or sound denoting the presence of a squalid class, or any indication pointing to a higher or a ruling class.

"When it has once reached a certain level of well-being, a peasant proprietary is a good judge of what amount of population the land will bear, and just as it increases in wealth and comfort, and in the special knowledge of the capabilities of the soil, so it becomes alive to the danger of jeopardizing this prosperity by over-population."

He speaks of spontaneous and systematic emigration as the safety-valve. "The use of this regulation is best understood in the Rhine provinces, which is one of the best cultivated and most prosperous districts in Europe. The Palatinate peasant cultivates his land more with the passion of an artist than in the plodding spirit of a mere bread-winner."

Of Lombardy, we are told that "Public opinion holds that small proprietors are advantageous to our mountain soils, where the spur of ownership is required to compel production. From a social point of view the possession of freeholds may always be considered a benefit to the peasantry, and when *la petite culture* is possible it is favourable to agriculture."

<small>Results of Changes of Land Laws.</small>

There is no official report from Switzerland, but of the condition of the agricultural population we have abundant evidence from numerous writers who have studied that country, and who all unite in bearing testimony to the wonderful improvements which have been made of late years, to the marvellous industry and thrift of the small proprietors, and to the general diffusion of wealth, of comfort, and of intelligence. The Rev. Barham Zincke, who has written a most excellent account of this country, the result of many successive visits to it, says of the Canton de Vaud, "I saw no mansions in Switzerland, neither did I see scarcely any houses that with us would pass for cottages. What I did see was a surprising number of good comfortable small houses, which showed that the district was inhabited by a large number of well-to-do families . . . . It must be obvious that the yearly produce of these little reclaimed grass farms, in which every little patch and corner is made to support as many blades of grass as the most careful cultivation can force into existence, would not maintain in their present style of living all the families that reside in these comfortable houses.

Results of Changes of Land Laws. But the Swiss system suggests and encourages the practice of saving; and in most of these houses a capital fund has been accumulated, which so aids what these small farmers get during a year from their farms that their families are enabled to live with what is to them ease and comfort."

"It is an incidental and not unimportant result of this system that it works in the direction of enabling the population to provide themselves with better houses than under the territorial system they could rent from speculative builders of rows of cottages run up by contract on land let for the purpose on a ninety-nine years' lease. The comfortable little houses on the small farms throughout this district are the property of those who are living in them. That was the reason why they spent as much as they could spare in constructing them well, and in making them roomy and, in accordance with their ideas and wants, commodious."

"We may infer from the general condition of the Swiss that it is the possession of land, or the prospect of being able to acquire it, that saves a labouring class from sinking into a mob of pauperized drudges, and educates them into men."

How great is the difference between the state of the Swiss as regards their houses and the agricultural labourers of England as regards their cottages will hereafter appear; the difference between their occupiers is scarcely less.

It is not, however, necessary to go beyond the immediate possessions of the Crown of England for a conspicuous illustration of the results of a widely distributed ownership of land upon the production, the industry, the content, and the general well-being of a whole community. There is such a case close at hand in the Channel Islands. The people of those islands, since their union with England 800 years ago, have jealously preserved their local government and their distinctive laws. Chief among these distinctions are their land laws, which they have inherited from the common law of Normandy; these laws favour the dispersion of property, and forbid its accumulation by entail or primogeniture. The result is, that with an area no larger than hundreds of private estates in England and Ireland, the islands boast of not less than 4,000 landowners, cultivating in most cases their own property, and constituting a class of small yeomen.

Results of Changes of Land Laws.

The industrial results of these small yeomen are most remarkable; the island is cultivated to the highest point which it is capable of; the gross produce is extraordinary; there is a general diffusion of wealth; thrift and saving are conspicuous in every class; cottages such as we see in England and Ireland are unknown; the people are better housed than in any part of Europe; pauperism is almost unkown; everything testifies to the stimulus effected by the wide distribution of property, and

Results of Changes of Land Laws. by the fact that property is brought within the prospect of acquisition by every one.

The most enlightened people in the island, equally with public opinion, attribute these results to their distinctive land laws; to the fact that they have successfully resisted the introduction of English laws, which they believe would have an opposite tendency; and they significantly allege that if these laws had been introduced some centuries ago, the islands, by this time, would probably have been each owned by a single individual; and their cultivators might have been in the condition of the Irish tenants. As it is, a more prosperous, loyal, and contented class does not exist under the Crown of England than the small yeomen of the Channel Islands.

CHANGES OF LAW IN THE UNITED STATES.

Changes of Law in the United States. Our colonies have dealt not less rudely with the principles of English land laws. The various States of North America retained them for many years, so long as they remained colonies, but after separation from the mother-country, commenced to amend them. By their new constitution the subject of the land laws was left to the discretion of the State legislatures. It is strong testimony to the strength of public opinion against these laws, and also to the result of the change, that every

State has in succession abolished primogeniture and has so restricted the power of settlement that what we call entail is impossible. They have universally, however, retained the freedom of willing. They have rejected the French system of compulsory division of property. They have preserved the parental authority intact. The universal custom, however, of testators is to distribute property on death equally among their children. Any preference not justified by exceptional circumstances is most rare, is condemned by public opinion, and where attempted not unfrequently leads to the will being disputed and upset on the ground of undue influence. Land transfer is exceedingly simple and uncostly; mortgages, which are almost a necessity for the existence of small properties, are effected with the greatest ease and at a most trifling cost, and the whole process of dealing with land is assimilated to that of personal property. Any legislation which tends to the monopoly of land or to reduce or curtail the free rights and dominions of its owners has everywhere been repudiated.

Changes of Law in the United States.

Under this system, and under the influence of public opinion, there is no tendency to create landed estates on the English principle, and the country throughout its length and breadth is farmed by men owning their own land. Hence the multitude of owners of land. The relation of landlord and tenant of farming land is all but

Changes of Law in the United States. unknown. The general aspect of the country, especially in such states as New York, Pennsylvania, Maryland, and New England would surprise those who have not been out of England. The rural districts have a more populous appearance than even in this country. Every hundred to a hundred and fifty acres belong to a separate owner, who has a substantial house, and who farms the land himself. There are no large owners. The three millions of landowners are the foundation of the social system, are the cause of stability, are the conservative element in a system otherwise profoundly democratic, and are also the promoters of prosperity to the numerous cities and towns. The same condition of things is extending through the far West, hundreds of miles beyond Chicago, and will eventually, and at no distant day, stretch across the continent.

In a similar manner have our other Anglo-Saxon colonies cast off the old shell of our land-laws, as soon as they were endowed with the power to legislate. They seem to have found them an intolerable nuisance, wholly unsuited to modern life, and to the necessities of an industrial society, of which freedom of commerce in land is the very life breath. These changes have universally taken the same direction; the withdrawal of state sanction to accumulation or to the preference of one child over another; the assimilation of the law with respect to all kinds of property; the limitation of family settlements, and the prohibition of a family succession different from that of the state; the registration of titles; the simplification of transfer. *Changes of Law in the United States.*

CHANGES FAVOUR INDIVIDUALISM.

It is to be observed that these changes, alike in the old world and in the new, have been in the same direction and with the same object—to favour and strengthen individual property in land and to promote its distribution. There is not in any of the legislation alluded to the slightest trace of communism, or of any new-fangled ideas of property in land. No attempt has been made towards state appropriation of land. No step has been taken to secure to the community what is called the unearned increment. The individual owner is everywhere invested with full, absolute, and undisputed control of the land which he owns. Freedom of contract is nowhere interfered with. *Changes Favour Individualism.*

Mr. West says of France, "Proprietary rights can never be called in question. Whether a property consists of one acre or one hundred, the owner is absolute in all matters relating to possession. The legislature cannot interfere between him and the tenant on questions respecting compensation for improvements or indemnities. Tenant right and fixity of tenure are phrases scarcely ever heard of in France."

Changes Favour Individualism.

Monsieur de Lavelaye says of Flanders,[1] "The Flemish tenant, though ground down by the constant rise of rents, lives among his equals, peasants like himself, who have tenants whom they can use just as the large landowner does his. His father, his brother, perhaps the man himself, possesses something like an acre of land, which he lets at as high a rent as he can get. In the public-house, peasant proprietors will boast of the high rents they get for their lands, just as they might boast of having sold their pigs or potatoes very dear. . . .

"Thus the distribution of a number of small properties among the peasantry forms a kind of rampart and safeguard for the holders of large estates; and the peasant property may without exaggeration be called the lightning-conductor that averts from society dangers which might otherwise lead to catastrophes."

Let it not then be said that any legislation in the same direction, has any the slightest taint either of communism or confiscation. The one great object in view is not to destroy property, or to lessen its value and the sense of security which it gives, but to extend its influence as one of the strongest and best agents in promoting individual exertion, and as a spur to efforts to rise in the social scale, which is equally powerful with the

---

[1] See *System of Land Tenure*, published by the Cobden Club.

lowest as with the highest. It proceeds then on the principle of individualism as opposed to any principle of socialism or communism. *Changes Favour Individualism.*

If then a right view has been taken of the motives which have led to all the changes already described in other countries, and of the results attained, equally in the old world as in the new, it must be difficult to suppose that England can withdraw herself from the stream of modern life, can hope to live in an atmosphere of her own, resist all changes in her laws, and content herself with going onward in the old groove, and under the pleasing assurance of philosophers that land was intended as a luxury for the rich, and that no poor man need hope for a permanent interest in the soil of his country, other than perhaps so much as is covered by his hearth-stone when alive, and his grave-stone when dead.

To those who argue that it is an inevitable law of nature that land should in a wealthy country become the luxury only of the rich, and that the existing state of things in England is due to this and not to our positive laws, two questions may fairly be put with reference to the condition of other countries. The one is, whether they would really desire to substitute the English system of complete separation between the three classes of landowners, farmers, and labourers, for the yeoman and peasant proprietorship which so extensively prevails elsewhere? whether they would

M

Changes Favour Individualism. contemplate with pleasure the possibility, or whether they expect, that the three million farming owners of the United States, with the advancing wealth and population of that country, will gradually be merged in about one-twentieth of their number of landlords, and that the relation of landlord and tenant should be universally substituted there?—whether in France it would be better, or be desirable in any sense, that the five millions of peasant owners should be reduced to the position of tenants at will to about one-hundredth part of their number of landlords, and that the Irish system should prevail there and in the Channel Islands as well as in Ireland?

The other question is what, on the assumption that these changes are desirable and to be aimed at, should be the first steps taken with a view to this end, and with the object of facilitating and promoting the gradual accumulation of land in few hands, and the substitution of a class of large landowners, with farming tenants for the existing systems of widely distributed landownerships?

Would not the first measures, adopted with this object, be that their legislatures should again give the sanction of law to primogeniture, should again give facilities for the entail of landed property, and should again revert to a system of land laws which would make the title to land obscure and complicated, and its transfer therefore costly and difficult? And if this be conceded, how can it be doubted that these same laws and difficulties have in this country been mainly instrumental in producing the result which we now observe? *Changes Favour Individualism.*

ORIGIN OF THE ENGLISH LAND SYSTEM.

In England, as in most parts of the Continent, there existed, prior to the feudal system, a very different state of things to that since brought about. In Saxon times England was undoubtedly a country of very numerous landowners: they consisted of "eorls," or larger owners, who held under the Crown, and "ceorls," a very numerous class, tilling the land they owned, and answering to the modern class of yeomen, "the root," as Hallam says, "of a noble plant, the free-soccage tenants, or English yeomanry, whose independence stamped with peculiar features both our constitution and our national character." These two classes owned the cultivated land; beyond were the common lands and forests, then called "folk land," the land of the people, the property of which was vested in the village community, and where the villagers had the right to turn out their cattle, dig their turf, or cut firewood. The property laws of these people were not different from those now prevailing among our colonists. There was equal division of land upon death among the children; the power of alienation and of willing was fully conceded; there was a public register of all deeds *Origin of the English Land System.*

Origin of the English Land System. affecting land; alienation was simple and public. These distinctive features of the Anglo-Saxon land laws were swept away after the Conquest. In their place was introduced the feudal system of land tenure, with its web of relations between the sovereign, the nobles, the knights, the villeins, and the serfs. The greater part of the land of England was confiscated after the battle of Hastings, and was granted out by the Conqueror to his military chiefs. These chiefs or lords again, on their part, granted portions of the lordships thus confided to them to their principal knights and retainers below them, to be held on the condition of military service.

Some of the Saxon landowners survived this process of confiscation, and were brought under the system as free tenants of feudal superiors subject only to military service. Much greater numbers were relegated to the position of villeins in the feudal system, a position under which they continued to cultivate their lands for their own use, but subject to dues and services, mostly of a personal or agricultural character, to their lords, and were considered to have no rights as against such superiors. Below these was the class of serfs, or slaves, without any rights of property, the mere menial servants of their lords and masters. The feudal system being of military origin, founded on conquest and maintained against internal difficulties and foreign foes by force, had necessitated the maintenance of military commands, or fiefs, in strong hands; the principle of primogeniture, therefore, by which the fief was inherited by the eldest male descendant was also a necessity; and equally opposed to the system was the power of alienation, without the consent at least of the superior lord. *Origin of the English Land System.*

The general state of England, then, shortly after the Conquest, was this. The country was divided into a great number of separate lordships or manors. The lord of each manor cultivated a portion of the land, entitled his demesne, by himself or by his bailiff, partly by the assistance of the villeins or small farmers of his manor, who were bound to render him service—some of so many days' labour, and others of so many days of team work—and partly by the labour of serfs or slaves. The common lands, or wastes, were appropriated in a sense by the lords, but subject to the rights of the freehold and other tenants of the manor to turn out their cattle or dig their turf there.

Other portions of the land within the manor were owned by free tenants, who owed only military service, or in many cases fixed rents, to their superior lord, and who in every other sense were independent owners of their holdings. The remaining lands of the manor were held and cultivated by the class of villeins. Many of them had originally been owners of their lands, but by commendation

Origin of the English Land System. or confiscation they had been completely subjected to the will of their feudal lords, and had lost all rights as against them. In theory and often in practice they were completely at the mercy of their lords, "*taillable et corvéable sans merci ni miséricorde*" (subject to dues and burthens without mercy or pity), as the old lawyers describe them; they were, however, rarely or never disturbed in the occupation of their lands. They were allowed to alienate them with the consent of their lords, and to bequeath them to their children; and for a time at least the old Saxon principle of equal division among such children on death of the owner without a will was preserved. In those days the number of retainers a lord could muster was a source of power and strength to him. He had no object then in dispossessing the tenants of his manor, neither did he undertake for them any of the duties which pertain to the modern landlord, of building houses for his tenants or improving their land; when, therefore, the country became more settled and the lawyers began to study the Roman law, they drew principles from it which recognised the right of such tenants to what we should now call fixity of tenure, a right to continue in possession of their holdings upon payment of the customary dues, services, rents, or fines, and no longer to be merely tenants at the will of their lord.

Certain it is, that between the time of the

Conqueror and of Edward the Third these villeins acquired a clear and absolute right to their holdings, and as tenants on the Roll of the Manor, or copyholders, have ever since been recognised as having an interest scarcely inferior to that of freeholders. And it is this body of small owners who constituted a large proportion of the small proprietors, who at one time were the boast of this country.

Origin of the English Land System.

Domesday Book, the most valuable record of the state of landownership and of the relation of various classes of a population which any country has ever possessed, informs us that about twenty years after the Conquest the number of lords of manors holding directly from the Crown or indirectly from some superior lord, was 9,271; that the number of freeholders holding under these lords of manors by military service was 13,700; and that the number of freemen holding from lords of manors by fixed or determined rent service, was 30,831, a total of 53,802 freeholders. The number of villeins, as distinguished from burgesses and serfs, and who were therefore occupiers of land in rural districts, is stated to have been 108,407. The four northern counties and Wales, comprising one-fifth of the country, were not included in *Domesday*. Adding one-fifth then to the number, there must at this time have been not short of 200,000 heads of families interested in the soil either as freeholders or villeins. The relation of landlord

Origin of the English Land System. and tenant, such as we now know it, did not exist. There is little trace of land having been let on lease to farmers before the reign of Edward I. The principle of primogeniture did not in these early times apply to any property but fiefs, or lands held under fiefs by military service; it did not apply to that freehold property known as free-soccage land, which had escaped confiscation at the Conquest, nor did it apply to the property of villeins. It is clear, then, that between the date of *Domesday* and the time of Edward III. there must have been a great increase in the number of persons who had an absolute right in the soil of their native country. Certain it is, that Sir John Fortescue, writing in the time of Henry VI., about a hundred years later, speaks of the number of its freeholders being one of the chief boasts of England of his day. He adds, that although there were some noblemen of great estates, yet that between these estates there were great numbers of small freeholders. The number of parish churches, the entries in old registries, and many other indications, point to the fact of England being, before the Black Death, very thickly populated in its rural districts. And Professor Rogers, who has investigated many old records and manorial lists of the fourteenth century, has found that the land was greatly subdivided, and that most of the regular farm-servants of that time were owners of land.

It would be interesting to trace, through

succeeding periods, the gradual reduction of this element of English life. Statistics are at no period to be obtained, so that anything like an accurate tracing of the decline is impossible.

<small>Origin of the English Land System.</small>

It is worthy of notice, however, that, unlike most other countries in Europe, where the principle of primogeniture was confined to feudal fiefs and lordships of manors or to the property of the nobility, and was not applied to the property of inferior classes, in England this principle came to be applied to every species of landed property and to all classes of landowners, however small. It was probably extended to copyhold property about the time of Henry III.

THE HISTORY OF ENTAIL.

It is however to the principle of entail that we must mainly ascribe the reduction and disappearance of small owners. This principle was by no means one of the earliest features of feudalism. Fiefs and lordships of manors being in the first instance connected with military duties, even the hereditary principle was not at first recognised, and was for a time resisted by the feudal superiors; but when fully recognised every effort was made to secure the perpetuation of these functions and properties in the male line of the family. The Norman barons endeavoured to introduce this principle shortly after the Conquest, but they met with great resistance from the Crown and the Church.

<small>History of Entail.</small>

History of Entail.   The main object which the feudal chiefs had in view was to secure their fiefs and property to their successors free from the chance of forfeiture in case of treasonable acts of their own. Conviction for treason was followed by forfeiture of property. Entail would preserve the property for the family, though the present holder might suffer forfeiture during his lifetime.

On the other hand, the Sovereign, representing the principle of order and of imperial interests, as opposed to those of the feudal lords or petty local chiefs, was much concerned in maintaining the principle of forfeiture of property in case of treason, as one of the main securities against rebellion. Any reduction therefore of this penalty was to be resisted. A powerful ally in this instance was found in the Church. The principle of entail if once admitted would deprive the Church of the main source of its wealth, the gifts of land by its pious sons. The clerical lawyers therefore assisted the sovereign in his efforts to prevent the introduction of this principle, and we find that they borrowed principles from the Civil Law with great ingenuity to upset the grants which had been obtained by the nobles with the object of creating entails.

For the first 200 years after the Conquest, the nobles failed to secure their object, or to effect entails. During the whole of this time therefore land was practically alienable; and no doubt this contributed greatly to the increase in the number of owners of land. *History of Entail.*

In the year 1285, however, the nobles found themselves strong enough to force upon the Crown and the country a law, which overrode the interpretation which had been given by the lawyers to the words of entail, and practically enabled perpetual entails to be created. It is worthy of notice that this statute of Edward I. known as 'De Donis,' an Act still on the statute book and part of the law of this country, never obtained the consent of the Commons. This vicious principle of perpetual entail speedily came into common use, and it was not long before grave inconvenience and mischief arose from it, and from the consequent withdrawal of a great part of the landed property of the country from free commerce. The celebrated Lord Coke speaking of the statute 'De Donis,' said of it—

"The true policy of the common law was overturned by this statute, which established a perpetuity, by art for all those who had or would have it; by force, whereof all the possessions in England were entailed accordingly, which was the occasion and cause of divers other mischiefs; and the same was attempted to be remedied at divers Parliaments, and divers bills were exhibited accordingly, but they where always on one pretence or other rejected. But the truth was that the Lords and Commons, knowing that their estates in tail were not to be forfeited for felony or treason, as their estates of inheritance

History of Entail. were before the said Act, and finding that they were not answerable for the debts and incumbrances of their ancestors, and that the sales or alienations and leases of their ancestors did not bind them, they always rejected such bills."

The bad effects of this statute are also described by Blackstone in a well-known passage :—

"Children grew disobedient when they knew they could not be set aside; farmers were ousted of the leases made by tenants in tail; creditors were defrauded of their debts; innumerable latent clauses were produced to deprive purchasers of land they had bought and paid for, and treasons were encouraged as estates tail were not liable to forfeiture longer than for the tenant's life."

These evils continued without remedy for another period of 200 years. After this long interval the reviving power of the Crown and the ingenuity of the lawyers combined to upset these perpetual entails, and a method was discovered by which the celebrated statute of Edward I. was circumvented and defeated. The process by which this was arrived at, and carried out, was so subtle, technical, and ingenious, that it would be impossible to explain it in popular language, or to make it intelligible to others than lawyers and logicians. It is sufficient to say, that by a kind of collusion between the courts of law and the immediate holder of an entailed property, the object of the entail could be defeated, and landed property subject to it could be sold.

Later the Tudor kings, Henry VII. and Henry VIII., succeeded in inducing Parliament to give legislative sanction to this curious device of the lawyers, and also to deprive entailed estates of their freedom from forfeiture in the case of the treason of their holders. These acts again gave great freedom to the sale of land, and though entails were not wholly destroyed and were still valid for certain purposes, they were not effective to prevent the alienation of land. Thenceforward for another 200 years land again became freely alienable, and entails were practically rendered innocuous.

History of Entail.

It may be not unworthy of notice that these 200 years, when land was practically free from the shackles of entail, when the holders of estates were really their owners, and not merely the ostensible owners or temporary enjoyers of them, were not the least memorable years of English history or the least fruitful of great Englishmen. They embraced the Elizabethan era, and they spanned the lives of Bacon, Shakespeare, and Milton; of Sydney, Raleigh, and Blake; of Cecil and Walsingham, of Hampden and Pim, of Cromwell and Vane, of Strafford and Falkland. It does not appear that, even in those days, notwithstanding the absence of effective entail, men had any fear of being unable to hand down to a remote posterity the products of their fortunes in lands and houses. Burleigh, Hatfield, Longleat, Audley End, Holland House, and Bramshill, and

History of Entail. numerous other great mansions, were built in this period, and still survive as evidence that even in days when landowners were in full possession of their property, they did not fear to build for a long future.

Frequently during this interval attempts were made by clever lawyers to restore the principle of indefeasible entail; the courts of law, however, uniformly resisted such attempts; in a well-known case which came before them, and which was known as the "Perpetuities case," it was attempted to create an entail or settlement upon an unborn person, not dissimilar to our present family settlements, by giving a life-interest to a father and vesting the property in his unborn eldest son; the Judges however rejected the scheme, alleging that if this were permitted the following evils would arise:

1. That the owner of the property would be prevented providing for his widow and younger children in such proportion as he should think fit.

2. That the eldest son being certain of his inheritance, and therefore independent of his father, would not be subject to parental control.

3. That such settlements would lead to complexity of title, and therefore to uncertainty and expense of transfer.

It is most important to recollect these objections of the Judges to the introduction of the first germs of a system which afterwards unhappily was established, and which, as will be shown, has led to the very evils which were thus foretold.

History of Entail.

The period of freedom of land from entails lasted from the date of the discovery of the means of eluding the Statute de Donis, in 1472, till about the time of the great Rebellion, another period of nearly 200 years; it might possibly have lasted till our own time, but for the accidental effects of that great political crisis upon the views of lawyers and landowners. It again became a great object to the owners of land to protect their properties from the possible results of their acts if convicted of treason; and at a time when almost every landowner was forced, either by inclination or public opinion, to take one side or the other in the great national struggle, there was almost equal danger of the enforcement of this forfeiture for treason, on either side, as now one party and now the other prevailed.

It is interesting to observe that the lawyers and Judges who had previously favoured freedom of alienation, and had exercised all their ingenuity to prevent entails, or to find the means of eluding and breaking them, now shifted their advocacy, and lending their subtleties to the opposite principle, aided the landowners in protecting their family estates from forfeiture, and succeeded in forging the system of entail through family settlements, from which the country has ever since suffered.

A royalist lawyer, of great learning and in-

History of Entail. genuity, Sir Orlando Bridgeman, the ancestor of the Earls of Bradford, was the first to devise a plan, by which landed property could be settled upon an unborn eldest son, in such a way, as to elude both the statute law against entails, and the common law doctrine against perpetuities, and to lay the foundation for the family entails such as we now have them. It is said that Sir Orlando, whose reputation as a lawyer was so great that he became "the oracle of both parties, his very enemies not thinking their estates secure without his advice," himself assisted in giving currency to his own coinage, when he was raised to the Bench of Judges after the Restoration; in other words, he upheld, by decisions from the Bench the devices he had invented as a lawyer. However this may be, it is certain, that about this period there was invented by the lawyers and accepted by the judges as valid, a system of entailing property on unborn persons, wholly alien to the principle which had induced Parliament 200 years before to break the system of entails, and utterly opposed to the doctrine of freedom and alienability of land which had been the happy condition of the country during that period.

The essence of the new principle thus introduced was the settling of property upon an unborn person, against which the courts of law had previously struggled. The effect of thus permitting the vesting of property in the unborn was to convert the immediate possessors of properties hampered by these arrangements into mere life-holders, without any real power over the property, without power to sell, or even to lease for any period beyond their own lives, and without any power of bequest in favour of other children than the one named in the settlement. It had the great merit however, at such a period, of preventing the forfeiture of more than the life estate in the event of the life-holder being convicted of treason. *History of Entail.*

It would be difficult, if not impossible, to make intelligible to other than lawyers how this was effected, and how the old traditions and doctrines of the law were evaded, or to describe all the subtleties and difficulties which have since grown out of it. It is sufficient to say that it led directly to the system known as that of family entail under which landed properties are now generally held. It will be observed that this system has never received the assent of Parliament. It has never fairly been brought under review of the legislature. It was the invention of lawyers, and was sanctioned by the courts of law, but has never been subjected to popular control.

MODERN ENTAILS.

The general object of such family entails may be briefly stated as follows:—to secure that the landed property which is the subject of them *Modern Entails.*

<small>Modern Entails.</small> shall descend in the direct male line by the order of primogeniture, intact and undiminished, for as long a period as possible; to prevent the holder, the tenant for life, and successive tenants for life, from alienating the property, or bequeathing it to their children in such proportion as they may think fit.

It is customary for lawyers, in representing this system, to speak of it as very limited in its operation, and as tying up estates for a comparatively short period. They say that once in every generation it is possible to break the entail, and for the persons interested to join in freeing the property, and selling or disposing of it as they think fit. It is true that when the tenant in tail, as he is called, the unborn son in whom the property is ultimately vested, after the death of his father and perhaps his grandfather, reaches the age of twenty-one, he and his father can agree together to break up the entail, and to cut off all other contingent interests or collateral claims.

In fact, however, the system is so curiously and artfully devised, that when this climax is reached, when after the lapse of years there are co-existing two or more persons in different generations, who by agreeing together can cut off the entail, there arises out of the very nature of the arrangement the greatest inducement to all concerned in such a family settlement to take this opportunity, not to free the estate from its cumbrous shackles, but to prolong the entail, and to make a new settlement which will carry on the entail to another unborn generation. *Modern Entails.*

The process has thus been described by an eminent legal writer:

" Upon the majority or marriage of the son who is tenant in tail under a family settlement the estate is commonly re-settled, he receiving an immediate provision, and by his estate being reduced to a life-estate with remainder to his issue in tail, parting with his prospective powers of alienation. By such a process as is here roughly described, the bulk of family estates in this country are kept in settlement from one generation to another, the new fetter being added at that epoch at which the power of alienation arises."

And the late Lord St. Leonards, a powerful advocate of the system, spoke of it as " from its own nature leading to successive settlements." Although, therefore, in one sense, such settlements may appear to be limited in duration, the truer view is that they embody all the vicious principles of perpetual entail. They are intended to preserve the family property intact through successive generations, and to prevent the head of the family, at any time, from either reducing the corpus of the property, or from exercising any option in favour of a more equal distribution among his children; and subject to some perils, which will shortly be pointed out, they certainly succeed in doing this.

Modern Entails.

It has been already shown that from the time of the Norman conquest till the present time there have been four nearly equal periods of 200 years each. In the first 200 years entails could not be effected. In the next 200 years they were permitted by law, and their evils were notorious, and admitted to be most disastrous. In the third period the system was again broken down, entails were practically inoperative, landowners were again masters of their own property, and land was again brought into free commerce. In the last period entails have again been permitted, through the medium of family settlements which, if not perpetual as they were in the former period, have tended to perpetuities, as Lord St. Leonards has told us.

This power and the consequent custom to entail land has now existed for rather more than 200 years. It is commonly admitted that about three-fourths of the landed property of the country is subject to such entails. What effect have they had upon the distribution and ownership of property? Have they been the cause of the accumulation of land in few hands? Do they tend to prevent the application of capital to the land? Have they been in the interest of the families concerned? How have they affected the position and well-being of the labouring class?

EFFECT OF ENTAILS ON NUMBER OF LANDOWNERS.

Effect of Entails on number of Landowners.

It would be most interesting to trace the number of landowners through these periods, and to show the effect of these various changes upon the distribution of land. Unfortunately, however, from the *Domesday Book* till the return of four years ago we have no certain facts and no reliable statistics whatever. It has been already shown that at a very early period there was a very large number of small proprietors. It is probable that in the time of the Edwards their number was very much greater than at the present time, notwithstanding that the area of cultivated land has been greatly increased in the interval by the inclosure of commons and the clearing of forests. There is every reason to believe that a large majority of farmers were yeomen, that is, were owners of the land they farmed; and that a very large number of the labouring class were also owners of cottages and small plots of land. The records of copyhold manors give abundant proof of this; and all the testimony of early writers is to the same effect. How far this number was reduced or affected by the prevalence of entails between 1285 and 1470 we cannot tell, nor whether the greater freedom of the next period either tended to increase their

Effect of Entails on number of Landowners.

number or to stem the reduction which had been taking place. It is certain, however, that in the time of the civil war the number of freeholders in rural districts was considerable. It is matter of history that 6,000 freeholders rode up from Buckinghamshire to Westminster to petition Parliament against the arbitrary acts of Charles I., from which Clarendon dates the commencement of the civil war. It was from the yeomen that Cromwell mainly drew his forces. It was the county freeholders that formed the main support of the parliamentary party.

Lord Macaulay, speaking of the yeomen class of 200 years ago, says that they were "an eminently manly and true-hearted race. These small proprietors who cultivated their own fields, and enjoyed a modest competence, without affecting to have escutcheons or crests, or aspiring to sit on the bench of justice, then formed a much more important part of the nation than at present. If we may trust the best statistical writers of that age, not less than 160,000 proprietors, who with their families made up more than a seventh of the whole population, derived their subsistence from small freehold estates. .... It was computed that the number of persons who occupied their own land was far greater than of those who farmed the land for others. Great," he adds, "has since been the change in the rural life of England."

There are also in most parts of rural England

indications that in times not very remote the small squires and yeomen were much more numerous than at the present time. Great numbers of existing farmhouses have the appearance and tradition of having been the residences of owners and not of tenants. It is admitted that the yeomen class has all but disappeared from most parts of England, and that the labouring class has almost ceased to have any permanent interest in or connection with the soil of their native land. The number of squires has been also so reduced, that in large districts there are very few resident gentlemen, except the clergy. Inquiry on this point has shown that in the counties of Berkshire and Dorsetshire more than half the parishes have no gentlemen of the landowning class resident within them. Of the county of Nottingham it was reported that of 245 parishes in the eastern division only sixty-five have resident squires; and it was added, " the bankruptcy of one duke and the eccentricity of another have caused great depression in this part of the county." Everything, therefore, points to the reduction of the number of landowners of all classes, whether of the squire class, or of the yeomen class, or of the agricultural labourer.

Effect of Entails on number of Landowners.

A careful examination of the list of landowners will tend to the same conclusions. Of the 955 landowners of upwards of 10,000 acres each, and averaging 30,000 acres, about sixty appear to have

<small>Effect of Entails on number of landowners.</small> come into this category during the last thirty years; some few of their owners have bought out other large proprietors, but the greater part of them have been created by the extinction of many small proprietors; and probably an examination of the list of proprietors in the next rank would show a somewhat similar result. Of those who have existed more than thirty years a certain number have from one cause or other been compelled to sell portions of their properties, yet a greater number have increased their properties, either by marriage or by purchase; and the general result of an examination of the list must be the conviction that the number of large proprietors is steadily increasing at the expense of the smaller proprietors, and that the average holdings of land by these large owners is also increasing. It may be worthy of notice, that in the list of those who have risen into the first grade of landowners within the last thirty years by purchase, and not by marriage, there is not a single name distinguished for any great service to the State or to the public. The days when statesmen, like the Cecils or Walpoles, or when great lawyers like the Howards, the Cokes, or the Bridgemans, or great generals such as the Marlboroughs and Wellingtons, could acquire great properties of land and could found families in the first rank of landowners, seems to be past. The list consists almost wholly of successful merchants, manufacturers, brewers, coalowners,

ironmasters, or tradesmen; it is from these classes that families are now being founded, which it is hoped by means of entails to maintain for a long future among the landed magnates. Without wishing to depreciate the merits of such persons, or the services which they have rendered to the industry and commerce of the country while building up their own fortunes, it may be permitted to express a doubt whether society is much interested in affording them the machinery for securing that their names shall be escorted by landed property in perpetuity.

Effect of Entails on number of Landowners.

It will not be denied, however, that if of this class a certain number are continually pressing into the ranks of landowners, and if an equivalent number is not dropping off the list by the dispersion or division of the property, by will or by sale, the list of large owners must be continually increasing, and the number of small owners continually diminishing in greater proportion; and the time must come when the ideal of such a system will be reached, when the country will be divided among a comparatively few of the largest owners, and when small proprietors will have ceased to exist in rural districts or beyond the immediate neighbourhood of large towns.

DANGERS OF ENTAIL.

Dangers of Entail. But for one feature of entail by family settlements there cannot be a doubt that accumulation would be far greater than it has been. The one counteracting force is that they sometimes tend to defeat their own objects. The effect of the arrangement is to divest the present holder of the property of all real power over it, and to vest the remainder with full power in the eldest son when he shall attain the age of twenty-one and survive his father. If the son should not agree to re-settle the estate, as it is called, when he arrives at the age of twenty-one, or if the father should die before the son reaches this age, the property will ultimately vest in the son to do as he likes with it. The certainty of thus coming into possession of the estate leads not a few eldest sons into early extravagance; they not unfrequently fall a prey to the class of money-lenders who are always on the lookout for them, and who induce them to anticipate their inheritance by borrowing upon their expectations. A young man who begins in this way is speedily brought to the point when he has ruined his property even before he has come into possession of it, and many are the cases where family properties have been sacrificed and sold through anticipations of this kind, favoured, if not created, by the very arrangements which were intended to preserve them intact. The settlor of the property who thought to preserve the family estate for future generations of his family, and who deprived his son of the full dominion over it and of the power of free bequest, is defeated in his object, through having vested the remainder in an unborn grandson, of whom he could know nothing, and who turns out to be unworthy of the charge. *Dangers of Entail.*

Another feature of such family arrangements and artificial attempts to maintain property in the family, in successive generations of eldest sons, is the gradually accumulating debt upon the estate. Although the estate is settled on the eldest males in succession, there must be some provision for other members of the family. Widows must be provided with annuities, younger sons and daughters cannot be left without means, portions for them must be charged on the property, in many cases debts must be met by charges on the estate, generally by arrangement between father and son when the property is re-settled; the result is that charges gradually accumulate, and it is well recognised that few except the very largest properties will bear the burthens of this nature for two or three successive generations, unless marriage of the heir brings accession of wealth, or unless the property improves greatly in value from some adventitious circumstance; and it may be doubted whether in the long run more families are not ruined and

Dangers of Entail. brought down by such arrangements than are perpetuated and enriched by them.

The effect of these accumulating charges upon the condition of the property itself will shortly be alluded to; meanwhile it must be pointed out that the family settlement involves evils of no small magnitude to the family itself. It deprives the parent of the greater part of his parental control over his eldest son; the son is placed in a position independent of his father, almost superior to him, for nothing can be done to the estate without the son's consent; however unworthy he may prove to be, the property must descend to him; the father has no power of selection or veto; and no doubt many a father has had reason to curse the family arrangement under which his property is settled upon one who is unworthy to succeed him.

There are other causes at work which tend to a constant reduction in the number of small owners, and which add to the inducement to persons to enrol themselves in the list of great landowners, and retard their retirement from the rank by sale or otherwise. They are, however, closely allied to that which has been already pointed out, and it is difficult to determine whether they are not effects rather than causes of the system. Chief among them is the great political power which has been, for the last 200 years, conceded to the owners of landed property. One branch of the legislature has been wholly created from their ranks. A large

FREEDOM OF LAND. 189

landed property is admittedly the necessary quali- Dangers of Entail.
fication for a peerage; this rank is almost conceded
to an owner of over 20,000 acres. The English
county representation in the House of Commons is
also wholly at the command of the landowners.
They rarely look beyond their own ranks or beyond
their own county for a representative. The owner of
a certain standard number of acres, if of the right
side of politics, is almost certain of representing
his county. This command over the county representation is mainly secured through the tenant
farmers. It is also the passport not only to honours
of all kinds, but to political office, and to state
patronage. The local government of the rural
districts is wholly in the hands of the landowners;
the county magistracy is their recognised appanage.
The sports of country life are such as almost to necessitate large properties, and could not be so fully
indulged in if there were many small proprietors.

The sense of power created by the possession of
a large estate in a rural district is also great, and
is generally opposed to the existence of small ownerships within its range. Opportunities, therefore,
are seldom neglected of buying up smaller properties
where they are likely to interfere with this power.

In the neighbourhood of large towns, where
land has attained a building value, these forces
are counteracted by the personal interest of the
owners, tempted by high prices; special facilities
have been given to the owners of settled estates

<small>Dangers of Entail.</small> to avail themselves of this great demand for building land. But in rural districts there is no such counteracting influence.

While then, on the one hand, all these forces promote the creation and increase of large properties, on the other hand the difficulties of title in our most complicated system of land laws, and the consequent expense of transfer, and the cost of our system of mortgage, tell with infinitely greater effect upon small properties than on large, and act as a great discouragement to their purchase or continued existence. This is what Lord Hatherley said on this subject in 1859 :—

"Look how the limitations of your law affect the transfer of land. It is only on account of these that you have difficulties in title; because, if it were not for the complexity of limitations, a system of registration would long since have been established, which so far as fraud and rapidity of transfer was concerned would have freed us from any difficulty of title whatever. You have now the combined effect of fraud and the complicated investigations of title which operate in the most serious manner to prevent the free transfer of land in our community; what I wish for, and have long wished for, is a free transfer of land."

All other experience tends to show that a cheap and simple system of registration of title and mortgages is an essential condition of the existence of small properties.

On the one hand, therefore, we have every encouragement given by law, and by political and social arrangements, to the concentration of land in few hands; and on the other, every discouragement given to its purchase, and to dealing with it in small quantities, and by small people. What wonder then that we should find the number of proprietors continually diminishing, and that England presents an exception so striking to the rest of the civilised world.

Dangers of Entail.

RESULTS OF THE SYSTEM IN IRELAND.

The most serious effects of the system thus described have been exhibited in Ireland; and it is well to pass them under review, although the case of Ireland is very different from that of England and far more serious.

Results of the System in Ireland.

It has already been shown that the number of landowners in Ireland is proportionably far less than in England. The difference is even more striking than that already pointed out if we compare the number of small proprietors in the rural districts of both countries.

The three agricultural counties, Bedfordshire, Berkshire, and Buckinghamshire, with an area of 1,173,000 acres, may be fairly compared with the Irish counties Meath, Westmeath, and Cavan, with an area of 1,360,000 acres. In the English counties there are 6,412 owners of between 1 and

<small>Results of the System in Ireland.</small> 50 acres. In the Irish counties with a larger area there are only 612 such owners.

Or if we take the mountainous districts of Northumberland and Westmoreland, with an area of 1,736,000 acres, and compare them with Galway and Mayo, whose area is 2,760,000 acres, we find in the former 3,003 owners of small properties, in the latter only 225 such owners. It appears then that as compared with England, Ireland has less than one-tenth the number of small owners.

The difference between the two countries is the more remarkable as, whatever may be the case in England, it is certain that in Ireland land has not acquired an artificial value. The price of land in Ireland is very much below that of England; it does not average more than twenty-two years' purchase of the annual rental, and has only reached even this point within the last few years. At this rate money may be invested in land in Ireland to pay about $4\frac{1}{2}$ per cent.

The explanation of this great difference in the number of landowners in Ireland, is to be found in the early history of that country, in the fact that it never passed through the feudal system, that it was not thoroughly conquered by England until the feudal system had already disappeared from the latter. Under the feudal system, the occupiers of land in Ireland, who held under ancient customs which gave them an interest in the soil from which they could not be dispossessed, would most probably have obtained the same recognition and fixity of tenure as did the villeins or copyholders in England. The later English law treated them on the Conquest as mere tenants at will of those who acquired by grant the land of the dispossessed lords of the soil.

Results of the System in Ireland.

In later years the position was still further aggravated by the penal laws directed against the Roman Catholics which forbade their inheriting or acquiring land by purchase. When, added to these, we have the English land system tending to the aggregation of land, and offering every obstacle to its dispersion or easy transfer, we can well account for the paucity of landowners in Ireland; and for the fact that even when compared with England their number is so very limited.

None of the justifications which are claimed for the system of England apply to Ireland. The same laws and the same system has achieved results in the two countries as different as possible. England is in the main a country of large landowners and of large farm holdings. Ireland is a country, proportionally of even larger landowners, but of very small farm holdings. Of its 533,000 farm tenancies, 450,000 are of less than 50 acres, and 50,000 between 50 acres and 100 acres. It is, therefore, essentially a country of peasant cultivators. In England the custom is for the landowner to effect all the substantial improvements on the farm; to build the farm-houses and other buildings, to drain and fence the land. In Ireland the landlord as a general rule does none of these. It is the tenant who lays out what little capital is spent in this way, even to the building of the house. He does this under a tenancy which is rarely more than a yearly holding.

<small>Results of the System in Ireland.</small>

The condition of Ireland is still more remarkable, when we consider that all experience from the Continent shows that farming on a small scale can only answer when largely combined with ownership; that it is the magic of ownership only which gives the inducement to the industry necessary for very small farms. Being a country of small farms, it is free from the argument that large properties are necessary in order that farming may be carried out on a large scale. It is equally free from the argument that large properties are economically advantageous, as they result in capital being invested in the land by the owner, and in tenants being able to use the whole of their capital in farming. Here then, of all places in the world, one would expect to find a large class of small owners. Apart from the recent sales under the Irish Church Act, there are none. There are all the conditions of a peasant proprietary, without any proprietary rights, or any fixity of tenure. The condition of Ireland before the famine of 1848 closely resembled the condition of France as described by Arthur Young, immediately before the Revolution of 1789. On the one hand, a pauperised tenant class; and on the other great properties encumbered to a degree which made the owners mere ciphers in the hands of their creditors. This state of things was brought to a crisis by the potato famine. The consequent emigration relieved Ireland of its plethora of cottier tenants. The effort made by the imperial legislature was first directed to freeing property from its encumbrances; and the Encumbered Estates Court was brought into existence for the purpose of cutting the knots of these tangled interests in landed estates, and enabling them to be sold. It was believed and hoped that the land, thus freed from its bankrupt owners, would pass into the hands of capitalists, who would improve its condition by expending capital in buildings, drainage, &c. It is reckoned that one-fifth of the landed property of Ireland has passed through this Court, has changed hands, and the number of owners of such land has probably been increased threefold. Those however who devised this measure reckoned without taking into consideration Irish feelings and Irish customs. With rare exceptions, the new owners spent no more capital on the land than did their easy-going predecessors. When they attempted to improve, the tenants often resented the process. It was an assertion of complete ownership which did not tally with the ideas of Irish tenants, of their relations to their landlords. Whatever the English law

Results of the System in Ireland.

Results of the System in Ireland. might be, the traditions, customs, and ideas of Irish tenants involved a relation to their landlords far different from that which holds in England; they claimed a participation in the proprietary rights, which was in fact conceded to them by custom, and which prevented the lords of the soil from ejecting them without good cause, arbitrarily raising rents, or appropriating, in the shape of increased rent, the value of the tenants' improvements. The new purchasers entered upon their properties without any of these traditional feelings, without any sympathy for their tenants, without any knowledge of local customs, or hereditary practices. They too frequently applied to their new purchases the most extreme doctrines of proprietorship; they thought they were entitled to raise rents to the highest rack-rental that could be extracted, regardless of the previous history of the estate, or of the customs of the country.

It cannot be denied that many cases of great hardship and injustice arose to Irish tenants. What was intended for their benefit resulted not unfrequently in their ruin.

The result therefore of the Encumbered Estates Act was to intensify the demand for the recognition of tenant right, and to give a great impulse to political agitation in favour of fixity of tenure. England at last turned an ear to Irish grievances, and the Land Act of 1870 was framed, on the principle of applying to the Irish land question so much of Irish ideas as was not wholly incompatible with English doctrines. <small>Results of the System in Ireland.</small>

It gave legal recognition for the first time to local customs such as the Ulster Tenant Right, which had created a practical property in the tenant. It reversed the doctrine of English law, that improvements of all kinds are annexed absolutely to the land, and in default of actual agreement enure wholly to the benefit of the landlord. It recognised the fact that in the case of tenants of small farms there could be such a thing as an arbitrary and capricious ejectment, and it gave to the tenant, who was ejected, a claim for any improvements effected, and damages for capricious ejectment. It did not, however, go the length of interfering between landlord and tenant as to the amount of rent. It left to the landlord the power of raising the rent to a point, when the rent would practically swallow up the value of the tenant's improvements, but it left to the tenant the option of refusing this rent, of throwing up his farm, and of making his claim for the value of his improvements and for disturbance of the tenancy, to which he would be entitled.

It is unnecessary to pursue further the question of tenant right or the relations of Irish landlords and tenants; it is, however, important to notice the impulse given by the state to the extension of proprietorship in substitution for tenancy, and to the creation of a class of peasant

Results of the System in Ireland. proprietors, where none such existed previously. The framers of the Irish Land Act, and of the Church Disestablishment Act, under the influence and impulse mainly of Mr. Bright, recognised the grave deficiency of proprietary rights in Ireland, and the expediency of endeavouring to increase the number of proprietors, and of converting where possible, by agreement or purchase, tenants into owners. This might indeed be deemed an alternative process to that of fixity of tenure demanded by the tenants. It was, at all events, though novel in its application as a remedy, in harmony with the ideas of English law and English proprietors. However unwilling Parliament might be to adopt any such plan in England, Ireland, it thought, might be an exception without raising any precedent dangerous to the principle of property.

The proposals in this direction met with no opposition in either branch of the Legislature. It is also worthy of notice that the first attempt to extend proprietary rights followed the example of France and Prussia. It was the secularisation of Church property which gave the opportunity for first experimenting in this direction. It was probably felt that to sell the landed property of the Irish Church in the open market was to risk its falling into the hands of persons who would capriciously and arbitrarily raise rents; and it was thought not only fair to offer such land in the first instance to its tenants, but that the result of increasing the number of proprietors would be a gain to the cause of property in Ireland. The Irish Church Act, therefore, directed the Commissioners charged with the sale of Church lands to give preference to the tenants, and to charge the land sold to them with the repayment of three-fourths of the purchase-money by instalments spread over thirty-two years. *Results of the System in Ireland.*

The intentions of Parliament were admirably carried out by the Irish Church Commissioners. They have earned the gratitude of the Irish people by pointing the road where it is possible much further progress may hereafter · be made. They might have obstructed the policy of Parliament, or they might have neglected to make it known to the tenants. They have, on the contrary, used their endeavours to make the policy of Parliament intelligible and acceptable to the tenants.

Under this operation nearly 5,000 tenants of the Church property, of the smallest class, have found one-fourth of the purchase-money for their farms, and have become absolute owners in lieu of tenants; for thirty-two years they will be responsible for annual instalments of the principal and interest of the remainder of the purchase-money, which are about equivalent to their former rent. It is in evidence that these new purchasers have paid their interest with regularity and without fail, and that many of them have already been induced to effect great improvements on

<small>Results of the System in Ireland.</small> their holdings, the result of the feeling of security created by absolute ownership in place of yearly tenancy.

The Irish Land Act contained provisions known as "the Bright Clauses" in the same direction, and with the same object, that of creating a proprietary class among the peasant farmers of Ireland. Under these clauses the State undertakes to lend two-thirds of the purchase-money of any farm sold to a tenant, repayable, as in the case of the Church property, by instalments spread over a term of years. The Landed Estates Court (the successor of the Encumbered Estates Court), is directed by the Act to afford facilities to tenants to purchase their holdings, when estates are sold in that Court, and various other provisions are contained with the same object. Hitherto, however, but little result has followed. In the eight years which have elapsed since the passing of the Act, not more than 100 sales have been effected to tenants in each year under its provisions,—a result which, whether compared with the results of the Irish Church Act, or with the intention and wishes of the Legislature, is certainly most inadequate.

The attention of Parliament has recently been directed to the failure of the Act of 1871. A Committee was appointed in the session of 1877, to inquire into the working of the Bright clauses, and to report whether any further facilities should be given to promote the purchase of their holdings by the occupying tenants of Ireland. After taking evidence of numerous witnesses, the Committee reported in the session of 1878. Its members unanimously agreed to the expression of opinion that there is a great desire on the part of the occupying tenants to become owners by purchase, on sale of properties in Ireland, and that it is most desirable that further facilities should be accorded by the State with this object. There were differences in the Committee as to the mode in which this object should be carried out, but there was none as to the principle. In the past session (1879) a resolution was proposed in the House of Commons, and was carried without opposition and with the consent of the Government, to the effect that "in view of the expediency of a considerable increase in the number of owners of land in Ireland among the class of persons cultivating its soil, legislation should be adopted for the purpose of increasing the facilities offered by the State with this object, and of securing to the tenants the opportunity of purchase on the sale of property consistently with the interests of the owners thereof." A stronger resolution condemning the condition of landownership in Ireland, or more emphatically declaring the duty of the State to adopt effective measures for remedying this condition, could not easily be framed. It is certain therefore that the Government must speedily propose to Parliament some measure with this object.

Results of the System in Ireland.

The evidence given before the Committee on this

Results of the System in Ireland. subject in 1877-78 is eminently worthy of attention, as showing the great obstacles which the land system opposes to the purchase and ownership of land by the peasant cultivators of Ireland. It shows that as a rule the tenants are most desirous of becoming owners by purchase of their holdings, that they often give for the mere right of occupancy sums which are not much less than the value of the fee-simple of the land; that they are ready to give more than the average price given by outsiders; but that as a rule they never have or can have the opportunity of purchase. The cost of title, the difficulties of conveyance, and the delay and trouble to both vendor and purchaser, absolutely preclude the possibility of any separate transaction of sale as between landlord and tenant, for the purpose of taking advantage of the Act, however much either of them, or both, may wish it.

It was admitted by the officials of the Landed Estates Court, and by every witness examined before the Committee, that a single tenancy will never bear the cost of investigation of title, and that therefore sales by agreement to single farmers, with the object of carrying out the Act, were almost impossible. "A single tenancy," says Mr. McDonnell, one of the examiners of the Court, " will not bear the cost of the investigation of title; a gentleman is offered 2,000l. for a tenant's farm, and he would have to pay 200l. for the cost of showing title to it.

The smallest property cannot be passed through

the Court for a less cost than 100*l.* A small hold-ing of 10 acres is not worth more than 250*l.* The costs of the transfer would swallow up forty per cent. of the purchase-money. Results of the System in Ireland.

The only chance which the tenants have of becoming purchasers is where a whole estate is sold, and the lots can be so arranged as to enable the tenants to bid, and purchase either separately or jointly. The costs in such case are distributed over the property, and little extra cost is incurred by selling in smaller lots.

The importance of this evidence is the light it throws upon our system of land transfer, and the grave obstacle presented to any purchaser of a small holding. Landlord and tenant may be desirous of effecting the sale, but the costs of investigation of title make the transaction hopeless and impossible. Who can say, with this light thrown upon it, that the present state of landownership is the result of purely economic laws? With such difficulties opposed to the creation of small owners, what must not be the difficulties incurred by the small owner when brought into existence? Every dealing with his property is fraught with the expense and delay of a system the most antiquated and absurd. He cannot mortgage his property without great expense. The whole of our laws of inheritance and transfer are wholly unsuitable to small owners. Having called into existence a class of small owners, there is urgent need that the laws should

Results of the System in Ireland. be made suitable for their continued existence, and such as will enable them to deal with their land in a manner to prevent its being a burthen and expense to them.

Looking back to 1848, when the Imperial Parliament devised means for encumbered landowners to sell their properties, what might not have been the result by this time, if advantage had then been taken to promote the sale of such properties to their tenants? Many thousands of tenants might have been added to the class of owners of land by this process; and who can doubt what would be the result of such an accession to the class of persons permanently interested in the soil of their native country? The opportunity has been lost, but with our experience of the last eight years of what has been done under the Irish Church Act and the Land Act, it is still possible in the future to do much. Who can say that, with such experience, the creation of a class of peasant proprietors in Ireland is a mere dream? What has been achieved may be but the commencement of a new policy which shall favour the spread or creation of ownership rather than tenancy. Can it be doubted that good results would follow the creation of such a class in Ireland? Who can look at the state of ownership of landed property in that island without feeling how insecure is its basis--how limited is the class of persons who are interested in its rights? What would not be the advantage to

Ireland, if of its 550,000 peasant farmers, a fair proportion were owners as well as occupiers? They would be an element of security both in the political and social system. They would exercise a powerful influence in promoting industry and thrift. They would raise the standard of production. They would supply the step of the ladder by which the lowest might hope to arrive at the position of landowners. Is it possible to suppose that such a result is beyond the reach of political effort? The success of the experiment in the sale of Church lands forbids a negative to the answer, and raises every hope for further success in a direction so full of promise to Ireland.

<small>Results of the System in Ireland.</small>

It will be said, perhaps, in answer to this, that the economic condition of small farms is unsound —that a greater net produce would result, and a higher rent to the landlord, if a number of these small farms were thrown into one, and their tenants, with one exception, turned into day labourers. Whether this economic result would be produced is a matter open to doubt. In the opinion of many, small owners will hold their own in production against large farms. But even if it were not so, it may be confidently asked, whether any one would contemplate with pleasure the conversion of every twenty small Irish farms of fifteen acres each into large farms of 300 acres? Is the condition of the English labourer such that the Irish small farmer would envy his lot? Which is the

<small>Results of the System in Ireland.</small> superior in general status in the world? Which has the pleasanter lot and the better hope for the future? Which is the best member of society? Which has the best opportunity of rising?

Whatever, however, English economists and theorists may think upon the subject of small farms *versus* large farms, and small proprietors *versus* large proprietors, it will be impossible to persuade the Irish tenants to any other than one conclusion. Their instinct and their traditions are opposed to any conversion of small farmers into day labourers. There remains therefore the only alternative, to increase the productive power of the small farmers by offering to them the opportunity of converting themselves by purchase into owners, wherever this can be done without injury to the rights of property; and by throwing the influence, weight, and sanction of the State in favour of a widely-diffused ownership of land, as opposed to the opposite system which has been at work in Ireland since its subjection to the rule and law of England.

RESULTS OF THE SYSTEM IN ENGLAND.

<small>Results of the System in England.</small> The same laws with respect to inheritance and entail have led to the same general result as in Ireland in the distribution of landed property, although the circumstances of its early history were more favourable in England to the creation of small proprietors, who have not wholly dis-

appeared in some rural districts. It is admitted, however, that even these are destined to be merged in their larger neighbours under the present system. Results of the System in England.

A wholly different system, however, has prevailed in England as regards the management of landed property and the distribution of land among the tenants. It has been shown that Ireland is a country of peasant farmers, where the landlords do nothing as a general rule towards the improvement of the farms. In comparison, England is a country of large farms, and the custom is for all improvements to be effected by the landlord and not by the tenant.

It must not, however, be concluded that England is wholly a country of large farms. There are large numbers of small holdings. According to the Agricultural Returns, of 37,000,000 acres of land, 27,000,000 are cultivated and improved, the rest being mountain, heath, commons, woods, &c. The cultivated land may be thus divided into four classes of holdings :—

	Numbers.	Average in acres.	Total acreage.
Small holdings below 50 acres	333,630	12	4,181,346
Small farms from 50 to 100 acres	54,498	72	3,957,989
Medium-sized farms from 100 to 300 acres	65,766	170	11,183,618
Large farms above 300 acres	16,106	472	7,512,972
	470,000		26,835,925

Results of the System in England.

The number of agricultural labourers and shepherds is stated to be 787,897. It will be seen from this table that England is by no means so fully the country of large farms as it is often represented to be. About one-third of its area is held in small holdings and small farms, numbering about 388,000, and two-thirds in large farms, numbering about 82,000. How many of the small farms and holdings are owned by their cultivators we have no means of knowing; it is believed the number is very small, and is being gradually reduced. In lieu we have an admitted tendency to substitute for ownership the relation of landlord and tenant. How far then does this relationship satisfy the economic conditions for the best cultivation of the soil, and what are its effects upon the various classes of the community?

The ideal of the English system of large proprietors and of tenants hiring the land they farm in lieu of owning it, is where the landlord, being a capitalist, is able to relieve the tenant of all expenditure of a permanent character, and to leave him the full employment of his capital in his trade of farming, in stocking and cultivating the land. This ideal involves a considerable expenditure on the part of the landlord, in building farm-houses and farm-buildings, in draining and other permanent improvements, and in building labourers' cottages. If these functions are performed by the landlord, if he has the capital to expend and does what is recognised as a duty, nothing can be better from the economic point of view than the condition of the property and the relation of landlord, tenant, and labourer. {Results of the System in England.}

The farms in such a case are parcelled out in the size which is most suitable to the full development of the soil; the necessary capital of a permanent character is expended by the landlord; the capital of the tenant is set free to stock and cultivate the farm to the best advantage; the tenant, in order to pay full rent upon the capital laid out, must exert himself to the best of his efforts; if he prove a slovenly farmer, the landlord gets rid of him.

The labourers' cottages are built with due regard to the requirements of the property. Some of them are attached to the farm for the convenience of the tenant, who wishes for full control of those labourers who are most necessary to him; others are retained in possession of the landlord, that too much power over the labourers may not be vested in the farmer. The labourers themselves are stimulated to work by the certainty that they will lose their homes if negligent and idle.

From an economic point of view, then, the agricultural machine in which the landlord, farmer, and labourer play their respective parts, and the land, capital, and wages have their share in the produce, works to the best advantage. That there are many such cases no one can deny. That many landlords most fully recognise their duties, and act fully up

Results of the System in England.

to the highest ideal, cannot be doubted. Many, indeed, pinch themselves in other expenditure in order to perform their duty; and few there are who would not do it if they could.

If all estates were maintained up to this ideal, there would be little to say against the system from the economic point of view; though even then there might be something to allege in favour of more distributed ownership, and more independence of individuals, especially of the labourers, than is consistent with such an ideal system.

The whole system, however, depends upon the owner of the property being able to provide the capital for permanent improvements, such as buildings, drainage, and labourers' cottages. If this capital be not forthcoming the system breaks down at its central point, on which the economic success of the whole system hinges. If the landlord cannot provide the necessary capital for these permanent improvements, no one else will do so. The farming tenant cannot be expected to do so upon any length of lease which is ordinarily given to him, and still less can the labourer be expected to build or improve his cottage.

It has already been shown that it is of the essence of such family arrangements known as settlements and entails that they lead to encumbrances. The land goes to the eldest son, perhaps free from charge in the first instance; the personalty is divided among the other members of the family. In the next generation, however, the land must be charged for the benefit of other members of the family.

Results of the System in England.

It is also well recognised that the owner of a landed estate cannot do full justice to it, unless he is able to draw upon other property for its improvement. Sir Robert Peel used to say that every landowner ought to have at least as much property in consols or other securities, if he wished to do his best by the land. The meaning of this is, that there is a constant drain upon the landlord for fresh outlay for improvements or for the maintenance of previous improvements, if the machine is to be well worked.

What, however, is the condition in this respect of the average landowner? How many of them have other means in this proportion to their land? How many are unencumbered as regards their family estates? How many of them are able to do their duty by the land?

It is certain that the greater number of them are utterly unable to perform their duties. They are the ostensible and temporary owners of family estates, for the most part already heavily charged with debts, or with charges for other members of the family, and wholly unable to expend further sums in draining and improving, still less in building cottages, which at best give but a poor return on the outlay.

P 2

Results of the System in England. Most of them are in this false position, that as tenants for life only of their property they cannot expend capital on their estates without subjecting the money thus spent to the same entail as the estates themselves. The limited owners thus have the alternative before them either of neglecting their properties, or of spending money upon them which they would otherwise intend for their younger children, to the ultimate benefit of their eldest sons, who are already entitled to the estates. If such persons were absolute owners of their property, and without other means of improvement, they would probably be induced to sell outlying parts of the property, and invest the proceeds in draining and improving the main portion of the estate. They would gain in income by doing so. The investment in land, we are told, produces an average of only two per cent.; the produce of a sale if spent on drainage would entitle the owner to raise his rents so as to pay five per cent. or more on the outlay. But he is tenant for life only, and he can only sell with the consent of trustees and reversioners, to re-invest in other land, or to pay off mortgages.

Is it possible to conceive a system better calculated to prevent capital finding its way to the land? That it has this result can scarcely be doubted. This is what Mr. Caird said a few years ago on the subject in his *Agricultural Survey of England*:—" Much of the land of England, a far greater proportion of it than is generally believed, is in the possession of tenants for life, so heavily burthened with settlement encumbrances that they have not the means of improving the land which they are obliged to hold. It would be a waste of time to dilate on the public and private disadvantages thus occasioned, for they are acknowledged by all who have studied the subject." *Results of the System in England.*

A Committee of the House of Lords in 1873 upon the improvement of land, reported, that what had already been accomplished in the way of drainage and other improvements was "only a fraction of what still remained to be done."

Mr. Bailey Denton stated before this Committee, as the result of his calculations, that out of 20,000,000 acres of land requiring drainage in England and Ireland, only 3,000,000 had as yet been drained. Mr. Caird, before the same Committee, speaking not only of drainage, but of all kinds of improvements, estimated that only one-fifth of what required to be done was accomplished.

The improvements thus spoken of are of a remunerative kind; improvements such as drainage and farm-buildings are generally paid for by an increase of rent fully compensating for the outlay. Unfortunately, however, the building of labourers' cottages by landlords is a most unremunerative expenditure. It seldom returns more than two per cent. on the outlay, very often less. If, therefore, we find the outlay of capital for

Results of the System in England.

remunerative improvements very much in arrear, it is only too certain that it will be far worse in the case of cottages.

The Report of the Royal Commission of 1869, as to the condition of women and children employed in agriculture, contains the most full information on this subject. The evidence was collected by Assistant Commissioners who visited every part of the rural districts of England, and who are unanimous in their testimony.

Mr. Fraser, now Bishop of Manchester, who visited Norfolk, Essex, Gloucestershire, and Sussex, describes the cottages in one district as "miserable;" in a second as "deplorable;" in a third as "detestable;" in a fourth as "a disgrace to a Christian community." He says that "even where adequate in quality, they are inadequate in quantity; and some rich landowner, 'lord of all he surveys,' having exercised his lordship by evicting so much of his population as were an eyesore, or were likely to become a burthen to him—still employing their labour, but holding himself irresponsible for their domicile—has, by a most imperfect system of compensation, built a limited number of ornamental roomy cottages, which he fills with his own immediate dependents. Out of the 300 parishes which I visited I can only remember two where the cottage accommodation appeared to be both admirable in quality and sufficient in quantity. The majority of the cottages that exist in rural parishes are deficient in almost every requisite that should constitute a home for a Christian family in a civilised community. It is impossible," he adds, "to exaggerate the ill-effects of such a state of things in every respect—physical, social, economical, moral, intellectual. Physically a ruinous ill-drained cottage, 'cribbed, cabin'd, confined,' and overcrowded, generates any amount of disease —fevers of every type, catarrh, rheumatism—as well as intensifies to the utmost that tendency to scrofula and phthisis, which, from their frequent intermarriages and their low diet, abounds so largely among the poor. Economically, the imperfect distribution of cottages deprives the farmer of a large proportion of his effective labour power; when he gets his man, he gets him more or less enfeebled by the distance he has to travel to his work. The moral consequences are fearful to contemplate. Modesty must be an unknown virtue, decency an imaginable thing, where in one small chamber two, and sometimes three, generations are herded promiscuously, and where the whole atmosphere is sensual, and human nature is degraded into something below the level of the swine. It is a hideous picture, and the picture is drawn from the life."

Results of the System in England.

As to the deficiency of cottages, he mentions the parish of Spixworth, where "there are only three cottages to 1,200 acres, there might well be twenty-five; at Waterdon only two cottages to

<small>Results of the System in England.</small>

750 acres, fifteen would be no excessive supply; at Markshall only five to 830 acres, at the usual Essex rate there should be 25. At Buckenham Tofts there are only two resident labourers on 650 acres; at Didlington no more on 1,850 acres. At Sedgeford the Ecclesiastical Commissioners have an estate of 2,000 acres without a single cottage, and in this parish we hear of ten and eleven persons sleeping in a single room. At Titchwell, Magdalene College, Oxford, the chief owner and lord of the manor, has not a single cottage. At White Colne, in Essex, the chief landowner has not one either." "Instances," he adds, "of this kind could be accumulated *ad infinitum.*"

The Bishop recognised that a great deal had been done of late years, especially by the largest landowners. Unfortunately, however, the remedy did not rest with the wealthiest landowners. Many cottages belonged to proprietors too indigent to have any money to spare for their improvement; some to absentee and embarrassed landowners; some to mortgagees. Mr. Portman, another Assistant Commissioner, who reported upon Cambridgeshire and Yorkshire, says, " The opinion appeared to be universal that the bad state of the cottages and the overcrowding of the sleeping-rooms is the root of the demoralization of both sexes." He states that "one of the principal causes is 'absenteeism,' under which I include not merely non-residence of the owner in the county where his estate is situated, but that which is equally bad, viz., non-attention to the outlying portions of that estate. On many occasions when, being struck by the poor state of the dwellings, I have inquired who is the owner, I have been told he is some one living perhaps in the county, but rarely, if ever, visiting the village or taking any heed as to the condition of the people." Of one very large property he reports, "The tenements are wretched; although the rents paid are small, the whole repairs have to be done by the cottagers, and so the rents become in fact very high; and as one of them told me, 'The landlord does not care if they all tumble down.' On other portions of this estate there was a great want of cottages, many having been pulled down and scarcely a new one built." Of another parish in Wales he says, "No Irish property can present more wretched consequences of absenteeism than this. The only consideration the parish receives from the owners of property is the regular collection of rents." The statement of Mr. Portman as to absenteeism is important as confirming what has been already stated as to the number of parishes without resident landowners.

Mr. Edward Stanhope, now Under-Secretary of the India Office, reports also as to the general bad state of cottages, though making many exceptions, especially in Lincolnshire, the county where it may be observed small peasant owners most abound. Of Leicestershire he says, "The cottages must be

Results of the System in England.

<small>Results of the System in England.</small> described as generally bad." He adds, "There is a strong feeling in Lincolnshire that Government should give assistance in providing cottages for the labouring class, and especially on entailed estates."

Mr. Culley, another of the Assistant Commissioners, says, " There constantly arises to me, and, I doubt, not, to my colleagues, the feeling that in speaking of that state of the cottages, I am exhibiting a dark picture, as if it was the fault of a class, many of whom are powerless to change it, and few of whom are answerable for it."

"What has led to the state of the labourers' dwellings being such as to justify me in speaking of it as a national disgrace? And why are so many landowners now powerless to deal with it? If I were to answer these questions, judging from the history of the estates I have visited, I would answer at once—the encouragement given by law to the creation of limited interests in land, and the power of entailing burthened estates. What can the poor life-tenant, especially if his estates be burthened, do towards providing good cottages for his labourers? Nine times out of ten he strives to do his duty, and suffers fully as much as the ill-housed labourers on his estates. The unhappy propensity to create limited interests, and entailed and burthened estates, tells hardest against the small properties, while if the owner lives as all the world expects him to live, there is no margin left for estate improvement, especially cottage improvement. Even the large estates, by the time all is done for which farm tenants most loudly call, unless burthens be light or the owner unusually self-denying, there is very little left to expend in the expensive luxury of cottage building. The case of small estates, however, is the worst, and in spite of the supposed protection of the law of entail, they are being swallowed up by their larger neighbours, or passing into the hands of men whose sole means are not invested in land."

Results of the System in England.

Mr. Portman says upon the same subject, " I would venture to suggest, for your consideration, whether it is not expedient that legislation should take place in such a direction, as to bring into the market those tracts of encumbered land, enabling those who have capital to acquire such lands if they desire to do so, and conferring a boon on those who now possess them by giving them money to spend on such an amount of territory as they wish to concentrate round their homes, while at the time the curse of poverty and misery will be removed from these districts whence all the profit is drawn and to which none returns. Bad cottages would, I think, then become more rare ; a portion at least of the profits would be spent on the spot, a more contented race of farmers and of labourers would be found, and the education of the people, now flagging for want of funds, would progress. Some may say that this question of the dwellings of the

Results of the System in England.

poor in agricultural districts is a passing question of the hour, and that it is not really so great an evil as is represented. I would answer, Go into the country and see for yourself. Use your common sense, and call to mind the effect of absenteeism on Ireland; and say whether or not in those portions of England where poverty and misery arising from the same cause meet you at every step, there is not urgent reason for dealing with the evils now existing by some legislative enactment, which shall put an end to a state of apathy and indifference in many holders of encumbered estates, and open the doors for the spending of capital on lands by those who are able, in the place of those who are now unable, to do so."

It is only fair to add, that it is not only upon entailed properties that cottages are bad. Some of the worst cases are to be found on land which has been bought by speculators, and whole rows of cottages have been built of the most flimsy material with insufficient accommodation, without gardens, and which are let at exorbitant rents. Most of these cases have arisen in what are called open parishes, adjoining those close parishes where, before the alteration of the law which threw the burthen of the support of the poor upon the whole Union, it was the interest of landowners to neglect to provide cottages, or to pull down existing cottages, in order to avoid giving to the labourers a claim for settlement, which would throw the cost of maintaining them, when paupers, upon such parishes. *Results of the System in England.*

The Census of 1861 showed that in the previous ten years, in 821 English parishes, a decrease of houses was accompanied by an increase of population. The last census shows that this action has been stayed by the Union Chargeability Act, but there was nothing in the Act to undo the mischief which had already been effected.

Other bad cases are not rare, where cottages have been built upon patches of land cribbed from the waste of a manor, or roadside waste, and which the labouring occupiers claim as their own; these, however, are hardly fair cases of individual ownership.

Let it not also be said that all landowners are to blame for this state of things. Nothing could be more unfair. If they were absolute owners of their property, with power to sell or to charge their properties as they might wish, there would indeed be ground for complaint if such a state of things were allowed to remain unredressed. But the system under which the great bulk of them hold their properties as mere nominal owners without real power over them, is devised with the certain result that it can never be their interest to expend money on cottages, and rarely in their power to do so.

Many efforts have been made by Parliament to find a remedy for these evils, short of interfering

Results of the System in England.
with entails or simplifying the transfer of land. The tenant for life (the limited owner, as he is very significantly called) had originally no power to bind his successor, either by leases or by charges on the property for its improvement. Parliament, however, has interfered to give him these powers, subject to the approval of public bodies, who are to have regard to the interests of the reversioner.

Short leases for agricultural purposes can now be given by tenants for life. Longer leases can be given with the consent of the Court of Chancery. Charges can be made on the entailed property for certain improvements with the consent of the Inclosure Commissioners. The charge, however, must be made in such a way as to repay the principal by instalments in varying terms of years according to the nature of the improvement. The result is that drainage generally involves an annual charge of $7\frac{1}{2}$ per cent. on the outlay, as much or more than the tenant will pay in the shape of increased rent. The building of cottages involves an annual charge which averages three times the amount of the rent which can usually be obtained for them. Sales may also be effected upon applications to the courts of law, where there are no powers for this purpose contained in the settlement; but the consent of tenants for life and of reversioners must be obtained; the proceeds must be expended in paying off mortgages or in buying other land to be settled in the same manner, and can never be expended in agricultural improvements, however necessary. These, however, are mere palliatives, and not remedies. They have failed to effect any substantial result. They tend to substitute for the real owner of the property a Government department, a State inspector, or a judicial tribunal; they entail troublesome and expensive applications to courts of law and Government officials; they involve friction and delay. From their very nature they are destined to failure. The system, however, which needs such remedies stands condemned by their proposal, and, as the late Mr. Wren Hoskyns well said, "Wherever a series of supplementary devices is needed to meet a law at variance with the time, it indicates the undercurrent of another law struggling against worn-out barriers that will not long withstand it." *Results of the System in England.*

What is this other law, struggling against the worn-out system, which has thus signally failed to meet the demands of the country and the claims of the land for the outlay of capital? It is freedom of sale, the alienability of land, the free commerce of land; the principle that land shall be owned by those who can give full title for it, and who can either borrow for improvements or sell what they cannot improve; the principle that land shall belong to the present generation and not to an unborn generation; that landowners shall be full masters of their own property, and not be obliged to obtain the consent of the unborn for improve-

Results of the System in England. ments or sale, through the medium of courts of law and Government offices.

It must be here freely admitted, that some of the largest properties are exceptions to this general condemnation, both in respect of farm improvements, farm buildings, and labourers' cottages. Such properties as those of the Dukes of Bedford, Devonshire, and Northumberland, and others that could be named, are models of all that conscientious and intelligent landowners should aim at. It is obvious that as there is a limit to the possible personal expenditure of families with such great fortunes, the margin which is left for improvement of their properties must be greater in proportion than on smaller estates; it will generally be found also that these very great landed properties are supported by great incomes from other sources, such as house property or minerals. It is often argued from such examples, that the larger properties are, the better prospect there is of capital being expended on the land by their owners; and hence a conclusion that it is well to encourage the creation of large properties and to regard with indifference the disappearance of smaller properties. The argument, however, is a dangerous one; the logical conclusion of it is, that it might be well to merge all large proprietors into one still greater proprietor, namely, the State itself. If the State were sole and supreme landlord, it might spend all the rent in local improvements, in farm buildings and cottages; and in such a case the whole of the rent would remain on the land from which it is due. This is obviously a *reductio ad absurdum*, but it suggests to us the necessity for bearing in mind the principle on which alone private property in land exists and can be defended.

<small>Results of the System in England.</small>

If the English system fails in bringing to the land the capital which is so essential for its development, or for building cottages so necessary for the accommodation, comfort, and even decency of the labourer, what is its effect upon the labouring class? The failure to spend capital on the land to them means low wages; low wages and bad cottages combined means a poverty-stricken life, which tells upon the whole existence of the labourers.

It may be confidently said that the agricultural labourers are divorced from any permanent interest, however small, in the land, or even in the villages in which they live. With rare exceptions, it is impossible for them to become possessed of a plot of land or even of a cottage. The sense of property therefore never comes home to them.

Can we wonder, then, at the thriftless, hopeless, and aimless condition into which so large a proportion of them have drifted? The effect of the English system upon them may be best judged by the results in those counties in the south where it has been longest in existence, where it is carried out most fully, and where it is undisturbed by the growth of any adjoining industries; such counties

Results of the System in England.

as Sussex and Dorsetshire. Who can be satisfied with the condition of the agricultural labourers in these districts? or who can suggest any remedy consistent with the ideal of the present system? What hope for advancement is there in their own country? what prospect of rising from the lowest steps of the ladder to the higher? An impassable barrier separates the labourer from the farming class immediately above him, and a still wider gulf from the owner of land who crowns the social edifice. What wonder, then, that the labourers should be thriftless and without energy; that education only induces the best of them to leave the country districts for other employments, and that by a process of natural selection the average of those who remain is being gradually deteriorated?

This condition is not the result of a harsh Poor Law, nor of the want of charity. The Poor Law is in most agricultural districts administered with benevolence, and probably there is no other country where local endowments for the distribution of doles and charities, and where private charities, are so numerous and liberal. It is, however, confidently stated that in those parishes where charity is most frequent, where there are most endowments for the distribution of doles, where the clergy and squires, actuated by the best intentions, are most active in private charities, there the condition of the labourer is the most depressed, and the least satisfactory; and there *Results of the System in England.* also is least thrift, and least energy for self-help and independence; in too many of such parishes excessive charity has succeeded in undermining the self-help, thrift, and independence of the labourers, and has encouraged wastefulness and intemperance.

What then appears to be most needed in the agricultural districts of England is an element of independence, which can only be attained by the sense of property; and of all the means of giving this sense of property and this feeling of independence, the ownership of land, even though limited in extent, and the ownership of a house and home, with its garden, would be the most powerful and effective.

In what has been thus said, it is by no means intended to convey the expectation, promise, or even the hope, that England, under an altered system of law, will become a country of yeoman farmers or of peasant proprietors. In the main, and for such a period as any legislator can prospectively look forward to, it would be impossible to realize either of these subjects. England will certainly continue to be, as it has been in the past, a country in which there will be many large properties. Even if all landowners should have secured to them the full power to dispose of their property as they think fit among their children, it may be confidently expected that the great bulk of them will continue to leave the main portion to

Results of the System in England. their eldest sons; and it will be long before any custom of a different kind grows up in a country so essentially conservative. What we may look forward to is, a considerable increase in the number of landed proprietors of all classes, and especially of small owners. Without aiming at a system of ownership such as we see in France, and other countries organized on the same plan, it is not beyond reason to expect that some nearer approach may be made to the system which prevails in Germany, where, as already explained, although there are many large proprietors, there are also many small owners, where there is a large class of yeomen farmers, and where a very large proportion of the agricultural labourers are also owners of small holdings, varying from half an acre to five or six acres. Of the effect of this distributed ownership and this interest in the soil upon the labouring class generally, there cannot be doubt to any one who reads the reports from the countries where this prevails.

It is not too much to say that if landowners, who are unable to do justice to their properties, were empowered to sell, and should avail themselves of this power, in respect only of a small portion of their properties, a very great change might soon be effected in the state of landownership in England and Ireland, and the landowners themselves would be the first to benefit.

GENERAL CONCLUSIONS.

If then the arguments already adduced have any weight in them, the conclusions from them and the objects to be aimed at will not be doubtful. {General Conclusions.}

These are, that the distribution of ownership of land is such that it is held in amounts far beyond the average means of its holders to perform their duties according to the ideal of the English system, in the outlay of capital on it and the building of cottages; and that the most is not being made of the land as an incentive to individual exertion and as the most powerful agent for the promotion of individual industry and thrift.

It has also been shown, from experience drawn from every part of the world, equally from Europe as from countries of Anglo-Saxon descent, that land is not necessarily the luxury only of the rich, and that if it should be placed within the reach of other classes, and the means be given of dealing with it in a simple and expeditious manner, it will become the luxury of a much wider class, and indeed of all classes proportionate to their means. The same experience has also been gathered from recent experiments in Ireland. It has been shown that while in every part of the civilized world efforts have been made successfully to free land from the obstructions and impediments of an obsolete feudal system, to withdraw the sanction

General Conclusions.

of Law to its accumulation in few hands, and to place it, as far as is consistent with the rights of property, within the reach of all classes, and to promote its ownership by the many rather than the few, in this country little or nothing has been done in this direction; all the influence of the State and of society has been in favour of the concentration of land in few hands, our laws of tenure sanction and assist this, the system of transfer fosters it. It has been shown that as a result we have a state of landownership such as is almost unique in the civilized world.

The objects to be aimed at by any legislation are not novel or destructive; they are not opposed to the rights of property, but in support of them; they savour not of communism or socialism, but are on the lines of individualism; they seek to make the best of individual property, for all its functions, and in all its actions on the social system; they are such as other countries have pursued with success; they claim that the State has some control over its own destinies, some voice in the disposition of its area, and that society is not necessarily the sport of an economic law favouring only accumulation, which, however we may disapprove it, we are powerless to resist. The objects then to aim at, are a wider distribution of landed property, to the extent that it shall in the main be held by those who have the means of performing their duties, and that it shall be brought within the reach of all classes of the community according to their means. *General Conclusions.*

The means by which these objects may be attained may be summed up under the following heads :—

1. The withdrawal of the State sanction to the accumulation of land by the law of primogeniture.

2. The limitation of family settlements to the extent of prohibiting entails in the manner invented by Sir Orlando Bridgeman, by which property can be settled upon unborn persons, and a family law of primogeniture secured.

3. The requirement that there shall be for every property some person or persons who shall have full power of dealing with the property by sale or otherwise.

4. The assimilation of the law relating to land and other property, and the simplification of the law relating to land tenure, so that its transfer may become simple and inexpensive.

5. The withdrawal of all State influence and sanction in favour of accumulation of land, and the exercise of it in future in favour of a numerous proprietary of land, consistently with the full recognition of existing rights.

It can easily be shown that these measures hang together; and that the pivot of them all is the abolition of primogeniture.

(1.) By the abolition of primogeniture is meant the removal of the State sanction to an arrange-

<small>General Conclusions.</small> ment by which, in the absence of a will, property in land descends to the eldest son of the intestate to the exclusion of the other children, a law which seldom operates without producing injustice. It is not contemplated that the property shall be compulsorily divided among the children against the will of the parent. The freedom of willing would be retained and preserved; and any interference with it would, it is believed, be alien to the feelings of the great majority of Englishmen. It is only possible in France and other countries because, as already shown, the custom of equal division of property is so universal and so entwined in the feelings of the people, that it is scarcely possible for them to conceive an unequal distribution, and because public opinion considers that a parent who does not provide for all his children according to his means is neglectful of his parental duty. Where such is the public opinion compulsory division by law is possible; but that is very far from being the opinion of Englishmen in the existing social conditions of England, where historical and family traditions so largely affect the opinions and habits, not only of the wealthy, but of all classes, that it would be absurd to expect either that a custom of equal distribution would speedily grow up, or that a law compelling it would be acceptable. An historic family has to be maintained, an ancient residence in and about which the traditions of a family have centred has to be

preserved, the political institution of the peerage has to be regarded; these and many other causes will long sustain and probably justify the custom of making a difference in favour of eldest sons in many families; though possibly not to the extent which is now often the case. *General Conclusions.*

(2.) When it shall be determined that the law itself will not sanction or invite inequality, it will follow almost as a matter of course, that it must be forbidden to individuals to make a family law of succession different from that of the State. Freedom of willing will be permitted, and every person will be allowed to make what distinction he thinks right among his children or relatives, but he will not be permitted to transmit these distinctions to another unborn generation. If freedom of willing is conceded to him, he must not in his turn deprive the next generation of the same privilege. The freedom of willing is a part of the paternal authority, and no parent should be deprived of this power by an antecedent generation.

(3.) The last principle being decided on, the next one becomes easy of accomplishment. The distinction in favour of an unborn person being cut off and prohibited, it follows that the present generation must have more power over the property, and the power of sale is one of the first and most important attributes of property.

(4.) The two last principles are indispensable to the next, that of simplifying the transfer of land.

General Conclusions.

The main difficulty in the transfer of land arises out of the complications due to the law of settlement or entail; so long as these exist, and so long as ownership may be divided between the present and the future, between the living and the unborn, it is impossible to expect or to hope for simplicity of title. Even the late Lord St. Leonards has said that "no young State ought ever to be entangled in the complication of our law of real property."

Why then, it may be asked, should any old State maintain and preserve these entanglements? They are retained only because they are necessary for our present system of family settlements. It will be easy enough to get rid of these difficulties if we come to the conclusion that these entails are injurious equally to those who are the objects of them, and to the community.

(5.) But not less important than all these is it that the general influence of the State shall no longer be used in the direction of the accumulation of land. It is unnecessary to suggest the subjects where an opposite influence might be used, and where it will be possible for a very different policy to be pursued by Parliament than has hitherto been done.

The action taken under the Bright clauses in Ireland has already shown how it is possible with the unanimous consent of all parties to make a most important move in the direction of giving active assistance for the conversion of tenancies into ownerships. This particular method may not be applicable to England; but an altered public opinion on the subject may justify other measures ; and it need hardly be pointed out that the land held in mortmain in England and Wales amounts to 1,300,000 acres, of which no less than 500,000 belong to charities. *General Conclusions.*

As a preliminary, however, to any action, it is necessary that public opinion should pronounce itself strongly on the broad question, whether it is satisfied with the present condition of landownership in this country. Public opinion may even without a change of law produce considerable effect. It may induce not a few of those who have hitherto considered that the interests of a rural district are best concerned where all the land in a parish or district is concentrated in one hand, to change their opinion, and to hold that as a matter of safety to the owners of property generally, as well as in the interest of all classes around them, it will be wise to favour the multiplication of landowners, and to give facilities for the creation of small owners of all classes rather than continually to reduce them. Such public opinion can, however, only be formed by a full and free discussion of the subject.

Does the land of this country produce what may reasonably be expected of it by a proper outlay of capital and labour on it? Does it act to its full extent as a stimulus to industry, thrift, and

General Conclusions. prudence? Is it a stable and satisfactory state of society where land is, or is considered to be, only the luxury of the rich? Is it not expedient that land should be brought within the reach of all classes, even at the risk of losing something of its value as an article of luxury?

It has been attempted to answer these questions by arguments and illustrations drawn from the history and experience of this and other countries. It is believed that the result of all this experience is that a country is happiest, and its economical, social, and political condition most sound, where there is a numerous and varied proprietary of its land, and where no class is divorced from the soil. This state of things, it is believed, will and can only result where the trade in land is free; that is, where the transfer of land is simple and uncostly, where all dealings in it are reduced to their simplest form, where each successive generation has full and unrestricted dominion over it, where the State gives no sanction or facilities to an accumulation of land for successive generations, and where the laws give equal facility for its dispersion as for its acquisition. Under such conditions, when artificial stimulus is removed, free competition will have its full effect, and will on the one hand prevent the undue subdivision of land, and on the other its too great aggregation.

BRITISH COLONIAL POLICY.

BY

SIR DAVID WEDDERBURN, BART., M.P.

BRITISH COLONIAL POLICY.

THE relations between Great Britain and one of her most important Colonies are at present in a state of severe tension, and Englishmen of both the great political parties are fully persuaded by the course of events in South Africa that we have reached a new point of departure in our Colonial policy. We cannot in future allow ourselves to be dragged into costly and disastrous wars with African barbarians by the Government of the Cape Colony, over whose action we exercise no control, just as we cannot permit our treaty obligations towards the United States to be overridden, and our friendly relations to be imperilled, by an Act of the Legislature of Newfoundland. A new point of departure in our Colonial policy.

These Colonies are in the enjoyment of "responsible" Government, but they seem to have never yet realised their own responsibility, although in South Africa that realisation seems now likely to be effected after a very tragic fashion, and the Colonists may find that their unaided strength is not adequate to the struggle which their rashness has provoked in Basutoland.

When the Transvaal Territory was annexed it was asserted that the Native inhabitants desired protection against the Boers, while the Boers in their turn required protection against the Natives, and that all alike were prepared to welcome the British flag. Unfortunately British protection is so little appreciated by the Natives, that the most powerful tribes within our territory are in open revolt, and it is only too probable that the Boers may make common cause with the Natives against us.

The Home Government not primarily to blame. For the calamities which have recently occurred and are still impending in South Africa the Home Government is not primarily to blame. As happened so often in the early history of our Indian Empire, the most decisive steps, for good or ill, were taken by local officers without waiting for authority from home. There was no electric cable between Europe and South Africa until a few months ago; but now the telegraph has rendered it impossible for the future that England should find herself committed, without her own knowledge, to the destruction of a native kingdom or the annexation of an independent republic.

Fluctuation of British Colonial policy. The Colonial policy of British statesmen has from time to time undergone remarkable fluctuations. There was an early period when Colonists were regarded as mere dependents, to be governed for the exclusive benefit of the Mother-country, and to be taxed without their own consent, their duty being to take home manufactures, whether they wanted them or not, to send all their saleable produce into the home market, and to receive upon their shores the offscourings of the criminal population. This was the Spanish theory of Colonial obligations, and when it was rudely dispelled by the American war of Independence, the policy afterwards adopted by the British Government erred in the opposite extreme. The Colonists were allowed to enjoy the chief privileges of self-government, and were relieved of its most serious burdens; costly armaments being maintained at the charge of the British exchequer for the protection of the Colonies against all dangers, real or imaginary. This state of affairs could not be permanent: it was justly stigmatized as tending to make the Colonies a useless burden on the Mother-country, and even to produce, rather than to prevent, the risk of Colonial wars. Again a change took place, and those statesmen who withdrew the garrisons of imperial troops from the Australasian and North American Colonies were at first accused of wilfully promoting the disruption of the empire. But what have been the actual results? On *our* side the loss of a few healthy and agreeable military stations may be set off against a considerable reduction in the army estimates, as well as in the loss of men by desertion. On *their* side the Colonists have cheerfully recognised the obligation of prosperous, self-governing communities to provide for their own defence, and have made the important discovery that the presence of standing armies is not conducive to the maintenance of peace. In particular the white people of New Zealand have found, since the departure of the red-coats, that it is possible to settle without fighting their disputes with their Maori neighbours, and the two races are now living side by side on terms of political equality.

Success of the policy carried out in North America and elsewhere. If it were possible to carry out in other quarters of the globe the policy which has proved so successful in North America, in Australia, and in New Zealand, the prospects of the British Colonial Empire would indeed be bright. In those fortunate countries the Colonists are exempt alike from vexatious interference and enfeebling protection on the part of the Mother-country. They feel themselves to be a source of strength, instead of a burden, to their countrymen at home, and they cherish a proud loyalty for the British crown and flag, urging only the sentimental grievance that people in the old country do not take sufficient interest in Colonial affairs. Especially of Australasia can it truly be said that in the great islands of the Southern Ocean a Young England has arisen, cherishing for Old England the affection of a daughter, not the jealousy of a rival. A mighty nation has been already founded—a nation looking to England as a model in politics, in art, in literature, even in sports,—living our life, thinking our thoughts, reading our books, and gradually transforming, as far as nature will permit, the new world at the antipodes into the likeness of the old home-land. It is difficult to imagine any cause or pretext for severing a union based thus on mutual esteem, and imposing upon neither party any galling burden or restraint. The connection with the old country acts most beneficially in binding together Colonies whose jealousy of each other might otherwise result in actual hostilities, and which are, but for this common bond, as completely independent of each other as are the various republics of Spanish America. Gradually these Colonies, which display in the early stages of their career so strong a tendency towards separatism and home rule, may be brought into closer relationship with each other through their common regard for the Mother-country, and may come to appreciate the advantages of a federal union over a system of hostile tariffs and inter-colonial rivalry.

Sir James Mackintosh has enunciated in terse language his own system of Colonial policy :—" A full and efficient protection from all foreign influence ; full permission to conduct the whole of their own internal affairs ; compelling them to pay all the reasonable expenses of their own government, and giving them at the same time a perfect control over the expenditure of the money ; and imposing no restrictions of any kind upon the industry or traffic of the people." These maxims were stated in a speech delivered in the House

Sir James Mackintosh's system of Colonial policy.

of Commons, in 1828, on the civil government of Canada, and it may be fairly asserted that in accordance with them the Colonial policy of Great Britain has since that date been conducted, while the British Colonial Empire has attained its existing prosperity and grandeur.

The words of Sir James Mackintosh, when uttered, were especially applicable to our North American colonies, whose condition and circumstances he contrasts thus favourably with those of all other known countries:—" Exempt at once from the slavery of the West and the castes of the East,—exempt from the embarrassments of that great continent which we have chosen as a penal settlement,—exempt from all the artificial distinctions of the Old World and many of the evils of the New." Australia is now no longer a penal settlement; and New Zealand has sprung recently into political existence, giving to the maxims above quoted a far wider application at the present time than they had when enunciated in 1828.

General acceptance by the Liberal party of Mackintosh's principles.

During the half-century which has elapsed since that distinguished Liberal, Sir James Mackintosh, enunciated his principles of Colonial policy, they have found general acceptance with the Liberal party, under whose auspices the British Empire has been administered during the greater part of that period. It is hardly too much to say, that any marked departure from these principles has invariably resulted in serious difficulty, although the bitter lessons of the American war of independence have been well enough laid to heart to prevent the recurrence of any complete disaster.

Perhaps the most difficult question has been to determine how far the interference of the Mother-country is necessary or desirable, in order to protect the Colonies "from all foreign influence." The phrase employed by Sir J. Mackintosh appears indeed to be too comprehensive, seeing that " all foreign influence" need not be mischievous, and that in many instances the Colonies are now quite capable of affording themselves " a full and efficient protection." Occasionally we have had differences with various European Powers and with the United States of America, when the interests, real or supposed, of our Colonies have been concerned, and where Great Powers are implicated we are bound to take care that our Colonial fellow-countrymen get fair play. On the other hand, Imperial intervention is frequently unnecessary, and even mischievous, when the Colonists are involved in disputes with barbarian neighbours, whether within or without their own territorial limits. In such disputes there is great reason to fear that the consciousness of having overwhelming strength at their back has rendered the Colonial authorities far less reasonable and just than they would otherwise have been.

The most difficult question.

The Colonial policy of the Beaconsfield Government.

The Colonial policy of Lord Beaconsfield's Government was in marked opposition to that which was advocated by Sir James Mackintosh. The Colonists were not encouraged to develop their internal resources by peaceful industry, and to expend their revenues upon improvements within their own borders, such as new countries most urgently require. They were rather encouraged in aggressions upon the territory of their neighbours, although possessing far more territory than they could fully occupy, while all the naval and military resources of the empire were devoted to the conquest and annexation of new countries.

During Lord Beaconsfield's tenure of power the Fiji Islands were annexed, Cyprus was occupied, and a large portion of Afghanistan was seized; but it was in South Africa that the most extensive additions to the empire were made, and it is difficult as yet to say exactly how many new subjects, or how much territory, may have there been acquired. In round numbers, however, the British Empire now extends over nine millions of square miles, and contains 300,000,000 inhabitants, surpassing even the Russian Empire in area, and rivalling even the Chinese in population. If increased extent, rather than increased prosperity and power, be the great desideratum for the empire, then the policy lately in fashion has been eminently successful. None, however, of these recent acquisitions seem likely to become true self-supporting colonies, and they must remain for a long period, if not permanently, a drag upon the resources of the home-country. As regards Cyprus, it will hardly be disputed that this island can never become a British Colony in the true sense of the term. Intended originally to be made, like Gibraltar and Malta, " a strong place of arms," Cyprus has been already, to all intents and purposes, evacuated by the British troops. It possesses no natural harbours; it is denuded of timber; and it is liable, like the neighbouring coasts of Syria and Cilicia, to be scourged at particular seasons with a wasting and deadly fever. In course of time, if the country were completely under British rule, and if a large amount of British money were spent upon its improvement, Cyprus would doubtless regain a portion of the prosperity which it enjoyed before it fell into the power of the Ottomans; but to England it will never be anything but an encumbrance. Neither the method by which Cyprus was obtained, nor the tenure by which it is held, under the *suzeraineté* of the Sultan, can be regarded as satisfactory, and the only apparent reason for keeping it is the difficulty of finding any one to take it off our hands. With regard to Fiji, on the other hand, it may be hoped that this new dependency will prosper, founded as it has been under favourable auspices, in close proximity to the great self-governing colonies of Australia. The Home

Government, however, must be prepared for strong pressure on the part of the colonists, who will certainly urge further annexations in New Guinea and throughout Polynesia. No risk of invasion by savage neighbours can well be alleged in these cases, but there is of course the "christianising and civilising mission" to be carried out—a mission which always in Australasia has resulted in the gradual extinction of the native races. Not a few of the most eager annexationists will also probably be found to have speculated on the rise in value of landed property, which the hoisting of the British flag is certain to produce.

Important consideration. In considering any proposed annexation of territory, it is most important to realise the fact that Englishmen resident on the spot are almost all interested personally in promoting annexation. On the frontier of every new country are to be found many enterprising and energetic individuals, with little to lose and much to gain by the results of a "forward" policy. These pioneers of civilisation are eager for employment, and quite ready to fight; so that the expenditure of imperial funds on a colonial frontier is always popular, either in peace or war.

India. It is impossible to omit India altogether in considering the colonial policy of Great Britain, for India is a country occupied and governed by Englishmen; it is a "Crown Colony" upon an enormous scale, and may be classed along with

Ceylon, Hong Kong, or Jamaica, however greatly it may exceed them in size and importance. To these so-called Crown Colonies the maxims of Sir James Mackintosh do not apply in their entirety, and in the case of India their application has been very partial and unfair, particularly of late years. India has no "permission to conduct her own internal affairs;" she has no "control over the expenditure of money" by her own government, although she is "compelled to pay all such expenditure," whether "reasonable" or not. As for "protection from all foreign influence," India has been repeatedly involved in trouble beyond her own frontiers upon quarrels with which she had no direct concern, and disputes in which she had no voice. She has contributed men and money to wars in China, in Abyssinia, in Afghanistan—wars into which she has been dragged by Imperial, not by Indian, statecraft.

In thus treating India we have not acted up to the lofty standard of policy usually professed in dealing with our dependencies. We cannot, indeed, at present give to the natives of India a "perfect control over their own internal and financial affairs," although considerable reforms in that direction might even now be effected. While India, however, is compelled to pay all her own expenses, it is only fair to her, and to her rulers, that those who are responsible for Indian finance should have the direction of Indian policy, and that Indian tax-payers should never have burdens cast upon them with the view of enhancing British prestige abroad, or of conciliating British electors at home. But after all India stands entirely separate from our other dependencies, and cannot well be included in a general scheme of British Colonial policy.

Increase of responsibilities. Within the last few years, while a "forward" policy has been in favour, we, the people of Great Britain, have had our actual responsibilities alarmingly increased, and obligations have been incurred on our behalf of such a nature that they cannot well be repudiated with honour, although the burden of attempting to fulfil them may become altogether intolerable. Our position is that of an embarrassed landowner, unable to do justice to his vast estates, because of his multifarious liabilities, yet grasping at every parcel of land within his reach, and mortgaging deeper and deeper his ancestral property in order to provide the purchase money.

In Asia we have indefinite obligations connected with the Anglo-Turkish convention, while the "strong, friendly, and independent Afghanistan" has been "shattered like an earthen pipkin" (to use Lord Lytton's own words) into fragments which prove very awkward indeed to handle. In Africa also a well-established native dynasty has been destroyed, and Zululand has been reduced to a condition of anarchy which can hardly fail to result in ultimate annexation, while additional territory, involving fresh risks of collision with the natives, is even now in course of acquisition upon various parts of the western coast.

Surely the time has come for the people of Great Britain to speak out distinctly, and to say that they will do their best to manage the possessions they hold already, but that British blood and treasure shall no longer be poured out like water in order that white adventurers may speculate successfully in land purchases, and may obtain greater facilities for selling rum to the blacks, or even in order that Christian missionaries may be protected from the consequences of their own rashness in playing the part of rulers and belligerents. *The time come for the people of Great Britain to speak out plainly.*

It is indeed certain that a large proportion of our conquests and annexations would never have been made, if the British nation, or even the British Government, had been fairly consulted in the matter. Again and again we have found ourselves involved in a course of action contrary alike to our notions of justice and of expediency, through the rash precipitancy, or even the deliberate disobedience, of officials whose distance from headquarters has enabled them to defy control, until irremediable errors have been committed.

The most serious error recently committed in Colonial policy has been the annexation of the Transvaal Territory, an act for which it would be difficult, if not impossible, to find any precedent *The most serious error.*

in the long history of British conquest and colonisation. We have often conquered during war the territories of other civilised nations, and have retained them after peace was concluded; we have often also seized and annexed the lands of troublesome barbarian neighbours, being sometimes driven to take such a course as a simple measure of self-defence. We have never before, in time of peace, appropriated forcibly the territory of an independent civilised community. The rights frequently denied to heathens with dark faces have hitherto been recognised in the case of white men, professing the Christian religion, and speaking a language kindred to our own.

The Boers of the Transvaal. The Boers of the Transvaal are not mere savages: their forefathers were Dutch Calvinists and French Huguenots, who carried into South Africa the sturdy courage and love of independence which characterised them in Europe. Unwilling to live under foreign rule, they have already twice abandoned their settlements, and plunged boldly into the wilderness beyond the ever-advancing British frontier. Now for the third time they have been overtaken, and the territory which they have occupied and colonized is declared to be British.

The motive for this high-handed proceeding on the part of the English Cabinet appears to have been the vain hope of promoting a federation of all the European settlements in South Africa, similar to that of the British Colonies in North America. There certainly was no lack of unprofitable territory, of native troubles, or of financial responsibilities in South Africa before the Transvaal was annexed, and all these are now largely increased, so far as the Colonial Office is concerned, without any apparent compensation.

It may be readily conceded that the position of Great Britain is strengthened, and her dignity is enhanced, by the development of free communities under her flag, cherishing her institutions, although not sharing her burdens. But neither strength nor dignity can be derived from the compulsory subjection of the South African Boers, whose territory is to us valueless, and with whom we need not have any cause of quarrel whatever. Possibly they may offer no serious armed resistance to overwhelming force; they may even "trek" once more towards the north, leaving to our army of occupation the lands which they have acquired by the usual rough methods of frontier pioneers in a barbarous country. If they depart, a "damnosa hæreditas" will be left to us; if they remain, even passive disaffection on their part will be a formidable matter for the British Government, and they will have the active sympathy of their numerous Dutch kindred within the Cape Colony itself. Happily the blunder committed in the annexation of the Transvaal Republic is not yet irreparable; it has caused *as yet* no bloodshed,[1] and

Neither strength nor dignity to be derived from the subjection of the Boers.

[1] Since the above has been in type this has unhappily ceased to be true.

what has been destroyed by the stroke of a pen may be restored by the same agency. A certain amount of magnanimity is required to acknowledge in a practical manner that an injustice has been done, but after all we may fairly claim to be a magnanimous nation, and have repeatedly proved ourselves capable of similiar acts of restitution. On the tomb of William the Taciturn, at Delft in Holland, hangs a wreath of immortelles dedicated by the Dutch " South African Republics" to the great Prince of Orange. One of these Republics has now lost the independence so dear to all Dutchmen, and our old allies of the Netherlands would thoroughly appreciate the justice and magnanimity which the restoration of that independence involves.

Importance of insularity and geographical position.

In considering the question as to how far the British Colonies would be a help or a hindrance to Great Britain in the event of a struggle with any first-class Power, the most important point seems to be their geographical position and their degree of insularity. The British Empire is essentially insular, or at least peninsular, and continental possessions can only be a source of weakness. Happily we possess little *continental* territory (as distinguished from *peninsular*), except in America, where our frontier for thousands of miles is conterminous with that of a very powerful neighbour, against whom it is absolutely indefensible. Elsewhere the ocean or the desert separates our territory from that of all our rivals, and upon the ocean we are still supreme; even in India the natural boundaries of the great peninsula are marked with singular clearness, and the highest mountain range in the world separates it from the rest of Asia. Australia is a continent in point of size, but an island in position. Africa remains, however, the hopeless land upon which European civilisation can make no permanent impression, where white men can never be more than conquerors and masters among a vastly preponderating multitude of coloured races, where slavery, *mutato nomine*, exists in reality, demoralizing the white master no less than the black bondsman. Difficulties may from time to time arise in any one of the numerous and extensive colonies of Great Britain, but the prospect in general is full of hope, and the mother country finds herself gradually relieved of burdens and responsibilities as her Colonial offspring becomes stronger and more independent. But South Africa is an "enfant terrible" in every sense of the word, and is likely in the immediate future to cause more trouble than all the others together.

In most of our self-governing Colonies the native population has either disappeared entirely, or has become peaceably merged in a preponderating mass of European descent; so that the Australian Blacks, the Red Indians of North America, and even the Maoris of New Zealand, have ceased to impede the spread of free representative institutions. Even in

Disappearance of native populations in most of our Colonies.

India itself, where we rule over a vast subject population, the worst features of modern "imperialism" do not manifest themselves readily among a docile race, with an ancient civilisation, and long accustomed to subjection.

South Africa an exception. It is far otherwise where, as in South Africa, a few conquering white men find themselves surrounded by swarms of natives, warlike and uncivilised, incapable of self-government according to European notions, dangerous as independent neighbours, and still more dangerous as disaffected subjects. The conquerors are rendered cruel by their own fear of the conquered, slavery in some form or other inevitably results, and the development of a prosperous free community is rendered well-nigh impossible. In the "Dark Continent" of Africa the natives do not recede before the white man, and the extent of country peopled with warlike savages is almost boundless; each new conquest or annexation brings us face to face with fresh complications, of which it is impossible to see the end.

The British settlers in South Africa a mere handful. In all our African possessions the British settlers are a mere handful, and it seems as if that country can never become an important field for European emigration. It would indeed be well for England, if her territory at the Cape of Good Hope were limited, as at Gibraltar, Aden, or Singapore, to a coaling station, a fortress, and a free port.

During the last few years the military cost

of our Colonial Empire has varied but little <small>Cost of our Colonial Empire.</small> in amount: the annual sum has been about 2,000,000*l*., one-half of which has been expended upon the four great military and naval stations, Gibraltar, Malta, Bermuda, and Hong Kong, and cannot fairly be regarded as Colonial expenditure. The free Colonies of Australia and New Zealand now demand no military outlay whatever from the British exchequer; and the same may be said of North America, with the single exception of Halifax in Nova Scotia. The military expenses for the West India Islands are not heavy, and tend to diminish. In short, the only true *Colonies*, which involve serious charges for military purposes upon the Imperial treasury are those in South Africa, and there the evil has greatly increased of late years. The Australian Colonies are disposed to squander their own money in fortifications and defences against a purely visionary foe, and we may admire their public spirit and patriotism while deprecating their needless extravagance. The same may be said as to the Dominion of Canada, with this addition, that warlike demonstrations against the United States tend to create a real danger, which would not otherwise exist. In Australia and America the colonists are perhaps pugnacious, but they are not aggressive, and, like our own Volunteers, they might take for their motto, "Defence, not Defiance." Difference of circumstances produces an entirely different policy in Africa, where wars of aggression are never ending, although each in turn is described as being necessary to maintain the very existence of the British settlements in that unfortunate country.

Confederation the new panacea. The new panacea for African troubles is Confederation, and we have been assured that it overrides in importance every other consideration. Doctrinaire statesmen may point to North America with triumph, and may ask: Why should not we carry out in another continent with success a similar scheme of confederation? The answer is simple enough: None of the conditions favourable to confederation exist in South Africa. Here is no group of free self-governing communities, acknowledging the same sovereign and the same flag, undisturbed by barbarian subjects or neighbours, and interested mainly for fiscal reasons in promoting a union. In South Africa there is only one British dependency enjoying responsible government, viz., the Cape Colony proper, with a population at the census of 1875 amounting to 720,000, less than one-third of whom are whites. The dependencies of the Cape Colony, all annexed within the last fifteen years, include British Kaffraria, Basutoland, Griqualand East, Griqualand West, and the Transvaal, with a population equal to that of the Colony proper, and almost entirely black, with the exception of the Boers. Then there is Natal, a British colony, with a population of 325,000, less than 23,000 of whom are of European descent.

Lastly comes the independent Dutch republic, or Orange Free State. Thus there are only three communities, which can possibly confederate at present, and the Orange Free State, over which we have no legal control whatever, is one of them. In the other two countries, which are under the British flag, there are more than a million of inhabitants, but only one quarter of these are of European descent, and of that quarter of a million the majority are not British, but are of Dutch, French, or German origin. In other words, the English settlers are a mere handful among a numerous population of alien whites and a far more numerous population of blacks, even within our own territory, while beyond those limits stretches a vast continent, more or less densely peopled with blacks, over which continent the red line of British dominion tends to advance with alarming rapidity. Confederation under such conditions is an absurdity, and can mean nothing more than the assumption by the Cape colonists of a task far beyond their powers, viz., that of administering unaided a territory which threatens to rival India in extent, if not in population.

Such an undertaking can only result in disastrous failure, if attempted by a feeble and divided Colony under the form of free institutions; it will test the wisdom and experience of the Home Government, backed by the whole power of the British Empire.

Disastrous failure a certain result.

Probable result of withdrawal of authority of mother country.

If the authority of the mother country be withdrawn from South Africa, it is only too probable that the result will be the establishment of a slaveholding oligarchy, in whose constitution and laws slavery will be the essential principle, although the name will not appear. In the Southern States of the American Union the Federal authority alone prevents the negroes from being to all intents and purposes re-enslaved. Coloured persons in various parts of the world are "apprenticed," or "held to labour" as coolies, although it is illegal to sell them as slaves; while in South Africa black women and children are "given out," and slavery exists under thinly disguised forms. The question now is whether the people of Great Britain are prepared to hand over the territories and the tribes conquered by them and at their cost, to be ruled by the handful of white men at the Cape, in Natal, and in the Transvaal. The responsibilities incurred by conquest and annexation cannot be so easily shuffled off, and in England, as in Rome of old, there will be "always news from Africa."

The African race the grand difficulty of the European.

The African race in both hemispheres seems destined to be the grand difficulty of the European, and the condition of affairs in the late Slave States of the American Union presents a strong analogy to that which prevails at the Cape. Confederation in the latter case will be as difficult a scheme as "Reconstruction" in the former, and "Reconstruction" has recently been described by a powerful American writer as "A Fool's Errand." "Slavery as a formal state of society was at an end; as a force, a power, a moral element, it was just as active as before. Its conscious evils were obliterated; its unconscious ones existed in the dwarfed and twisted natures which had been subjected for generations to its influences, master and slave alike. As a form of society it could be abolished by proclamation and enactment; as a moral entity it was indestructible as the souls on which it has left its mark."

It is true that the blacks of South Africa have not been bought and sold like chattels within the memory of the present generation, nor are they liable to the lash of the task-master as a legalised punishment; but they are in the position of serfs, and they can truly say, like their brethren in the old Slave States, "Niggers never can have a white man's chance here." *The South African blacks in the position of serfs.*

"The remedy is one that must be applied from the outside. The South will never purge itself of the evils which affect it. Its intellect, its pride, its wealth, in short, its power, is all arrayed against even the slow and tedious development which time and semi-barbarism would bring. Hour by hour, the chains will be riveted closer. Look at the history of slavery in our land. See how the law-makers, the courts, public sentiment, and all the power of the land grew year by year more harsh and oppressive *The remedy.*

on the slave and his congener, the 'free person of colour,' in all the Slave States. In direct conflict with all the predictions of statesmen, the thumb-screws of oppression were given a new and sharper turn with every passing year. The vestiges of liberty and right were shred away by legislative enactment, and the loopholes of mercy closed by judicial construction, until only the black gulf of hopeless servitude remained.

<small>The remedy from without, not from within.</small>

"The remedy is not from within. The minority knows its power, and the majority realizes its weakness so keenly as to render that impossible. That which has made 'bulldozing' possible renders progress impossible. *It must be from without. The remedy for darkness is light; for ignorance, knowledge; for wrong, righteousness.* Let the nation undo the evil it has permitted and encouraged. Let it educate those whom it made ignorant, and protect those whom it made weak."[1]

If the Mother Country were to make over the destinies of the vast coloured population in the British African Colonies to the tender mercies of the white colonists, the result would probably be much the same as if the freedmen of the former American Slave States were left, unprotected by the Republicans of the North, to settle their political status with their former masters in the South. The responsible Government conferred

[1] "A Fool's Errand," by One of the Fools.

upon the Cape Colony unfortunately restricts the effective intervention of the Colonial Office to the territories lying beyond the present boundaries of that Colony.

In the meantime we must beware of extending the area of *nominal* self-government by bestowing absolute power upon a small minority of whites over a subject black population. The experiment of a representative Government under such conditions failed in Jamaica, and, warned by this failure, we can now see that the independence of the few implies the subjection of the many, and that even the nominal enfranchisement of the ignorant blacks does not enable them efficiently to protect themselves. In Barbados and in Natal the problem of constitutional reform is rendered well-nigh insoluble, and the Transvaal question is complicated by the same difficulty.

The area of nominal self-Government should not be extended.

H. E. Captain Strahan, C.M.G., Governor of the Windward Islands, in the address with which he opened the Legislative session in Barbados, on the 12th of December, 1877, uses these words :—
"The late unhappy disturbances have attracted public attention very strongly to the question whether the constitution of Barbados requires amendment, either by extending the franchise or by establishing that direct protection by the Crown of the unrepresented classes which takes the place of representation, and which is afforded by the constitution of a Crown Colony."

He further speaks of the Barbados constitution as "conferring singularly independent powers upon a small minority of the people," but protests against the idea of any large extension of the franchise among the negro population.

<small>Sir Garnet Wolseley on a "responsible" Goverment for Natal.</small> Sir Garnet Wolseley, on the 13th of February, 1880, in a despatch to Sir Michael Hicks-Beach, the Secretary of State for the Colonies, writes from Pietermaritzburg, Natal, on the subject of creating a "responsible" Government in that Colony, an address praying for such a form of Government having been forwarded to Her Majesty from the Legislative Council of Natal. He uses these words :—"In a colony where the voters or, in other words, the grown-up males of European descent are only about 4,100, any attempt to create a constitution on such a very narrow basis, in imitation of that which we possess in England, would be as futile as it would be dangerous. The whole white population of Natal does not amount to 22,300 souls, while the Kaffir population is said to be nearly 400,000. You will remark that under the proposed constitution it is not intended that the natives should have any voice in public affairs, or that they should be directly represented in either of the two Councils. To give over the government of this Colony into the hands of the very small number of white people in it would, in my opinion, be as unjust to the large number of natives living within its borders, as it would be

dangerous to the peace of South Africa. I believe that one of the principal and earliest products of responsible Government in Natal would be an endeavour, in one way or another, to set up little by little the compulsory relation of master and servant, employer and employed, between the white population and the black; and I can foresee the gravest and most disastrous consequences as the almost certain outcome of any such attempt, were it permitted by the Mother Country." Sir Garnet Wolseley goes on to mention, "The white man who hungers for the possession of farms beyond the existing boundary of the Colony," and to describe the native policy, which finds favour with the colonists of Natal, as "a policy of annexation and of interference in native affairs beyond their own borders, a policy of which war sooner or later must be the result." And he adds:—"To the colonists war means the spreading amongst them of millions of money drawn from the English treasury; and the crime of bringing about a native war does not so clearly appear to the Natal colonist, who thinks he may rely always upon the aid of British battalions to save him from the adverse consequences of a conflict which he may have himself provoked."

What Sir G. Wolseley says of Natal is true of all Colonies existing under similar conditions, and the practice (loudly denounced when attributed to the Dutch Boers) of "indenturing" natives, especially women, for long periods of compulsory service, has already called forth remonstrances from the Home Government, addressed to the authorities of the Cape Colony. In South Africa every native war results in confiscation of native lands, with the virtual reduction to servitude of the natives themselves. Thus the frontier farmers obtain land and labour at the same time, while responsibilities and burdens are cast upon the Home Government and the British taxpayer. Such has been the course of events hitherto; but it may be hoped that a change has recently taken place, and that the Basuto war, now raging in South Africa, may teach a salutary lesson to all concerned.

Decline of the importance of the Colonial Department. The recent transfer of Cyprus from the control of the Foreign to that of the Colonial Office is apparently a prudent proceeding. The latter Department of State has declined greatly in relative importance to the other first-class Departments, as one Colony after another has been emancipated from the control of the Mother Country and entrusted with powers of self-government. In fact, the Colonial Office has ceased to be a first-class Department, and the population under its immediate jurisdiction is now comparatively small. While the India Office is responsible, according to the most recent census, for a population of 191,000,000 in British India, besides 48,000,000 in the Protected Native States, the Colonial Office has, in round numbers, 5,000,000 subjects, besides

1,000,000, whose position of partial subordination may be compared with that of the Indian Feudatories.

But although the Colonial Department is insignificant in magnitude when contrasted with India, it is far more successful in its administration, if financial prosperity may be taken as an evidence of success. Except in the case of military and naval stations, maintained for the advantage, real or supposed, of the empire generally, the colonies impose no burden of any consequence upon the British exchequer, and those countries which are under the jurisdiction of the Colonial Office can exhibit a most satisfactory balance-sheet, with annual surplus and insignificant debt. It is, indeed, otherwise with the free constitutional colonies; but for their finance the Home Government is in no sense responsible.

Successful administration of the Colonial Department.

Grants in aid are still made from the civil estimates for salaries of governors, and other special purposes, but they are small in amount, and are gradually diminishing; so that the British Colonial Empire is really self-supporting, as regards all civil and internal administration.

The British Colonies are divisible into three distinct classes. First, *Crown Colonies*, where legislation and administration are alike under the control of the Home Government, by whom all public officers are appointed. Not one of these Crown Colonies is of first-class importance

The Colonies divisible into three classes.—First class.

(India of course being excepted), and some of them are merely military garrisons, naval stations, or trading settlements. The most populous are Ceylon, Jamaica, Mauritius, the Gold Coast, and the Straits Settlements; and their aggregate population amounts, including Cyprus, to considerably more than four millions and a half.

Second class. Secondly, Colonies where *Representative Institutions* exist, and where the Crown exercises only a veto on legislation, but the Home Government has retained the control of the executive, and the appointment of public officers. Such Colonies are Natal, Western Australia, Barbados, Malta, Leeward Islands, Bahamas, Bermudas, and British Guiana. The population of the "Representative" Colonies is somewhat greater than one million.

Third class. The third class includes all the most important Colonies, those enjoying *Responsible Government*. Over these the Home Government possesses no control beyond the appointment of a constitutional Governor as representative of the British Crown, and a veto upon legislation very rarely exercised. In this category are Newfoundland, the Dominion of Canada, the Cape of Good Hope, New Zealand, Tasmania, and the four principal Colonies of the Australian continent. Their population amounts, according to the latest returns, to seven millions and a half, nearly all of whom, except in the Cape

Colony and its dependencies, are of European race ; whereas, in the other two classes of colony, the white inhabitants form a minority quite insignificant in numbers. The Colonial Office, therefore, exercises complete control over 5,000,000, partial control over 1,000,000, and merely nominal control over 7,500,000, the total being 13,500,000 persons. The different classes of Colonies differ greatly as to their financial position. The constitutional Colonies have fallen into errors natural to young and prosperous communities, and have failed to profit either by the example of the Mother Country, or by that of the United States. They alienate the public lands with reckless rapidity, they hamper trade with protective tariffs, and they raise loans for the "development of the country," while they disburse as ordinary revenue, rather than as capital, the produce of the public land sales.

Great Britain has adopted a free trade policy, by virtue of which she has acquired enormous wealth ; but she makes no serious effort to reduce her national debt, even in times of peace and prosperity, leaving it as a permanent burden to future generations, for whose supposed benefit so much of it has been contracted, but who will certainly find it a disastrous inheritance, and will probably have enough to do in meeting the obligations and liabilities arising in their own times. *Great Britain's free trade policy, non-reduction of national debt.*

The United States, on the other hand, have

The United States, its protective policy, but rapid discharge of national liabilities.

hitherto favoured protection of home industries—a policy which, in their case, has proved less mischievous than usual, on account of their vast territory and the varied resources existing within their own limits. The Americans are increasing rapidly in numbers and in wealth; they might fairly argue that their descendants will be better able than they are to bear the burdens incurred in the great civil war which put an end to slavery, but they do not favour this indefinite postponement of national liabilities, and are paying off at the cost of the present generation the debt which this generation has incurred.

Principal Colonies falling into double error.

Our principal Colonies are falling into the double error of hampering their commerce and postponing their liabilities; they accept alike the American policy of protection and the British policy of indebtedness, reducing both *ad absurdum*. Each colony maintains a hostile tariff, not only against the Mother Country, but against its Colonial neighbours; so that Australia, with a population smaller than that of single American States, has half-a-dozen distinct fiscal systems, framed in a spirit of mutual jealousy, and seriously impeding the commercial development of the country.

The Australian Colonies.

The six Australian colonies (including Tasmania) are rapidly outstripping the Old Country in the matter of indebtedness. The oldest of them had not a single British settler a century ago; their aggregate population in 1878 was a little over two millions, while their aggregate public debt was 45,000,000*l*. New Zealand, with a population (including Maoris) of less than half a million, had in 1878 a public debt of 22,608,311*l*., and New Zealand has not yet existed forty years as a separate colony. The annual expenditure of these colonies continues to exceed their income; and the consequent increase of indebtedness is not the worst feature of the case, for a large proportion of the revenue is derived from land sales—a source of supply liable to exhaustion in all colonies, and in certain colonies already almost exhausted.

Thus in 1877 the gross amount of public revenue for the Australasian Colonies was 17,800,000*l*., of that amount rather less than one-third being raised by actual taxation. In 1878 the "ordinary" expenditure of New Zealand, in a time of profound peace, exceeded the revenue by nearly 200,000*l*. while the expenditure out of "loans for public works" was 1,786,992*l*.

New Zealand has a great future before her, but that future has been gravely compromised by a reckless financial policy, which has already expended a large portion of her splendid patrimony, the public lands, and has saddled the community with a public debt just twice as heavy per head as that of the United Kingdom.

In fact, the most promising of all our Colonies,

on account of natural advantages, is now, in proportion to population, the most heavily indebted country in the world. The "*net indebtedness*" of the Colony, including the old Provincial Government loans, has been stated by the Agent-General for New Zealand as amounting on the 30th June, 1879, to 21,513,303*l*. 14*s*. 5*d*.

<small>The most promising Colony the most heavily indebted.</small>

Ten millions sterling of this money have been expended on railways constructed and in course of construction, and five millions upon other public works, including roads, harbours, lighthouses, and telegraphs. Upon immigration 3,770,000*l*. have been spent, and 1,470,000*l*. upon the purchase of native lands. All of these are doubtless objects involving a certain outlay, which, if made judiciously, will prove beneficial in the future, and which need not have been made entirely out of current revenue. But, in estimating the financial extravagance which has piled up so large a debt in so short a time, it must be borne in mind that an additional sum of 10,763,577*l*. has been spent by the Colony of New Zealand, being the amount realised from public lands granted and sold down to the end of 1878. Now this large sum, amounting to one-half of the entire public debt, ought surely to have been regarded as capital, and not as current income; it ought to have been applied either to the reduction of the permanent debt, or it should have been set apart for special contingencies; but nothing of the sort has been

<small>Nature, objects, and extent of expenditure.</small>

done. The annual charge for interest of debt and sinking fund is stated in 1879 at 1,200,000*l*., but the total sinking fund accrued at that date has been only 1,709,000*l*., reducing the net indebtedness to twenty-one and a half millions sterling, as above mentioned. For the last ten years the revenue of New Zealand has been divided into "consolidated" and "land" revenue, the former having increased gradually and steadily during that period from one million to more than two millions and a half, while the annual revenue from sales of land has fluctuated between 208,000*l*. and 1,586,500*l*.

This highest figure was reached in 1877—78, and it is noticeable that from various causes the land revenue has in the following year shown a falling off to the amount of nearly one-half. It is somewhat difficult to reconcile the details of the statistics furnished by the Agent-General for New Zealand with those given in the Statistical Abstract recently laid before Parliament, but it is clear enough that, while the land revenue has been spent from year to year, the public permanent debt has been trebled since 1869.

Increase of permanent debt.

Hitherto no check has been placed upon such reckless extravagance by the pressure of direct taxation, but this will not be the case in future, and a heavy tax upon property has been imposed within the last few months. It may be hoped that the effect of this impost will be to open the eyes of the New Zealand people, and

Check upon extravagance.

T

to bring about economy and retrenchment. Their Agent-General boasts that their public works are not constructed for the present population only, but for many times the number. Whence are these multitudes to come? The country wants European immigrants, but its great distance from Europe places it at a woeful disadvantage compared with America as a field for emigration. If, in addition to this disadvantage, New Zealand is to be handicapped with heavy taxation, even the present scanty stream of immigration will be turned away from her shores, and she will have to depend solely upon the natural increase of her existing population. Meanwhile the evil done is by no means irreparable: the public credit of New Zealand is still justly high; the larger portion of the lands of the colony is still unalienated, while the railways constitute a really valuable property, already producing, at least in the Middle Island, a net return of three per cent. upon the cost.

Analogy between New Zealand and Victoria. The peculiarities which characterise the finance of New Zealand are found also in that of Victoria to a considerable extent. If the five years from 1873—74 to 1877—78 be considered, the revenue is found to vary between four millions sterling and four millions and three-quarters, while the expenditure for each year, except 1876—77, considerably exceeds the revenue. Out of this revenue only a portion, far less than the moiety, is raised by taxation.

In 1877—78 out of four and a half millions sterling one million seven hundred thousand, or 38 per cent., resulted from taxation, almost entirely from customs, although a land tax was then imposed for the first time. In that year 756,000*l.* was realised from land sales, 1,202,000*l.* from railways, 239,000*l.* from posts and telegraphs, besides large sums from rent of Crown lands, water supply, fines, forfeitures, &c. All these sources of income are steady, some of them are increasing, and all, except land sales, may be regarded as legitimate revenue. From other Australian Colonies reports of budget statements reach us, showing that financial difficulties are now seriously felt, and it is a very hopeful sign that recourse is being generally made to direct taxation. Financial reform and retrenchment are probably not far distant, when self-governing communities, whose public income has been hitherto derived from land sales and protective import duties, begin to feel the pinch of direct taxes.

At present the Australians are inclined to boast of their large revenues, and the Victorian Year-Book for 1878—79, para. 160, says, "Not one country (in the world) raises so much per head as any of the Colonies on the Australian continent, or as New Zealand." The very next paragraph, however, shows that in the case of Victoria the proportion of revenue *raised by taxation* is only 38 per cent., while it is rather less than one-third of the total revenue for all the Australasian Colonies.

Australian inclination to boast of their revenues.

Indebtedness of Canada, Newfoundland, and the Cape.

The Dominion of Canada has not displayed quite so serious a case of youthful extravagance as have the Australasian Colonies. The total "net liabilities" of the Dominion and Provincial Governments was in 1878 just under 30,000,000*l.* for a population of less than four millions. This gives a degree of public indebtedness per head of population corresponding closely to that of the United States, and considerably less than half that of the United Kingdom. Canada has never been burdened with the costs of a great civil war, but it is a significant fact that whereas the receipts annually exceed the expenditure by a very large sum in the United States, and the public debt diminishes steadily, the Dominion debt displays an opposite tendency, and in 1878 the expenditure exceeded the revenue by 235,000*l.*, besides a sum of 1,386,916*l.* expended from "Loans on Public Works." Newfoundland has held aloof from the rest of British North America, and is quite independent of the Dominion. Her public debt is as yet small, but here as elsewhere the tendency is to increase, the deficit in 1878 being 27,000*l.* on a total expenditure of less than a quarter of a million sterling. The only other important self-governing Colony is that of the Cape, where the public debt is growing rapidly, having increased between 1870 and 1878 from little more than one million to nearly seven millions sterling, a sufficiently alarming figure for a country where the white population does not yet equal a quarter of a million; but this debt must be largely increased by the wars in which the Colony is now engaged.

A good example of financial economy is given by the Orange Free State, which declares a very small debt, and a surplus of annual revenue over expenditure. In this respect the little Dutch Republic stands alone among the numerous self-governing communities founded by European settlers beyond the limits of Europe. <small>A good example.</small>

But, while the "Responsible" Colonies are thus plunging headlong into debt, and mortgaging their future prosperity, the two other classes display a far more satisfactory balance-sheet, notwithstanding the large staff of salaried officials which they usually maintain. The Governor of Jamaica has recently called attention to the flourishing finances of that important island, where debt has been largely reduced of late years, without any increase in taxation, and where the amount of revenue in 1878 was 539,000*l.*, exceeding the expenditure by 35,000*l.*, so that Jamaica is now almost free from public debt. <small>Satisfactory financial condition of Crown Colonies.—Jamaica.</small>

Barbados stands in a still more satisfactory position, as in 1878 the public debt was only 25,000*l.*, and the revenue for the year exceeded the expenditure by 7,000*l.* Trinidad in 1878 shows a debt not much greater than half the annual revenue, which is very largely in excess of the expenditure. In the Leeward Islands the revenues exceed the <small>Barbados.</small>

expenditure, and the public debt is inconsiderable. In the Bahamas and the Bermudas a fair equilibrium seems to be maintained between incomings and outgoings; while Tobago returns almost precisely the same figures for revenue as for expenditure.

West Indies. Thus the British possessions in the West Indies set an excellent example in finance to the more independent and progressive Colonies, and it is gratifying to find that these comparatively humble dependencies are now so well administered as to be able to pay their own way, and to meet all their liabilities with ease. The same holds good of the Crown Colonies in other parts of the world: except such as are mere garrisons, none are a burden on the British taxpayers, and, except the great Indian empire, none are bowed down beneath a weight of debt.

Ceylon. Ceylon in 1878 was practically free from debt, and the revenue exceeded the expenditure by 95,000*l*. Mauritius had then a debt of 700,000*l*, less by 90,000*l*. than the revenue for that year, which also exceeded the annual expenditure by 55,000*l*. Of the other dependencies of the British Crown, viz. Hong Kong, Straits Settlements, Labuan, Guiana, it may be said that they are all solvent and prosperous in their fiscal affairs.

Malta and Gibraltar. Malta and Gibraltar are able to defray without difficulty all necessary expenses of civil government. Heligoland has a small annual surplus, and a trifling debt. Even such settlements as British Honduras, the Falkland Islands, and St. Helena contrive to pay their own way fairly well; while the West African Settlements, the Gold Coast Colony, and Lagos are prosperous financially, notwithstanding their insalubrious climate.

The financial prosperity of the British Crown Colonies is thus in marked contrast to the indebted condition of civilised communities in general, not excepting some of the wealthiest and most powerful European empires (with which it is useless to compare them), while Switzerland alone can display an equally favourable balance sheet. If, however, they contrast favourably in this respect with British Constitutional Colonies, much more favourable is the contrast as regards most of the independent communities which have arisen from the ruins of the Spanish American Empire: the Argentine Republic, Colombia, Mexico, Peru, Paraguay, Uruguay, Venezuela, and Central America vie with each other in deficit and debt. *Financial prosperity of Crown Colonies in marked contrast to civilized communities in general.*

Altogether the result of an inquiry into the financial condition of the British Colonies and their pecuniary relations to the Mother Country is by no means unsatisfactory, always excepting India, and perhaps South Africa.

The aggregate revenue of the British Dominions is, by the latest returns, upwards of 160,000,000*l*. One-half of this enormous sum is raised in Europe, and one-third in Asia. Of the remaining sixth *Aggregate revenue of British Dominions.*

nearly two-thirds are raised in Australasia, leaving only one twenty-fifth of the total for America and one-fiftieth for Africa.

<small>Relative importance of British possessions.</small>

If the relative importance of the British possessions in the five divisions of the globe be estimated by their respective incomes, then, taking one hundred as the total, Europe is represented by fifty, Asia by thirty-three, Australasia by eleven, America by four, and Africa by two. If population, or area, be taken as the standard of comparison, very different results are obtained.

As regards population their order of magnitude is—Asia, Europe, America, Australasia; and as regards area, it is—America, Australasia, Asia, Europe. In both respects Africa is now quite indeterminate.

<small>A class of politicians to be on our guard against.</small>

We cannot be too much upon our guard against that class of politicians who believe that the strength and resources of the British empire necessarily increase with its territorial extension, and who regard all conquests or annexations of rival nations as affording just cause for alarm. They appear to think that every barbarous country, and especially every island, all over the globe, belongs, or ought to belong, to England. If a rumour gets abroad that the Americans propose to purchase a naval station near Honolulu, or that a couple of German war-vessels have been lying for a considerable time at the Samoa group of islands, these "patriots" are frantic with jealousy, lest another Great Power should do *once* what England has done over and over again, and should attempt to share the British monopoly in civilizing aboriginals off the face of the earth. It is true that, when a country inhabited by savages has once been invaded by white settlers, the only chance of protection for the natives is under the flag of a civilized Power, and in their choice of evils the British flag is probably the least; but our hands are already too full, and we cannot do justice to our vast possessions. If other great nations are willing to undertake a share in the task of civilizing Africa or Asia, a far-sighted policy dictates ready acquiescence on our part in what is merely the imposition of a burden on the shoulders of a possible rival. Thanks to her naval supremacy, England has already secured all the best available territory for colonization, and that which remains unappropriated is not very likely to "pay."

When the French undertook the expedition that finally resulted in the conquest and annexation of Algiers, great jealousy and alarm were excited in this country, and many persons actually believed that British interests would suffer, if a stable, civilized Government were substituted in North Africa for chronic piracy and misrule. France was then the "bête noire," or bugbear, of so-called British patriots, who are now able to perceive— what the French tax-payer has long ago discovered

Jealousy and alarm at foreign conquests and annexations are groundless.

—that Algeria has profited more than France by the hoisting of the tricolor upon the shores of Africa. At the present day Russia is exhausting her imperfectly developed resources in subjugating the wild hordes of Central Asia, and again it is imagined that British interests are menaced, and that all Russian action is directed by hostility to England. Surely these patriots, who regard the strength and prosperity of neighbouring nations as necessarily disastrous to themselves must rejoice when that strength is expended, and that prosperity is diminished in carrying out the "mission" of subduing barbarians and unbelievers. Enlightened selfishness should prompt Englishmen not to restrain suspected rivals from distant conquests, but rather to encourage them in squandering their forces over the surface of the globe. Experience has taught us in many wars, that remote colonies and possessions are a serious encumbrance to a belligerent of inferior maritime force, and in particular it has been proved again and again, that all islands occupied by the rivals of Great Britain are simply hostages placed in the hands of that Power which so long has ruled the seas. During the wars waged with other European nations by England, since the destruction of the Spanish Armada inaugurated her naval supremacy, the enemy's settlements and garrisons, isolated and cut off from reinforcement, have invariably fallen one after another into British hands. The Dutch in particular were almost everywhere explorers and pioneers to the British, and the names of New Holland, New Zealand, and Van Diemen's Land sufficiently indicate that Australasia, as well as South Africa and Ceylon, would have been Dutch, if England had not finally triumphed over Holland, her determined maritime rival. The ocean does not separate outlying possessions from a mother-country that has undisputed command of the waves. The Mediterranean bound together the widely-scattered provinces of the Roman Empire, in the centre of which lay the city of Rome. The British Isles lie in the centre of the land surface of the globe, and are united to remote dependencies by the same salt waves that part them from neighbouring rivals. After Rome had vanquished Carthage, her only maritime rival, she flourished for many centuries, having none to make her afraid; but Italy is not an island, or Rome might have continued, like Venice amidst the lagoons, to defy the barbarians for many centuries more.

The Roman poet might well lament that the sound of Italian wars was audible alike to Medes and to Africans, and might ask what fields were not enriched with Latin blood—

> "Qui gurges aut quæ flumina lugubris
> Ignara belli? Quod mare Dauniæ
>   Non decoloravere cædes?
>   Quæ caret ora cruore nostro?"[1]

---

[1] Horatii Flacci Carminum, lib. ii., Ode i.

In a yet wider sense the question has been asked—

> "Sons of the Ocean Isle !
> Where sleep your mighty dead?"

And the answer is :—

> "Wave may not foam, nor wild wind sweep,
> Where rest not England's dead."

The sea, whose shores have been enriched with English blood, spreads far beyond the Pillars of Hercules, and the existence of our vast empire is due to our command of that grand highway of nations, far more than to any superiority over other races, either as conquerors or as colonists. Not without reason is the British navy popular, giving, as it does, security at home and empire abroad, without menacing liberty or unduly burdening the exchequer.

Value of the navy. At the present period no portion of the empire, except India, would be seriously imperilled, if we did not possess any regular army at all, and if the defence of the whole were entrusted to a powerful navy, with a well-organized local militia in each colony, as well as in the United Kingdom. Even India, it must be remembered, was conquered from the seaboard, and our maritime supremacy alone enabled us there to crush our French rivals. Without that supremacy we could hardly hold the country for a year, while with the sea open to our transport vessels, and India garrisoned by a localised European force, no enemy exists that need alarm the most timid of patriots. For us the "gates of India" are on the Suez Canal, and Egypt is the only *land*, beyond the limits of India proper, the possession of which would strengthen our Eastern Empire.

The case of Great Britain is indeed without a parallel in history: her empire stretches over "regions Cæsar never knew," and her colonies have never been rivalled in extent by those of any nation except Spain. The "red line" of British dominion continues to encroach upon all other colours over the map of the globe, including ever more and more territory, until it seems as if the empire must crumble away from its own weight and want of cohesion. Unlike Rome, England is surrounded by many independent nations, several of them surpassing her in military power, although she might almost cope singly with the united naval forces of all. If all England's vast empire were in truth a "Greater Britain," contributing willingly in men and money to the maintenance of English rule, then indeed she might defy the world in arms; but, as Mr. Gladstone has most truly said, her rule has to be maintained "with the strength that lies within the narrow limits of these shores." The self-governing Colonies of British origin have ceased to be a burden: they pay their own way, and might even become a support in any time of dire emergency; but they contribute neither to the

The case of Great Britain unparalleled.

imperial forces nor to the imperial exchequer. India has paid her own way hitherto; but the first grant in aid has already been made to her by England, in the form of a loan without interest.

<small>Heavy responsibilities.</small> The remainder of the empire, including all the African possessions, must be regarded as entailing heavy responsibilities upon the people of the United Kingdom, without adding to the strength necessary for discharging those responsibilities. To acquire more possessions of this nature, whether in Zululand, in Afghanistan, or in Asia Minor, simply means casting fresh burdens, military and financial, not upon the empire at large, but upon the 33,000,000 inhabitants of Great Britain and Ireland, who bear bravely the load already on their shoulders, but certainly feel that they have got about as much as they can well carry. Practice in carrying weights doubtless develops strength up to a certain point, but there is a limit even for the strongest, and that limit we seem now to have reached; but still, such is the energy of the race, that there are Englishmen who continue to cry out for more dusky subjects, more barren territories, more wars, and more debts!

<small>A large proportion of the empire an unpeopled waste.</small> We possess already the most extensive empire that has ever existed on this globe, and a large proportion of this is still an unpeopled waste, requiring capital and labour to develop its splendid resources, and to support millions where now

only thousands are found. There is an ample field for all our national energy within our own existing borders, and the Englishman who advocates the wider extension of those borders, far from the sea our own element, into the heart of Africa or Asia, is no true friend to his country.

It has been stated that our imperial burdens are borne by the inhabitants of the United Kingdom; but at the present time this statement is hardly correct, for Ireland is now an additional burden on the military strength of the empire, and, until Ireland is pacified by just legislation, England has only Scotland to assist her in sustaining "the too vast orb of her fate."

Yet statesmen like Sir Bartle Frere continue to advocate the retention of Kandahar, and the extension of a British protectorate over the whole of South Africa, and, unless British electors and taxpayers speak out strongly against such a policy of "force, folly, and fraud," they will find themselves saddled with ever more and more useless and costly possessions. In her future competition with other nations Great Britain is already handicapped quite seriously enough with her enormous public debt, from which encumbering weight her most formidable rival is rapidly shaking herself free. Is there no lesson to be learnt by us from the policy of civilised nations at the present day, as well as from that of Rome or Spain in the past? *Necessity for British electors to speak out.*

Two notable examples. Two notable examples are before us—Germany and the United States of America. Both of these nations doubtless have a great future before them, but which of them is pursuing the policy best calculated to raise it to the foremost place? Germany annexes valuable provinces, contracts powerful alliances, increases her army, and takes upon herself to become the arbiter of Europe. The Americans leave other nations to manage their own affairs, reduce their military expenditure to the lowest possible figure, and direct their indomitable energy to the reduction of their public liabilities and to the development of their internal resources. They abstain, in spite of great provocation, from farther encroachment upon Mexico; they decline to be tempted even by so glittering a bait as Cuba, the "Pearl of the Antilles;" they refuse to become an "imperial" race ruling over subject nationalities, or to burden themselves with outlying possessions, easy to attack, and difficult to defend. They have their reward: they are indeed a mighty nation, compact and self-governing, free from burdens and liabilities, strong in their position, their wealth, their numbers, and their energy, without an unwilling subject or a foreign enemy, at once the most powerful and the most peaceable nation on the face of the earth. Are we to follow their example, or that of Germany? Are we to thrust ourselves into every European quarrel, as well as to carry fire and sword through Africa and

Asia? Are we to increase continually our public debt, as well as the number of our discontented subjects and unprofitable possessions? The industrial Commonwealth is clearly outstripping the military Empire in all that makes life worth having, and German emigrants are pouring into America by hundreds of thousands. England has, like America, a secure position, immense territories, and free institutions; let her compete in the rivalry of peace and progress, rather than in that of spoliation and conquest.

The "forward" Colonial policy, of which Sir Bartle Frere is the chief apostle, has had a fair trial, and it has brought upon us, in Zululand and in Afghanistan, the two most serious military reverses ever sustained by the British arms in battle with a barbarian foe. These defeats have indeed been "avenged," but there is little glory or satisfaction to be gained in the punishment of men, whose crime is to have fought bravely and successfully in defence of their native land against unprovoked invasion. *(The results of a fair trial of the "forward" policy.)*

Of the wars that have arisen, and are likely to arise, out of this disastrous policy it is impossible now to foresee the end, even if the present Liberal Government should display a greater readiness than they have hitherto done to break the continuity of disaster, by dismissing all the agents whose conduct produced the original mischief, and employing men in sympathy with a policy of *(Impossible to see the end of wars arising out of this policy.)*

peace and conciliation, such men as Sir Henry Bulwer, late Governor of Natal.

Duty of Liberals. If the Liberals really believe that rash and unjust acts have been committed by their predecessors in office, why can they not make manifest their belief by deeds as well as by words? How can those who condemn the seizure of the Transvaal against the will of its inhabitants treat the Boers as *rebels* for attempting to resist annexation? Is it impossible, or absurd, for a great nation to acknowledge a blunder, and make restitution for a wrong? If Liberal Ministers content themselves with censuring, instead of altering, the Colonial policy of the Conservatives, they will have themselves only to thank, when they reap the fruits of that policy.

Scope for the energy of Colonial Office. Even within the limits of its present jurisdiction the Colonial Office may find scope for considerable energy. The Crown Colonies are financially prosperous, but important reforms are lacking in many, if not all of them, and it is possible that in some cases administrative economy has been carried too far. From Ceylon come eager demands for railway extension and for ecclesiastical disestablishment and disendowment. From Malta there is a cry for representative reform; from Cyprus and Honduras there are petitions for important constitutional amendments.

Objects of our future Colonial policy. Our future Colonial policy must be to reform the institutions and develop the resources of those countries for whose administration we are really responsible; to divest ourselves of all liability for the action of those Colonies over whose government we exercise no power of control; and, above all, to put an end to the system of "filibustering" by officials, traders, or missionaries under shelter of the British flag.

DAVID WEDDERBURN.

THE END.

LONDON:
R. CLAY, SONS, AND TAYLOR,
BREAD STREET HILL.

BEDFORD STREET, STRAND, LONDON, W.C.
February, 1880.

MACMILLAN & CO.'S CATALOGUE of Works in the Departments of History, Biography, Travels, Critical and Literary Essays, Politics, Political and Social Economy, Law, etc.; and Works connected with Language.

HISTORY, BIOGRAPHY, TRAVELS, &c.

Albemarle.—FIFTY YEARS OF MY LIFE. By GEORGE THOMAS, Earl of Albemarle. With Steel Portrait of the first Earl of Albemarle, engraved by JEENS. Third and Cheaper Edition. Crown 8vo. 7s. 6d.

"*The book is one of the most amusing of its class.* ... *These reminiscences have the charm and flavour of personal experience, and they bring us into direct contact with the persons they describe.*"—EDINBURGH REVIEW.

Anderson.—MANDALAY TO MOMIEN; a Narrative of the Two Expeditions to Western China, of 1868 and 1875, under Colonel E. B. Sladen and Colonel Horace Browne. By Dr. ANDERSON, F.R.S.E., Medical and Scientific Officer to the Expeditions. With numerous Maps and Illustrations. 8vo. 21s.

"*A pleasant, useful, carefully-written, and important work.*"—ATHENÆUM.

Appleton.—Works by T. G. APPLETON :—

A NILE JOURNAL. Illustrated by EUGENE BENSON. Crown 8vo. 6s.

SYRIAN SUNSHINE. Crown 8vo. 6s.

Arnold (M.)—ESSAYS IN CRITICISM. By MATTHEW ARNOLD. New Edition, Revised and Enlarged. Crown 8vo. 9s.

Arnold (W. T.)—THE ROMAN SYSTEM OF PROVINCIAL ADMINISTRATION TO THE ACCESSION OF CONSTANTINE THE GREAT. Being the Arnold Prize Essay for 1879. By W. T. Arnold, B.A. Crown 8vo. 6s.

Atkinson.—AN ART TOUR TO NORTHERN CAPITALS OF EUROPE, including Descriptions of the Towns, the Museums, and other Art Treasures of Copenhagen, Christiania, Stockholm, Abo, Helsingfors, Wiborg, St. Petersburg, Moscow, and Kief. By J. BEAVINGTON ATKINSON. 8vo. 12s.

Bailey.—THE SUCCESSION TO THE ENGLISH CROWN. A Historical Sketch. By A. BAILEY, M.A., Barrister-at-Law. Crown 8vo. 7s. 6d.

Baker (Sir Samuel W.)—Works by Sir SAMUEL BAKER, Pacha, M.A., F.R.S., F.R.G.S.:—

CYPRUS AS I SAW IT IN 1879. With Frontispiece. 8vo. 12s. 6d.

"*From the first page to the last the reader is engrossed in the story, the interest of which never for a moment flags. In every line we find information, in every chapter instruction, skilfully intermingled with amusing anecdotes. . . . The work may be viewed under two distinct aspects; its importance as a contribution to scientific and political knowledge, and its interest as a book of travel and adventure. It is equally good from both points.*"—MORNING POST.

ISMAILÏA: A Narrative of the Expedition to Central Africa for the Suppression of the Slave Trade, organised by Ismail, Khedive of Egypt. With Portraits, Map, and Numerous Illustrations. New Edition. Crown 8vo. 6s.

"*Well written and full of remarkable adventures.*"—PALL MALL GAZETTE. "*Reads more like a romance . . . . incomparably more entertaining than books of African travel usually are.*"—MORNING POST.

THE ALBERT N'YANZA Great Basin of the Nile, and Exploration of the Nile Sources. Fifth Edition. Maps and Illustrations. Crown 8vo. 6s.

"*Charmingly written;*" says the SPECTATOR, "*full, as might be expected, of incident, and free from that wearisome reiteration of useless facts which is the drawback to almost all books of African travel.*"

THE NILE TRIBUTARIES OF ABYSSINIA, and the Sword Hunters of the Hamran Arabs. With Maps and Illustrations. Sixth Edition. Crown 8vo. 6s.

The TIMES *says: "It adds much to our information respecting Egyptian Abyssinia and the different races that spread over it. It contains, moreover, some notable instances of English daring and enterprising skill; it abounds in animated tales of exploits dear to the heart of the British sportsman; and it will attract even the least studious reader, as the author tells a story well, and can describe nature with uncommon power.*"

Bancroft.—THE HISTORY OF THE UNITED STATES OF AMERICA, FROM THE DISCOVERY OF THE CONTINENT. By GEORGE BANCROFT. New and thoroughly Revised Edition. Six Vols. Crown 8vo. 54s.

HISTORY, BIOGRAPHY, TRAVELS, ETC.   3

Barker (Lady).—Works by LADY BARKER :—
A YEAR'S HOUSEKEEPING IN SOUTH AFRICA. With Illustrations. New and Cheaper Edition. Crown 8vo. 6s.

"*We have to thank Lady Barker for a very amusing book, over which we have spent many a delightful hour, and of which we will not take leave without alluding to the ineffably droll illustrations which add so very much to the enjoyment of her clear and sparkling descriptions.*"—MORNING POST.

Beesly.—STORIES FROM THE HISTORY OF ROME. By Mrs. BEESLY. Extra fcap. 8vo. 2s. 6d.

"*A little book for which every cultivated and intelligent mother will be grateful for.*"—EXAMINER.

Bismarck—IN THE FRANCO-GERMAN WAR. An Authorized Translation from the German of Dr. MORITZ BUSCH. Two Vols. Crown 8vo. 18s.

The TIMES *says :*—"*The publication of Bismarck's after-dinner talk, whether discreet or not, will be of priceless biographical value, and Englishmen, at least, will not be disposed to quarrel with Dr. Busch for giving a picture as true to life as Boswell's 'Johnson' of the foremost practical genius that Germany has produced since Frederick the Great.*"

Blackburne.—BIOGRAPHY OF THE RIGHT HON. FRANCIS BLACKBURNE, Late Lord Chancellor of Ireland. Chiefly in connexion with his Public and Political Career. By his Son, EDWARD BLACKBURNE, Q.C. With Portrait Engraved by JEENS. 8vo. 12s.

Blanford (W. T.)—GEOLOGY AND ZOOLOGY OF ABYSSINIA. By W. T. BLANFORD. 8vo. 21s.

Brontë.—CHARLOTTE BRONTË. A Monograph. By T. WEMYSS REID. With Illustrations. Third Edition. Crown 8vo. 6s.

Brooke.—THE RAJA OF SARAWAK: an Account of Sir James Brooke, K.C.B., LL.D. Given chiefly through Letters or Journals. By GERTRUDE L. JACOB. With Portrait and Maps. Two Vols. 8vo. 25s.

Bryce.—Works by JAMES BRYCE, D.C.L., Regius Professor of Civi Law, Oxford :—
THE HOLY ROMAN EMPIRE. Sixth Edition, Revised and Enlarged. Crown 8vo. 7s. 6d.

"*It exactly supplies a want: it affords a key to much which men read of in their books as isolated facts, but of which they have hitherto had no connected exposition set before them.*"—SATURDAY REVIEW.

Bryce.—*continued.*

TRANSCAUCASIA AND ARARAT: being Notes of a Vacation Tour in the Autumn of 1876. With an Illustration and Map. Third Edition. Crown 8vo. 9s.

"*Mr. Bryce has written a lively and at the same time an instructive description of the tour he made last year in and about the Caucasus. When so well-informed a jurist travels into regions seldom visited, and even walks up a mountain so rarely scaled as Ararat, he is justified in thinking that the impressions he brings home are worthy of being communicated to the world at large, especially when a terrible war is casting a lurid glow over the countries he has lately surveyed.*"—ATHENÆUM.

Burgoyne.—POLITICAL AND MILITARY EPISODES DURING THE FIRST HALF OF THE REIGN OF GEORGE III. Derived from the Life and Correspondence of the Right Hon. J. Burgoyne, Lieut.-General in his Majesty's Army, and M.P. for Preston. By E. B. DE FONBLANQUE. With Portrait, Heliotype Plate, and Maps. 8vo. 16s.

Burke.—EDMUND BURKE, a Historical Study. By JOHN MORLEY, B.A., Oxon. Crown 8vo. 7s. 6d.

Burrows.—WORTHIES OF ALL SOULS: Four Centuries of English History. Illustrated from the College Archives. By MONTAGU BURROWS, Chichele Professor of Modern History at Oxford, Fellow of All Souls. 8vo. 14s.

"*A most amusing as well as a most instructive book.*—GUARDIAN.

Cameron.—OUR FUTURE HIGHWAY. By V. LOVETT CAMERON, C.B., Commander R.N. With Illustrations. 2 vols. Crown 8vo. 21s.

Campbell.—LOG-LETTERS FROM THE "CHALLENGER." By LORD GEORGE CAMPBELL. With Map. Fifth and cheaper Edition. Crown 8vo. 6s.

"*A delightful book, which we heartily commend to the general reader.*"—SATURDAY REVIEW.

"*We do not hesitate to say that anything so fresh, so picturesque, so generally delightful, as these log-letters has not appeared among books of travel for a long time.*"—EXAMINER.

Campbell.—MY CIRCULAR NOTES: Extracts from Journals; Letters sent Home; Geological and other Notes, written while Travelling Westwards round the World, from July 6th, 1874, to July 6th, 1875. By J. F. CAMPBELL, Author of "Frost and Fire." Cheaper Issue. Crown 8vo. 6s.

HISTORY, BIOGRAPHY, TRAVELS, ETC.

Campbell.—TURKS AND GREEKS. Notes of a recent Excursion. By the Hon. DUDLEY CAMPBELL, M.A. With Coloured Map. Crown 8vo. 3s. 6d.

Carpenter.—LIFE AND WORK OF MARY CARPENTER. By the Rev. J. E. CARPENTER. With Portrait. Crown 8vo. 10s. 6d.

Carstares.—WILLIAM CARSTARES: a Character and Career of the Revolutionary Epoch (1649—1715). By ROBERT STORY, Minister of Rosneath. 8vo. 12s.

Chatterton: A BIOGRAPHICAL STUDY. By DANIEL WILSON, LL.D., Professor of History and English Literature in University College, Toronto. Crown 8vo. 6s. 6d.

Chatterton: A STORY OF THE YEAR 1770. By Professor MASSON, LL.D. Crown 8vo. 5s.

Clark.—MEMORIALS FROM JOURNALS AND LETTERS OF SAMUEL CLARK, M.A., formerly Principal of the National Society's Training College, Battersea. Edited with Introduction by his WIFE. With Portrait. Crown 8vo. 7s. 6d.

Clifford (W. K.)—LECTURES AND ESSAYS. Edited by LESLIE STEPHEN and FREDERICK POLLOCK, with Introduction by F. POLLOCK. Two Portraits. 2 vols. 8vo. 25s.

The TIMES *of October* 22, 1879, *says:*—"*Many a friend of the author on first taking up these volumes and remembering his versatile genius and his keen enjoyment of all realms of intellectual activity must have trembled lest they should be found to consist of fragmentary pieces of work, too disconnected to do justice to his powers of consecutive reasoning and too varied to have any effect as a whole. Fortunately those fears are groundless . . . . It is not only in subject that the various papers are closely related. There is also a singular consistency of view and of method throughout . . . . It is in the social and metaphysical subjects that the richness of his intellect shows itself most forcibly in the variety and originality of the ideas which he presents to us. To appreciate this variety, it is necessary to read the book itself, for it treats, in some form or other, of nearly all the subjects of deepest interest in this age of questioning.*"

Combe.—THE LIFE OF GEORGE COMBE, Author of "The Constitution of Man." By CHARLES GIBBON. With Three Portraits engraved by JEENS. Two Vols. 8vo. 32s.

"*A graphic and interesting account of the long life and indefatigable labours of a very remarkable man.*"—SCOTSMAN.

Cooper.—ATHENÆ CANTABRIGIENSES. By CHARLES HENRY COOPER, F.S.A., and THOMPSON COOPER, F.S.A. Vol. I. 8vo., 1500—85, 18s.; Vol. II., 1586—1609, 18s.

Correggio.—ANTONIO ALLEGRI DA CORREGGIO. From the German of Dr. JULIUS MEYER, Director of the Royal Gallery, Berlin. Edited, with an Introduction, by Mrs. HEATON. Containing Twenty Woodbury-type Illustrations. Royal 8vo. Cloth elegant. 31s. 6d.

Cox (G. V.)—RECOLLECTIONS OF OXFORD. By G. V. Cox, M.A., New College, late Esquire Bedel and Coroner in the University of Oxford. *Cheaper Edition.* Crown 8vo. 6s.

Cunynghame (Sir A. T.)—MY COMMAND IN SOUTH AFRICA, 1874—78. Comprising Experiences of Travel in the Colonies of South Africa and the Independent States. By Sir ARTHUR THURLOW CUNYNGHAME, G.C.B., then Lieutenant-Governor and Commander of the Forces in South Africa. Third Edition. 8vo. 12s. 6d.

The TIMES *says:—"It is a volume of great interest, ... full of incidents which vividly illustrate the condition of the Colonies and the character and habits of the natives..... It contains valuable illustrations of Cape warfare, and at the present moment it cannot fail to command wide-spread attention."*

"Daily News."—THE DAILY NEWS' CORRESPONDENCE of the War between Germany and France, 1870—1. Edited with Notes and Comments. New Edition. Complete in One Volume. With Maps and Plans. Crown 8vo. 6s.

THE DAILY NEWS' CORRESPONDENCE of the War between Russia and Turkey, to the fall of Kars. Including the letters of Mr. Archibald Forbes, Mr. J. E. McGahan, and other Special Correspondents in Europe and Asia. Second Edition, enlarged. Cheaper Edition. Crown 8vo. 6s.

FROM THE FALL OF KARS TO THE CONCLUSION OF PEACE. Cheaper Edition. Crown 8vo. 6s.

Davidson.—THE LIFE OF A SCOTTISH PROBATIONER being a Memoir of Thomas Davidson, with his Poems an Letters. By JAMES BROWN, Minister of St. James's Stree Church, Paisley. Second Edition, revised and enlarged, wit Portrait. Crown 8vo. 7s. 6d.

Deas.—THE RIVER CLYDE. An Historical Description of the Rise and Progress of the Harbour of Glasgow, and of the Improvement of the River from Glasgow to Port Glasgow. By J. DEAS, M. Inst. C.E. 8vo. 10s. 6d.

Denison.—A HISTORY OF CAVALRY FROM THE EARLIEST TIMES. With Lessons for the Future. By Lieut.-Col. GEORGE DENISON, Commanding the Governor-General's Body Guard, Canada, Author of "Modern Cavalry." With Maps and Plans. 8vo. 18s.

Dilke.—GREATER BRITAIN. A Record of Travel in English-speaking Countries during 1866-7. (America, Australia, India. By Sir CHARLES WENTWORTH DILKE, M.P. Sixth Edition. Crown 8vo. 6s.

"Many of the subjects discussed in these pages," says the DAILY NEWS, *"are of the widest interest, and such as no man who cares for the future of his race and of the world can afford to treat with indifference."*

Doyle.—HISTORY OF AMERICA. By J. A. DOYLE. With Maps. 18mo. 4s. 6d.

"Mr. Doyle's style is clear and simple, his facts are accurately stated, and his book is meritoriously free from prejudice on questions where partisanship runs high amongst us."—SATURDAY REVIEW.

Drummond of Hawthornden: THE STORY OF HIS LIFE AND WRITINGS. By PROFESSOR MASSON. With Portrait and Vignette engraved by C. H. JEENS. Crown 8vo. 10s. 6d.

Duff.—Works by M. E. GRANT-DUFF, M.P., late Under Secretary of State for India:—
NOTES OF AN INDIAN JOURNEY. With Map. 8vo. 10s. 6d.
MISCELLANIES POLITICAL AND LITERARY. 8vo. 10s. 6d.

Eadie.—LIFE OF JOHN EADIE, D.D., LL.D. By JAMES BROWN, D.D., Author of "The Life of a Scottish Probationer." With Portrait. Second Edition. Crown 8vo. 7s. 6d.

"An ably written and characteristic biography."—TIMES.

Elliott.—LIFE OF HENRY VENN ELLIOTT, of Brighton. By JOSIAH BATEMAN, M.A. With Portrait, engraved by JEENS. Extra fcap. 8vo. Third and Cheaper Edition. 6s.

Elze.—ESSAYS ON SHAKESPEARE. By Dr. KARL ELZE. Translated with the Author's sanction by L. DORA SCHMITZ. 8vo. 12s.

English Men of Letters. Edited by JOHN MORLEY. A Series of Short Books to tell people what is best worth knowing as to the Life, Character, and Works of some of the great English Writers. In crown 8vo. Price 2s. 6d. each.

I. DR. JOHNSON. By LESLIE STEPHEN.

"The new series opens well with Mr. Leslie Stephen's sketch of Dr. Johnson. It could hardly have been done better; and it will convey to the readers for whom it is intended a juster estimate of Johnson than either of the two essays of Lord Macaulay"—PALL MALL GAZETTE.

English Men of Letters.—*continued.*

II. SIR WALTER SCOTT. By R. H. HUTTON.
"*The tone of the volume is excellent throughout.*"—ATHENÆUM.
"*We could not wish for a more suggestive introduction to Scott and his poems and novels.*"—EXAMINER.

III. GIBBON. By J. C. MORISON.
"*As a clear, thoughtful, and attractive record of the life and works of the greatest among the world's historians, it deserves the highest praise.*"—EXAMINER.

IV. SHELLEY. By J. A. SYMONDS.
"*The lovers of this great poet are to be congratulated on having at their command so fresh, clear, and intelligent a presentment of the subject, written by a man of adequate and wide culture.*"—ATHENÆUM.

V. HUME. By Professor HUXLEY.
"*It may fairly be said that no one now living could have expounded Hume with more sympathy or with equal perspicuity.*"—ATHENÆUM.

VI. GOLDSMITH. By WILLIAM BLACK.
"*Mr. Black brings a fine sympathy and taste to bear in his criticism of Goldsmith's writings as well as in his sketch of the incidents of his life.*'—ATHENÆUM.

VII. DEFOE. By W. MINTO.
"*Mr. Minto's book is careful and accurate in all that is stated, and faithful in all that it suggests. It will repay reading more than once.*"—ATHENÆUM.

VIII. BURNS. By Principal SHAIRP, Professor of Poetry in the University of Oxford.
"*It is impossible to desire fairer criticism than Principal Shairp's on Burns's poetry . . . . None of the series has given a truer estimate either of character or of genius than this little volume . . . . and all who read it will be thoroughly grateful to the author for this monument to the genius of Scotland's greatest poet.*"—SPECTATOR.

IX. SPENSER. By the Very Rev. the DEAN OF ST. PAUL'S.
"*Dr. Church is master of his subject, and writes always with good taste.*"—ACADEMY.

X. THACKERAY. By ANTHONY TROLLOPE.
"*Mr. Trollope's sketch is excellently adapted to fulfil the purpose of the series in which it appears.*"—ATHENÆUM.

XI. BURKE. By JOHN MORLEY.
"*Perhaps the best criticism yet published on the life and character of Burke is contained in Mr. Morley's compendious biography. His style is vigorous and polished, and both his political and personal judgment, and his literary criticisms are just, generous, subtle, and in a high degree interesting.*"—SATURDAY REVIEW.

HISTORY, BIOGRAPHY, TRAVELS, ETC.   9

English Men of Letters.—*continued.*
XII. MILTON. By MARK PATTISON. Crown 8vo. 2s. 6d.
"*The writer knows the times and the man, and of both he has written with singular force and discrimination.*"—SPECTATOR.
XIII. HAWTHORNE. By HENRY JAMES. Crown 8vo. 2s. 6d.
"*Probably no one living could have done so good a book on Hawthorne as he has done.*"—SATURDAY REVIEW.
XIV. SOUTHEY. By Professor DOWDEN. Crown 8vo. 2s. 6d.
XV. BUNYAN. By J. A. FROUDE. Crown 8vo. 2s. 6d.
CHAUCER. By Professor WARD.
COWPER. By GOLDWIN SMITH.   } [*In preparation.*]
WORDSWORTH. By F. W. H. MYERS.
Others in preparation.

Eton College, History of. By H. C. MAXWELL LYTE, M.A. With numerous Illustrations by Professor DELAMOTTE, Coloured Plates, and a Steel Portrait of the Founder, engraved by C. H. JEENS. New and cheaper Issue, with Corrections. Medium 8vo. Cloth elegant. 21s.
"*We are at length presented with a work on England's greatest public school, worthy of the subject of which it treats.... A really valuable and authentic history of Eton College.*"—GUARDIAN.

European History, Narrated in a Series of Historical Selections from the best Authorities. Edited and arranged by E. M. SEWELL and C. M. YONGE. First Series, crown 8vo. 6s.; Second Series, 1088-1228, crown 8vo. 6s. Third Edition.
"*We know of scarcely anything,*" says the GUARDIAN, *of this volume,* "*which is so likely to raise to a higher level the average standard of English education.*"

Faraday.—MICHAEL FARADAY. By J. H. GLADSTONE, Ph.D., F.R.S. Second Edition, with Portrait engraved by JEENS from a photograph by J. WATKINS. Crown 8vo. 4s. 6d.
PORTRAIT. Artist's Proof. 5s.

Forbes.—LIFE AND LETTERS OF JAMES DAVID FORBES, F.R.S., late Principal of the United College in the University of St. Andrews. By J. C. SHAIRP, LL.D., Principal of the United College in the University of St. Andrews; P. G. TAIT, M.A., Professor of Natural Philosophy in the University of Edinburgh; and A. ADAMS-REILLY, F.R.G.S. 8vo. with Portraits, Map, and Illustrations, 16s.

Freeman.—Works by EDWARD A. FREEMAN, D.C.L., LL.D.:—
HISTORICAL ESSAYS. Third Edition. 8vo. 10s. 6d.
CONTENTS:—*I. "The Mythical and Romantic Elements in Early English History;" II. "The Continuity of English History;" III. "The Relations between the Crowns of England and Scotland;" IV.*

Freeman—*continued.*
"*St. Thomas of Canterbury and his Biographers;*" V. "*The Reign of Edward the Third:*" VI. "*The Holy Roman Empire;*" VII. "*The Franks and the Gauls;*" VIII. "*The Early Sieges of Paris;*" IX. "*Frederick the First, King of Italy;*" X. "*The Emperor Frederick the Second;*" XI. "*Charles the Bold;*" XII. "*Presidential Government.*"

HISTORICAL ESSAYS. SECOND SERIES. 8vo. 10s. 6d.
The principal Essays are:—"*Ancient Greece and Mediæval Italy:*" "*Mr. Gladstone's Homer and the Homeric Ages:*" "*The Historians of Athens:*" "*The Athenian Democracy:*" "*Alexander the Great:*" "*Greece during the Macedonian Period:*" "*Mommsen's History of Rome:*" "*Lucius Cornelius Sulla:*" "*The Flavian Cæsars.*"

HISTORICAL ESSAYS. Third Series. 8vo. 12s.
CONTENTS:—"*First Impressions of Rome.*" "*The Illyrian Emperors and their Land.*" "*Augusta Treverorum.*" "*The Goths at Ravenna.*" "*Race and Language.*" "*The Byzantine Empire.*" "*First Impressions of Athens.*" "*Mediæval and Modern Greece.*" "*The Southern Slaves.*" "*Sicilian Cycles.*" "*The Normans at Palermo.*"

COMPARATIVE POLITICS.—Lectures at the Royal Institution. To which is added the "Unity of History," the Rede Lecture at Cambridge, 1872. 8vo. 14s.

THE HISTORY AND CONQUESTS OF THE SARACENS. Six Lectures. Third Edition, with New Preface. Crown 8vo. 3s. 6d.

HISTORICAL AND ARCHITECTURAL SKETCHES: chiefly Italian. With Illustrations by the Author. Crown 8vo. 10s. 6d.

HISTORY OF FEDERAL GOVERNMENT, from the Foundation of the Achaian League to the Disruption of the United States. Vol. I. General Introduction. History of the Greek Federations. 8vo. 21s.

OLD ENGLISH HISTORY. With *Five Coloured Maps.* New Edition. Extra fcap. 8vo., half-bound. 6s.
"*The book indeed is full of instruction and interest to students of all ages, and he must be a well-informed man indeed who will not rise from its perusal with clearer and more accurate ideas of a too much neglected portion of English history.*"—SPECTATOR.

HISTORY OF THE CATHEDRAL CHURCH OF WELLS, as illustrating the History of the Cathedral Churches of the Old Foundation. Crown 8vo. 3s. 6d.
"*The history assumes in Mr. Freeman's hands a significance, and, we may add, a practical value as suggestive of what a cathedral ought to be, which make it well worthy of mention.*"—SPECTATOR.

HISTORY, BIOGRAPHY, TRAVELS, ETC.

Freeman—*continued*.

THE GROWTH OF THE ENGLISH CONSTITUTION FROM THE EARLIEST TIMES. Crown 8vo. 5s. Third Edition, revised.

GENERAL SKETCH OF EUROPEAN HISTORY. Being Vol. I. of a Historical Course for Schools edited by E. A. FREEMAN. New Edition, enlarged with Maps, Chronological Table, Index, &c. 18mo. 3s. 6d.

"*It supplies the great want of a good foundation for historical teaching. The scheme is an excellent one, and this instalment has been accepted in a way that promises much for the volumes that are yet to appear.*"—EDUCATIONAL TIMES.

THE OTTOMAN POWER IN EUROPE : its Nature, its Growth, and its Decline. With Three Coloured Maps. Crown 8vo. 7s. 6d.

Galileo.—THE PRIVATE LIFE OF GALILEO. Compiled principally from his Correspondence and that of his eldest daughter, Sister Maria Celeste, Nun in the Franciscan Convent of S. Matthew in Arcetri. With Portrait. Crown 8vo. 7s. 6d.

Geddes.—THE PROBLEM OF THE HOMERIC POEMS. By W. D. GEDDES, LL.D., Professor of Greek in the University of Aberdeen. 8vo. 14s.

Gladstone—Works by the Right Hon. W. E. GLADSTONE, M.P. :—
JUVENTUS MUNDI. The Gods and Men of the Heroic Age. Crown 8vo. cloth. With Map. 10s. 6d. Second Edition.

"*Seldom,*" *says the* ATHENÆUM, "*out of the great poems themselves, have these Divinities looked so majestic and respectable. To read these brilliant details is like standing on the Olympian threshold and gazing at the ineffable brightness within.*"

HOMERIC SYNCHRONISM. An inquiry into the Time and Place of Homer. Crown 8vo. 6s.

"*It is impossible not to admire the immense range of thought and inquiry which the author has displayed.*"—BRITISH QUARTERLY REVIEW.

Goethe and Mendelssohn (1821—1831). Translated from the German of Dr. KARL MENDELSSOHN, Son of the Composer, by M. E. VON GLEHN. From the Private Diaries and Home Letters of Mendelssohn, with Poems and Letters of Goethe never before printed. Also with two New and Original Portraits, Facsimiles, and Appendix of Twenty Letters hitherto unpublished. Crown 8vo. 5s. Second Edition, enlarged.

" . . . *Every page is full of interest, not merely to the musician, but to the general reader. The book is a very charming one, on a topic of deep and lasting interest.*"—STANDARD.

Goldsmid.—TELEGRAPH AND TRAVEL. A Narrative of the Formation and Development of Telegraphic Communication between England and India, under the orders of Her Majesty's Government, with incidental Notices of the Countries traversed by the Lines. By Colonel Sir FREDERIC GOLDSMID, C.B., K.C.S.I., late Director of the Government Indo-European Telegraph. With numerous Illustrations and Maps. 8vo. 21s.

Gordon.—LAST LETTERS FROM EGYPT, to which are added Letters from the Cape. By LADY DUFF GORDON. With a Memoir by her Daughter, Mrs. Ross, and Portrait engraved by JEENS. Second Edition. Crown 8vo. 9s.

"*The intending tourist will not, if he is well advised, grudge a place in his portmanteau to this book.*"—TIMES.

Gray.—CHINA. A History of the Laws, Manners, and Customs of the People. By the VENERABLE JOHN HENRY GRAY. LL.D., Archdeacon of Hong Kong, formerly H.B.M. Consular Chaplain at Canton. Edited by W. Gow Gregor. With 150 Full-page Illustrations, being Facsimiles of Drawings by a Chinese Artist. 2 Vols. Demy 8vo. 32s.

"*Its pages contain the most truthful and vivid picture of Chinese life which has ever been published.*"—ATHENÆUM.

"*The only elaborate and valuable book we have had for many years treating generally of the people of the Celestial Empire.*"—ACADEMY.

Gray, (Mrs.).—FOURTEEN MONTHS IN CANTON. By Mrs. GRAY. With Illustrations. Crown 8vo. 9s.

"*Everybody ought to read Mrs. Gray's book.*"—GRAPHIC.

"*The book will be found readable and interesting, both to old residents in China and strangers to the 'Heathen Chinee.'*"—LONDON AND CHINA EXPRESS.

Green.—Works by JOHN RICHARD GREEN :—

HISTORY OF THE ENGLISH PEOPLE. Vol. I.—Early England—Foreign Kings—The Charter—The Parliament. With 8 Coloured Maps. 8vo. 16s. Vol. II.—The Monarchy, 1461—1540 ; the Restoration, 1540—1603. 8vo. 16s. Vol. III. —Puritan England, 1603—1660 ; the Revolution, 1660—1688. With 4 Maps. 8vo. 16s. [*Vol. IV. in the press.*

"*Mr. Green has done a work which probably no one but himself could have done. He has read and assimilated the results of all the labours of students during the last half century in the field of English history, and*

Green.—*continued.*

has given them a fresh meaning by his own independent study. He has fused together by the force of sympathetic imagination all that he has so collected, and has given us a vivid and forcible sketch of the march of English history. His book, both in its aims and its accomplishments, rises far beyond any of a similar kind, and it will give the colouring to the popular view to English history for some time to come."—EXAMINER.

A SHORT HISTORY OF THE ENGLISH PEOPLE. With Coloured Maps, Genealogical Tables, and Chronological Annals. Crown 8vo. 8s. 6d. Sixty-third Thousand.

" *To say that Mr. Green's book is better than those which have preceded it, would be to convey a very inadequate impression of its merits. It stands alone as the one general history of the country, for the sake of which all others, if young and old are wise, will be speedily and surely set aside.*"

STRAY STUDIES FROM ENGLAND AND ITALY. Crown 8vo. 8s. 6d. Containing: Lambeth and the Archbishops—The Florence of Dante—Venice and Rome—Early History of Oxford—The District Visitor—Capri—Hotels in the Clouds—Sketches in Sunshine, &c.

" *One and all of the papers are eminently readable.*"—ATHENÆUM.

Guest.—LECTURES ON THE HISTORY OF ENGLAND. By M. J. GUEST. With Maps. Crown 8vo. 6s.

" *The book is pleasant reading, it is full of information, much of it is valuable, most of it is correct, told in a gossipy and intelligible way.*"—ATHENÆUM.

Hamerton.—Works by P. G. HAMERTON :—

THE INTELLECTUAL LIFE. With a Portrait of Leonardo da Vinci, etched by LEOPOLD FLAMENG. Second Edition. Crown 8vo. 10s. 6d.

" *We have read the whole book with great pleasure, and we can recommend it strongly to all who can appreciate grave reflections on a very important subject, excellently illustrated from the resources of a mind stored with much reading and much keen observation of real life.*"—SATURDAY REVIEW.

THOUGHTS ABOUT ART. New Edition, revised, with an Introduction. Crown 8vo. 8s. 6d.

"*A manual of sound and thorough criticism on art.*"—STANDARD.

Hill.—THE RECORDER OF BIRMINGHAM. A Memoir of Matthew Davenport Hill, with Selections from his Correspondence. By his Daughters ROSAMOND and FLORENCE DAVENPORT-HILL. With Portrait engraved by C. H. JEENS. 8vo. 16s.

Hill.—WHAT WE SAW IN AUSTRALIA. By ROSAMOND and FLORENCE HILL. Crown 8vo. 10s. 6d.
"*May be recommended as an interesting and truthful picture of the condition of those lands which are so distant and yet so much like home.*"—SATURDAY REVIEW.

Hodgson.—MEMOIR OF REV. FRANCIS HODGSON, B.D., Scholar, Poet, and Divine. By his Son, the Rev. JAMES T. HODGSON, M.A. Containing numerous Letters from Lord Byron and others. With Portrait engraved by JEENS. Two Vols. Crown 8vo. 18s.
"*A book that has added so much of a healthy nature to our knowledge of Byron, and that contains so rich a store of delightful correspondence.*"—ATHENÆUM.

Hole.—A GENEALOGICAL STEMMA OF THE KINGS OF ENGLAND AND FRANCE. By the Rev. C. HOLE, M.A., Trinity College, Cambridge. On Sheet, 1s.

A BRIEF BIOGRAPHICAL DICTIONARY. Compiled and Arranged by the Rev. CHARLES HOLE, M.A. Second Edition. 18mo. 4s. 6d.

Hooker and Ball.—MAROCCO AND THE GREAT ATLAS: Journal of a Tour in. By Sir JOSEPH D. HOOKER, K.C.S.I., C.B., F.R.S., &c., and JOHN BALL, F.R.S. With an Appendix, including a Sketch of the Geology of Marocco, by G. MAW, F.L.S., F.G.S. With Illustrations and Map. 8vo. 21s.
"*It is long since any more interesting book of travels has issued from our press.*"—SATURDAY REVIEW. "*This is, without doubt, one of the most interesting and valuable books of travel published for many years.*"—SPECTATOR.

Hozier (H. M.)—Works by CAPTAIN HENRY M. HOZIER, late Assistant Military Secretary to Lord Napier of Magdala :—

THE SEVEN WEEKS' WAR; Its Antecedents and Incidents. *New and Cheaper Edition*. With New Preface, Maps, and Plans. Crown 8vo. 6s.

THE INVASIONS OF ENGLAND : a History of the Past, with Lessons for the Future. Two Vols. 8vo. 28s.

Hübner.—A RAMBLE ROUND THE WORLD IN 1871. By M. LE BARON HÜBNER, formerly Ambassador and Minister. Translated by LADY HERBERT. New and Cheaper Edition. With numerous Illustrations. Crown 8vo. 6s.
"*It is difficult to do ample justice to this pleasant narrative of travel . . . . it does not contain a single dull paragraph.*"—MORNING POST.

HISTORY, BIOGRAPHY, TRAVELS, ETC. 15

Hughes.—Works by THOMAS HUGHES, Q.C., Author of "Tom Brown's School Days."
ALFRED THE GREAT. New Edition. Crown 8vo. 6s.
MEMOIR OF A BROTHER. With Portrait of GEORGE HUGHES, after WATTS. Engraved by JEENS. Crown 8vo. 5s. Sixth Edition.
"*The boy who can read this book without deriving from it some additional impulse towards honourable, manly, and independent conduct, has no good stuff in him.*"—DAILY NEWS.

Hunt.—HISTORY OF ITALY. By the Rev. W. HUNT, M.A. Being the Fourth Volume of the Historical Course for Schools. Edited by EDWARD A. FREEMAN, D.C.L. 18mo. 3s.
"*It is a book which may be safely recommended to others besides schoolboys.*"—JOHN BULL.

Hutton.—ESSAYS THEOLOGICAL AND LITERARY. By R. H. HUTTON, M.A. Cheaper issue. 2 vols. 8vo. 18s.

Irving.—THE ANNALS OF OUR TIME. A Diurnal of Events, Social and Political, Home and Foreign, from the Accession of Queen Victoria to the Peace of Versailles. By JOSEPH IRVING. *Fourth Edition.* 8vo. half-bound. 16s.
ANNALS OF OUR TIME. Supplement. From Feb. 28, 1871, to March 19, 1874. 8vo. 4s. 6d.
ANNALS OF OUR TIME. Second Supplement. From March, 1874, to the Occupation of Cyprus. 8vo. 4s. 6d.
"*We have before us a trusty and ready guide to the events of the past thirty years, available equally for the statesman, the politician, the public writer, and the general reader.*"—TIMES.

James.—Works by HENRY JAMES, Jun. FRENCH POETS AND NOVELISTS. Crown 8vo. 8s. 6d.
CONTENTS:—*Alfred de Musset; Théophile Gautier; Baudelaire; Honoré de Balzac; George Sand; The Two Ampères; Turgenieff, &c.*

Johnson's Lives of the Poets.—The Six Chief Lives—Milton, Dryden, Swift, Addison, Pope, Gray. With Macaulay's "Life of Johnson." Edited, with Preface, by MATTHEW ARNOLD. Crown 8vo. 6s.

Killen.—ECCLESIASTICAL HISTORY OF IRELAND, from the Earliest Date to the Present Time. By W. D. KILLEN, D.D., President of Assembly's College, Belfast, and Professor of Ecclesiastical History. Two Vols. 8vo. 25s.
"*Those who have the leisure will do well to read these two volumes. They are full of interest, and are the result of great research. . . . We*

have no hesitation in recommending the work to all who wish to improve their acquaintance with Irish history."—SPECTATOR.

Kingsley (Charles).—Works by the Rev. CHARLES KINGSLEY, M.A., Rector of Eversley and Canon of Westminster. (For other Works by the same Author, *see* THEOLOGICAL and BELLES LETTRES Catalogues.)

ON THE ANCIEN RÉGIME as it existed on the Continent before the FRENCH REVOLUTION. Three Lectures delivered at the Royal Institution. Crown 8vo. 6*s*.

AT LAST : A CHRISTMAS in the WEST INDIES. With nearly Fifty Illustrations. Sixth Edition. Crown 8vo. 6*s*.
Mr. Kingsley's dream of forty years was at last fulfilled, when he started on a Christmas expedition to the West Indies, for the purpose of becoming personally acquainted with the scenes which he has so vividly described in "Westward Ho!" These two volumes are the journal of his voyage. Records of natural history, sketches of tropical landscape, chapters on education, views of society, all find their place. "We can only say that Mr. Kingsley's account of a 'Christmas in the West Indies' is in every way worthy to be classed among his happiest productions."—STANDARD.

THE ROMAN AND THE TEUTON. A Series of Lectures delivered before the University of Cambridge. New and Cheaper Edition, with Preface by Professor MAX MÜLLER. Crown 8vo. 6*s*.

PLAYS AND PURITANS, and other Historical Essays. With Portrait of Sir WALTER RALEIGH. New Edition. Crown 8vo. 6*s*.
In addition to the Essay mentioned in the title, this volume contains other two—one on "Sir Walter Raleigh and his Time," and one on Froude's "History of England."

Kingsley (Henry).—TALES OF OLD TRAVEL. Re-narrated by HENRY KINGSLEY, F.R.G.S. With *Eight Illustrations* by HUARD. Fifth Edition. Crown 8vo. 5*s*.
"We know no better book for those who want knowledge or seek to refresh it. As for the 'sensational,' most novels are tame compared with these narratives."—ATHENÆUM.

Lang.—CYPRUS : Its History, its Present Resources and Future Prospects. By R. HAMILTON LANG, late H.M. Consul for the Island of Cyprus. With Two Illustrations and Four Maps. 8vo. 14*s*.
"The fair and impartial account of her past and present to be found in these pages has an undoubted claim on the attention of all intelligent readers."—MORNING POST.

HISTORY, BIOGRAPHY, TRAVELS, ETC.

Laocoon.—Translated from the Text of Lessing, with Preface and Notes by the Right Hon. SIR ROBERT J. PHILLIMORE, D.C.L. With Photographs. 8vo. 12s.

Leonardo da Vinci and his Works.—Consisting of a
Life of Leonardo Da Vinci, by MRS. CHARLES W. HEATON, Author of "Albrecht Dürer of Nürnberg," &c., an Essay on his Scientific and Literary Works by CHARLES CHRISTOPHER BLACK, M.A., and an account of his more important Paintings and Drawings. Illustrated with Permanent Photographs. Royal 8vo, cloth, extra gilt. 31s. 6d.

Liechtenstein.—HOLLAND HOUSE. By Princess MARIE LIECHTENSTEIN. With Five Steel Engravings by C. H. JEENS, after Paintings by WATTS and other celebrated Artists, and numerous Illustrations drawn by Professor P. H. DELAMOTTE, and engraved on Wood by J. D. COOPER, W. PALMER, and JEWITT & Co., about 40 Illustrations by the Woodbury-type process, and India Proofs of the Steel Engravings. Two vols. medium 4to. half morocco elegant. 4l. 4s.

Lloyd.—THE AGE OF PERICLES. A History of the Arts and Politics of Greece from the Persian to the Peloponnesian War. By W. WATKISS LLOYD. Two Vols. 8vo. 21s.

"*No such account of Greek art of the best period has yet been brought together in an English work. . . . Mr. Lloyd has produced a book of unusual excellence and interest.*"—PALL MALL GAZETTE.

Loch Etive and the Sons of Uisnach.—With Illustrations. 8vo. 14s.

"*Not only have we Loch Etive of the present time brought before us in colours as true as they are vivid, but stirring scenes which happened on the borders of the beautiful lake in semi-mythical times are conjured up with singular skill. Nowhere else do we remember to have met with such a well-written account of the invasion of Scotland by the Irish.*"—GLOBE.

Loftie.—A RIDE IN EGYPT FROM SIOOT TO LUXOR, IN 1879; with Notes on the Present State and Ancient History of the Nile Valley, and some account of the various ways of making the voyage out and home. By the Rev. W. J. LOFTIE. With Illustrations. Crown 8vo. 10s. 6d.

"*We prophesy that Mr. Loftie's little book will accompany many travellers on the Nile in the coming winters.*"—TIMES.

Lubbock. — ADDRESSES, POLITICAL AND EDUCATIONAL. By Sir JOHN LUBBOCK, Bart., M.P., D.C.L., F.R.S. 8vo. 8s. 6d.

Macdonell.—FRANCE SINCE THE FIRST EMPIRE. By JAMES MACDONELL. Edited with Preface by his Wife. Crown 8vo. 6s.

Macarthur.—HISTORY OF SCOTLAND, By MARGARET MACARTHUR. Being the Third Volume of the Historical Course for Schools, Edited by EDWARD A. FREEMAN, D.C.L. Second Edition. 18mo. 2s.

"*It is an excellent summary, unimpeachable as to facts, and putting them in the clearest and most impartial light attainable.*"—GUARDIAN.
"*No previous History of Scotland of the same bulk is anything like so trustworthy, or deserves to be so extensively used as a text-book.*"—GLOBE.

Macmillan (Rev. Hugh).—For other Works by same Author, see THEOLOGICAL and SCIENTIFIC CATALOGUES.

HOLIDAYS ON HIGH LANDS; or, Rambles and Incidents in search of Alpine Plants. Second Edition, revised and enlarged. Globe 8vo. cloth. 6s.

"*Botanical knowledge is blended with a love of nature, a pious enthusiasm, and a rich felicity of diction not to be met with in any works of kindred character, if we except those of Hugh Miller.*"—TELEGRAPH.

Macready.—MACREADY'S REMINISCENCES AND SELECTIONS FROM HIS DIARIES AND LETTERS. Edited by Sir F. POLLOCK, Bart., one of his Executors. With Four Portraits engraved by JEENS. New and Cheaper Edition. Crown 8vo. 7s. 6d.

"*As a careful and for the most part just estimate of the stage during a very brilliant period, the attraction of these volumes can scarcely be surpassed. . . . Readers who have no special interest in theatrical matters, but enjoy miscellaneous gossip, will be allured from page to page, attracted by familiar names and by observations upon popular actors and authors.*"—SPECTATOR.

Mahaffy.—Works by the Rev. J. P. MAHAFFY, M.A., Fellow of Trinity College, Dublin :—

SOCIAL LIFE IN GREECE FROM HOMER TO MENANDER. Third Edition, revised and enlarged, with a new chapter on Greek Art. Crown 8vo. 9s.

"*It should be in the hands of all who desire thoroughly to understand and to enjoy Greek literature, and to get an intelligent idea of the old Greek life, political, social, and religious.*"—GUARDIAN.

HISTORY, BIOGRAPHY, TRAVELS, ETC. 19

Mahaffy.—*continued.*
RAMBLES AND STUDIES IN GREECE. With Illustrations. Crown 8vo. 10s. 6d. New and enlarged Edition, with Map and Illustrations.
"*A singularly instructive and agreeable volume.*"—ATHENÆUM.

"Maori."—SPORT AND WORK ON THE NEPAUL FRONTIER; or, Twelve Years' Sporting Reminiscences of an Indigo Planter. By "MAORI." With Illustrations. 8vo. 14s.
"*Every day's adventures, with all the joys and perils of the chase, are told as only a keen and cunning sportsman can tell them.*"—STANDARD.

Margary.—THE JOURNEY OF AUGUSTUS RAYMOND MARGARY FROM SHANGHAE TO BHAMO AND BACK TO MANWYNE. From his Journals and Letters, with a brief Biographical Preface, a concluding chapter by Sir RUTHERFORD ALCOCK, K.C.B., and a Steel Portrait engraved by JEENS, and Map. 8vo. 10s. 6d.
"*There is a manliness, a cheerful spirit, an inherent vigour which was never overcome by sickness or debility, a tact which conquered the prejudices of a strange and suspicious population, a quiet self-reliance, always combined with deep religious feeling, unalloyed by either priggishness, cant, or superstition, that ought to commend this volume to readers sitting quietly at home who feel any pride in the high estimation accorded to men of their race at Yarkand or at Khiva, in the heart of Africa, or on the shores of Lake Seri-kul.*"—SATURDAY REVIEW.

Markham.—NORTHWARD HO! By Captain ALBERT H. MARKHAM, R.N., Author of "The Great Frozen Sea," &c. Including a Narrative of Captain Phipps's Expedition, by a Midshipman. With Illustrations. Crown 8vo. 10s. 6d.
"*Captain Markham's interesting volume has the advantage of being written by a man who is practically conversant with the subject.*"—PALL MALL GAZETTE.

Martin.—THE HISTORY OF LLOYD'S, AND OF MARINE INSURANCE IN GREAT BRITAIN. With an Appendix containing Statistics relating to Marine Insurance. By FREDERICK MARTIN, Author of "The Statesman's Year Book." 8vo. 14s.

Martineau.—BIOGRAPHICAL SKETCHES, 1852—1875. By HARRIET MARTINEAU. With Additional Sketches, and Autobiographical Sketch. Fifth Edition. Crown 8vo. 6s.

Masson (David).—For other Works by same Author, *see* PHILOSOPHICAL and BELLES LETTRES CATALOGUES.

Masson (David).—*continued.*

CHATTERTON: A Story of the Year 1770. By DAVID MASSON, LL.D., Professor of Rhetoric and English Literature in the University of Edinburgh. Crown 8vo. 5s.

THE THREE DEVILS: Luther's, Goethe's, and Milton's; and other Essays. Crown 8vo. 5s.

WORDSWORTH, SHELLEY, AND KEATS; and other Essays. Crown 8vo. 5s.

Mathews.—LIFE OF CHARLES J. MATHEWS, Chiefly Autobiographical. With Selections from his Correspondence and Speeches. Edited by CHARLES DICKENS.

"*One of the pleasantest and most readable books of the season. From first to last these two volumes are alive with the inimitable artist and comedian.... The whole book is full of life, vigour, and wit, and even through some of the gloomy episods of volume two, will repay most careful study. So complete, so varied a picture of a man's life is rarely to be met with.*"—STANDARD.

Maurice.—THE FRIENDSHIP OF BOOKS; AND OTHER LECTURES. By the REV. F. D. MAURICE. Edited with Preface, by THOMAS HUGHES, Q.C. Crown 8vo. 10s. 6d.

Mayor (J. E. B.)—WORKS edited by JOHN E. B. MAYOR, M.A., Kennedy Professor of Latin at Cambridge:—

CAMBRIDGE IN THE SEVENTEENTH CENTURY. Part II. Autobiography of Matthew Robinson. Fcap. 8vo. 5s. 6d.

LIFE OF BISHOP BEDELL. By his SON. Fcap. 8vo. 3s. 6d.

Melbourne.—MEMOIRS OF THE RT. HON. WILLIAM, SECOND VISCOUNT MELBOURNE. By W. M. TORRENS, M.P. With Portrait after Sir. T. Lawrence. Second Edition. 2 Vols. 8vo. 32s.

"*As might be expected, he has produced a book which will command and reward attention. It contains a great deal of valuable matter and a great deal of animated, elegant writing.*"—QUARTERLY REVIEW.

Mendelssohn.—LETTERS AND RECOLLECTIONS. By FERDINAND HILLER. Translated by M. E. VON GLEHN. With Portrait from a Drawing by KARL MÜLLER, never before published. Second Edition. Crown 8vo. 7s. 6d.

"*This is a very interesting addition to our knowledge of the great German composer. It reveals him to us under a new light, as the warmhearted comrade, the musician whose soul was in his work, and the home-loving, domestic man.*"—STANDARD.

Merewether.—BY SEA AND BY LAND. Being a Trip through Egypt, India, Ceylon, Australia, New Zealand, and America—all Round the World. By HENRY ALWORTH MEREWETHER, one of Her Majesty's Counsel. Crown 8vo. 8s. 6d.

Michael Angelo Buonarotti ; Sculptor, Painter, Architect. The Story of his Life and Labours. By C. C. BLACK, M.A. Illustrated by 20 Permanent Photographs. Royal 8vo. cloth elegant, 31s. 6d.

"*The story of Michael Angelo's life remains interesting whatever be the manner of telling it, and supported as it is by this beautiful series of photographs, the volume must take rank among the most splendid of Christmas books, fitted to serve and to outlive the season.*"—PALL MALL GAZETTE.

Michelet.—A SUMMARY OF MODERN HISTORY. Translated from the French of M. MICHELET, and continued to the present time by M. C. M. SIMPSON. Globe 8vo. 4s. 6d.

Milton.—LIFE OF JOHN MILTON. Narrated in connection with the Political, Ecclesiastical, and Literary History of his Time. By DAVID MASSON, M.A., LL.D., Professor of Rhetoric and English Literature in the University of Edinburgh. With Portraits. Vol. I. 18s. Vol. II., 1638—1643. 8vo. 16s. Vol. III. 1643—1649. 8vo. 18s. Vols. IV. and V. 1649—1660. 32s. Vol. VI. With Portrait. 21s. [*Index Volume in preparation.* This work is not only a Biography, but also a continuous Political, Ecclesiastical, and Literary History of England through Milton's whole time.

Mitford (A. B.)—TALES OF OLD JAPAN. By A. B. MITFORD, Second Secretary to the British Legation in Japan. With upwards of 30 Illustrations, drawn and cut on Wood by Japanese Artists. New and Cheaper Edition. Crown 8vo. 6s.

"*These very original volumes will always be interesting as memorials of a most exceptional society, while regarded simply as tales, they are sparkling, sensational, and dramatic.*"—PALL MALL GAZETTE.

Monteiro.—ANGOLA AND THE RIVER CONGO. By JOACHIM MONTEIRO. With numerous Illustrations from Sketches taken on the spot, and a Map. Two Vols. crown 8vo. 21s.

Morison.—THE LIFE AND TIMES OF SAINT BERNARD, Abbot of Clairvaux. By JAMES COTTER MORISON, M.A. New Edition. Crown 8vo. 6s.

Moseley.—NOTES BY A NATURALIST ON THE *CHALLENGER*: being an Account of various Observations made during the Voyage of H.M.S. *Challenger*, Round the World, in 1872–76. By H. N. MOSELEY, F.R.S., Member of the Scientific Staff of the *Challenger*. 8vo. with Maps, Coloured Plates, and Woodcuts. 21*s*.

"This is certainly the most interesting and suggestive book, descriptive of a naturalist's travels, which has been published since Mr. Darwin's '*Journal of Researches*' appeared, more than forty years ago."—NATURE. "We cannot point to any book of travels in our day more vivid in its powers of description, more varied in its subject matter, or more attractive to every educated reader."—SATURDAY REVIEW.

Murray.—ROUND ABOUT FRANCE. By E. C. GRENVILLE MURRAY. Crown 8vo. 7*s*. 6*d*.

"These short essays are a perfect mine of information as to the present condition and future prospects of political parties in France. . . . It is at once extremely interesting and exceptionally instructive on a subject on which few English people are well informed."—SCOTSMAN.

Napier.—MACVEY NAPIER'S SELECTED CORRESPONDENCE. Edited by his Son, MACVEY NAPIER. 8vo. 14*s*.

The TIMES says:—"It is replete with useful material for the biographers of many distinguished writers of the generation which is passing away. Since reading it we understand several noteworthy men, and Brougham in particular, far better than we did before." "It would be useless to attempt within our present limits to give any adequate idea of the abundance of interesting passages which meet us in the letters of Macaulay, Brougham, Carlyle, Jeffrey, Senior, and many other well-known writers. Especially piquant are Jeffrey's periodical criticisms on the contents of the Review which he had formerly edited."—PALL MALL GAZETTE.

Napoleon.—THE HISTORY OF NAPOLEON I. By P. LANFREY. A Translation with the sanction of the Author. 4 vols. 8vo. Vols. I. II. and III. price 12*s*. each. Vol. IV. With Index. 6*s*.

The PALL MALL GAZETTE says it is "one of the most striking pieces of historical composition of which France has to boast," and the SATURDAY REVIEW calls it "an excellent translation of a work on every ground deserving to be translated. It is unquestionably and immeasurably the best that has been produced. It is in fact the only work to which we can turn for an accurate and trustworthy narrative of that extraordinary career. . . . The book is the best and indeed the only trustworthy history of Napoleon which has been written."

Nichol.—TABLES OF EUROPEAN LITERATURE AND HISTORY, A.D. 200—1876. By J. NICHOL, LL.D., Professor of English Language and Literature, Glasgow. 4to. 6*s*. 6*d*.

TABLES OF ANCIENT LITERATURE AND HISTORY, B.C. 1500—A.D. 200. By the same Author. 4to. 4*s*. 6*d*.

HISTORY, BIOGRAPHY, TRAVELS, ETC. 23

Nordenskiöld's Arctic Voyages, 1858-79.—With Maps and numerous Illustrations. 8vo. 16s.

"*A volume of great interest and much scientific value.*"—NATURE.

Oliphant (Mrs.).—THE MAKERS OF FLORENCE: Dante Giotto, Savonarola, and their City. By Mrs. OLIPHANT. With numerous Illustrations from drawings by Professor DELAMOTTE, and portrait of Savonarola, engraved by JEENS. Second Edition. Medium 8vo. Cloth extra. 21s.

"*We are grateful to Mrs. Oliphant for her eloquent and beautiful sketches of Dante, Fra Angelico, and Savonarola. They are picturesque, full of life, and rich in detail, and they are charmingly illustrated by the art of the engraver.*"—SPECTATOR.

Oliphant.—THE DUKE AND THE SCHOLAR; and other Essays. By T. L. KINGTON OLIPHANT. 8vo. 7s. 6d.

"*This volume contains one of the most beautiful biographical essays we have seen since Macaulay's days.*"—STANDARD.

Otte.—SCANDINAVIAN HISTORY. By E. C. OTTE. With Maps. Extra fcap. 8vo. 6s.

Owens College Essays and Addresses.—By PROFESSORS AND LECTURERS OF OWENS COLLEGE, MANCHESTER. Published in Commemoration of the Opening of the New College Buildings, October 7th, 1873. 8vo. 14s.

Palgrave (R. F. D.)—THE HOUSE OF COMMONS; Illustrations of its History and Practice. By REGINALD F. D. PALGRAVE, Clerk Assistant of the House of Commons. New and Revised Edition. Crown 8vo. 2s. 6d.

Palgrave (Sir F.)—HISTORY OF NORMANDY AND OF ENGLAND. By Sir FRANCIS PALGRAVE, Deputy Keeper of Her Majesty's Public Records. Completing the History to the Death of William Rufus. 4 Vols. 8vo. 4l. 4s.

Palgrave (W. G.)—A NARRATIVE OF A YEAR'S JOURNEY THROUGH CENTRAL AND EASTERN ARABIA, 1862-3. By WILLIAM GIFFORD PALGRAVE, late of the Eighth Regiment Bombay N. I. Sixth Edition. With Maps, Plans, and Portrait of Author, engraved on steel by Jeens. Crown 8vo. 6s.

"*He has not only written one of the best books on the Arabs and one of the best books on Arabia, but he has done so in a manner that must command the respect no less than the admiration of his fellow-countrymen.*"—FORTNIGHTLY REVIEW.

Palgrave.—*continued.*
ESSAYS ON EASTERN QUESTIONS. By W. GIFFORD PALGRAVE. 8vo. 10s. 6d.

"*These essays are full of anecdote and interest. The book is decidedly a valuable addition to the stock of literature on which men must base their opinion of the difficult social and political problems suggested by the designs of Russia, the capacity of Mahometans for sovereignty, and the good government and retention of India.*"—SATURDAY REVIEW.

DUTCH GUIANA. With Maps and Plans. 8vo. 9s.

"*His pages are nearly exhaustive as far as facts and statistics go, while they are lightened by graphic social sketches as well as sparkling descriptions of scenery.*"—SATURDAY REVIEW.

Patteson.—LIFE AND LETTERS OF JOHN COLERIDGE PATTESON, D.D., Missionary Bishop of the Melanesian Islands. By CHARLOTTE M. YONGE, Author of "The Heir of Redclyffe." With Portraits after RICHMOND and from Photograph, engraved by JEENS. With Map. Fifth Edition. Two Vols. Crown 8vo. 12s.

"*Miss Yonge's work is in one respect a model biography. It is made up almost entirely of Patteson's own letters. Aware that he had left his home once and for all, his correspondence took the form of a diary, and as we read on we come to know the man, and to love him almost as if we had seen him.*"—ATHENÆUM. "*Such a life, with its grand lessons of unselfishness, is a blessing and an honour to the age in which it is lived; the biography cannot be studied without pleasure and profit, and indeed we should think little of the man who did not rise from the study of it better and wiser. Neither the Church nor the nation which produces such sons need ever despair of its future.*"—SATURDAY REVIEW.

Pauli.—PICTURES OF OLD ENGLAND. By Dr. REINHOLD PAULI. Translated, with the approval of the Author, by E. C. OTTÉ. Cheaper Edition. Crown 8vo. 6s.

Payne.—A HISTORY OF EUROPEAN COLONIES. By E. J. PAYNE, M.A. With Maps. 18mo. 4s. 6d.

The TIMES *says*:—"*We have seldom met with a historian capable of forming a more comprehensive, far-seeing, and unprejudiced estimate of events and peoples, and we can commend this little work as one certain to prove of the highest interest to all thoughtful readers.*"

Persia.—EASTERN PERSIA. An Account of the Journeys of the Persian Boundary Commission, 1870-1-2.—Vol. I. The Geography, with Narratives by Majors ST. JOHN, LOVETT, and EUAN SMITH, and an Introduction by Major-General Sir FREDERIC GOLDSMID, C.B., K.C.S.I., British Commissioner and Arbitrator.

HISTORY, BIOGRAPHY, TRAVELS, ETC. 25

With Maps and Illustrations.—Vol. II. The Zoology and Geology. By W. T. BLANFORD, A.R.S.M., F.R.S. With Coloured Illustrations. Two Vols. 8vo. 42s.
"*The volumes largely increase our store of information about countries with which Englishmen ought to be familiar. . . . . They throw into the shade all that hitherto has appeared in our tongue respecting the local features of Persia, its scenery, its resources, even its social condition. They contain also abundant evidence of English endurance, daring, and spirit.*"—TIMES.

Prichard.—THE ADMINISTRATION OF INDIA. From 1859 to 1868. The First Ten Years of Administration under the Crown. By I. T. PRICHARD, Barrister-at-Law. Two Vols. Demy 8vo. With Map. 21s.

Raphael.—RAPHAEL OF URBINO AND HIS FATHER GIOVANNI SANTI. By J. D. PASSAVANT, formerly Director of the Museum at Frankfort. With Twenty Permanent Photographs. Royal 8vo. Handsomely bound. 31s. 6d.
The SATURDAY REVIEW *says of them*, "*We have seen not a few elegant specimens of Mr. Woodbury's new process, but we have seen none that equal these.*"

Reynolds.—SIR JOSHUA REYNOLDS AS A PORTRAIT PAINTER. AN ESSAY. By J. CHURTON COLLINS, B.A. Balliol College, Oxford. Illustrated by a Series of Portraits of distinguished Beauties of the Court of George III.; reproduced in Autotype from Proof Impressions of the celebrated Engravings, by VALENTINE GREEN, THOMAS WATSON, F. R. SMITH, E. FISHER, and others. Folio half-morocco. £5 5s.

Rogers (James E. Thorold).—HISTORICAL GLEANINGS : A Series of Sketches. Montague, Walpole, Adam Smith, Cobbett. By Prof. ROGERS. Crown 8vo. 4s. 6d. Second Series. Wiklif, Laud, Wilkes, and Horne Tooke. Crown 8vo. 6s.

Routledge.—CHAPTERS IN THE HISTORY OF POPULAR PROGRESS IN ENGLAND, chiefly in Relation to the Freedom of the Press and Trial by Jury, 1660—1820. With application to later years. By J. ROUTLEDGE. 8vo. 16s.
"*The volume abounds in facts and information, almost always useful and often curious.*"—TIMES.

Rumford.—COUNT RUMFORD'S COMPLETE WORKS, with Memoir, and Notices of his Daughter. By GEORGE ELLIS. Five Vols. 8vo. 4l. 14s. 6d.

Seeley (Professor).—LECTURES AND ESSAYS. By J. R. SEELEY, M.A. Professor of Modern History in the University of Cambridge. 8vo. 10s. 6d.
CONTENTS:—*Roman Imperialism:* 1. *The Great Roman Revolution;* 2. *The Proximate Cause of the Fall of the Roman Empire; The Later Empire. — Milton's Political Opinions — Milton's Poetry — Elementary Principles in Art — Liberal Education in Universities — English in Schools — The Church as a Teacher of Morality — The Teaching of Politics: an Inaugural Lecture delivered at Cambridge.*

Shelburne.—LIFE OF WILLIAM, EARL OF SHELBURNE, AFTERWARDS FIRST MARQUIS OF LANSDOWNE. With Extracts from his Papers and Correspondence. By Lord EDMOND FITZMAURICE. In Three Vols. 8vo. Vol. I. 1737—1766, 12s.; Vol. II. 1766—1776, 12s.; Vol. III. 1776—1805. 16s.
"*Lord Edmond Fitzmaurice has succeeded in placing before us a wealth of new matter, which, while casting valuable and much-needed light on several obscure passages in the political history of a hundred years ago, has enabled us for the first time to form a clear and consistent idea of his ancestor.*"—SPECTATOR.

Sime.—HISTORY OF GERMANY. By JAMES SIME, M.A. 18mo. 3s. Being Vol. V. of the Historical Course for Schools. Edited by EDWARD A. FREEMAN, D.C.L.
"*This is a remarkably clear and impressive History of Germany.*"—STANDARD.

Squier.—PERU: INCIDENTS OF TRAVEL AND EXPLORATION IN THE LAND OF THE INCAS. By E. G. SQUIER, M.A., F.S.A., late U.S. Commissioner to Peru. With 300 Illustrations. Second Edition. 8vo. 21s.
The TIMES *says:*—"*No more solid and trustworthy contribution has been made to an accurate knowledge of what are among the most wonderful ruins in the world. The work is really what its title implies. While of the greatest importance as a contribution to Peruvian archæology, it is also a thoroughly entertaining and instructive narrative of travel. Not the least important feature must be considered the numerous well executed illustrations.*"

Strangford.—EGYPTIAN SHRINES AND SYRIAN SEPULCHRES, including a Visit to Palmyra. By EMILY A. BEAUFORT (Viscountess Strangford), Author of "The Eastern Shores of the Adriatic." New Edition. Crown 8vo. 7s. 6d.

Tait.—AN ANALYSIS OF ENGLISH HISTORY, based upon Green's "Short History of the English People." By C. W. A. TAIT, M.A., Assistant Master, Clifton College. Crown 8vo. 3s. 6d.

Tait.—CATHARINE AND CRAUFURD TAIT, WIFE AND SON OF ARCHIBALD CAMPBELL, ARCHBISHOP OF CANTERBURY : a Memoir, Edited, at the request of the Archbishop, by the Rev. W. BENHAM, B.D., Vicar of Margate, and One of the Six Preachers of Canterbury Cathedral. With Two Portraits engraved by JEENS. Crown 8vo. 12s. 6d.

"*The volume can scarcely fail to be read widely and with deep interest. . . . It is difficult to put it down when once taken in hand, still more difficult to get through it without emotion. . . . We commend the volume to those who knew Catharine and Craufurd Tait as one which will bring back to their minds recollections of their characters as true as the recollections of the faces brought back by the two excellent portraits which adorn the book; while to those who knew them not, we commend it as containing the record of two noble Christian lives, which it will be a pleasure to them to contemplate and an advantage to emulate.*"—TIMES.

Thomas.—THE LIFE OF JOHN THOMAS, Surgeon of the "Earl of Oxford" East Indiaman, and First Baptist Missionary to Bengal. By C. B. LEWIS, Baptist Missionary. 8vo. 10s. 6d.

Thompson.—HISTORY OF ENGLAND. By EDITH THOMPSON. Being Vol. II. of the Historical Course for Schools, Edited by EDWARD A. FREEMAN, D.C.L. New Edition, revised and enlarged, with Maps. 18mo. 2s. 6d.

"*Freedom from prejudice, simplicity of style, and accuracy of statement, are the characteristics of this volume. It is a trustworthy text-book, and likely to be generally serviceable in schools.*"—PALL MALL GAZETTE. "*In its great accuracy and correctness of detail it stands far ahead of the general run of school manuals. Its arrangement, too, is clear, and its style simple and straightforward.*"—SATURDAY REVIEW.

Todhunter.—THE CONFLICT OF STUDIES; AND OTHER ESSAYS ON SUBJECTS CONNECTED WITH EDUCATION. By ISAAC TODHUNTER, M.A., F.R.S., late Fellow and Principal Mathematical Lecturer of St. John's College, Cambridge. 8vo. 10s. 6d.

Trench (Archbishop).—For other Works by the same Author, *see* THEOLOGICAL and BELLES LETTRES CATALOGUES, and page 30 of this Catalogue.

GUSTAVUS ADOLPHUS IN GERMANY, and other Lectures on the Thirty Years' War. Second Edition, revised and enlarged. Fcap. 8vo. 4s.'

PLUTARCH, HIS LIFE, HIS LIVES, AND HIS MORALS. Five Lectures. Second Edition, enlarged. Fcap. 8vo. 3s. 6d.

LECTURES ON MEDIEVAL CHURCH HISTORY. Being the substance of Lectures delivered in Queen's College, London. Second Edition, revised. 8vo. 12s.

Trench (Maria).—THE LIFE OF ST. TERESA. By MARIA TRENCH. With Portrait engraved by JEENS. Crown 8vo, cloth extra. 8s. 6d.
"*A book of rare interest.*"—JOHN BULL.

Trench (Mrs. R.)—REMAINS OF THE LATE MRS. RICHARD TRENCH. Being Selections from her Journals, Letters, and other Papers. Edited by ARCHBISHOP TRENCH. New and Cheaper Issue, with Portrait. 8vo. 6s.

Trollope.—A HISTORY OF THE COMMONWEALTH OF FLORENCE FROM THE EARLIEST INDEPENDENCE OF THE COMMUNE TO THE FALL OF THE REPUBLIC IN 1831. By T. ADOLPHUS TROLLOPE. 4 Vols. 8vo. Half morocco. 21s.

Uppingham by the Sea.—A NARRATIVE OF THE YEAR AT BORTH. By J. H. S. Crown 8vo. 3s. 6d.

Victor Emmanuel II., First King of Italy.—HIS LIFE. By G. S. GODKIN. 2 vols., crown 8vo. 16s.
"*An extremely clear and interesting history of one of the most important changes of later times.*"—EXAMINER.

Wallace.—THE MALAY ARCHIPELAGO: the Land of the Orang Utan and the Bird of Paradise. By ALFRED RUSSEL WALLACE. A Narrative of Travel with Studies of Man and Nature. With Maps and numerous Illustrations. Sixth Edition. Crown 8vo. 7s. 6d.
"*The result is a vivid picture of tropical life, which may be read with unflagging interest, and a sufficient account of his scientific conclusions to stimulate our appetite without wearying us by detail. In short, we may safely say that we have never read a more agreeable book of its kind.*"— SATURDAY REVIEW.

Ward.—A HISTORY OF ENGLISH DRAMATIC LITERATURE TO THE DEATH OF QUEEN ANNE. By A. W. WARD, M.A., Professor of History and English Literature in Owens College, Manchester. Two Vols. 8vo. 32s.
"*As full of interest as of information. To students of dramatic literature invaluable, and may be equally recommended to readers for mere pastime.*"—PALL MALL GAZETTE.

Ward (J.)—EXPERIENCES OF A DIPLOMATIST. Being recollections of Germany founded on Diaries kept during the years 1840—1870. By JOHN WARD, C.B., late H.M. Minister-Resident to the Hanse Towns. 8vo. 10s. 6d.

Waterton (C.)—WANDERINGS IN SOUTH AMERICA, THE NORTH-WEST OF THE UNITED STATES, AND THE ANTILLES IN 1812, 1816, 1820, and 1824. With Original Instructions for the perfect Preservation of Birds, etc., for Cabinets of Natural History. By CHARLES WATERTON. New Edition, edited with Biographical Introduction and Explanatory Index by the Rev. J. G. WOOD, M.A. With 100 Illustrations. Cheaper Edition. Crown 8vo. 6s.

Wedgwood.—JOHN WESLEY AND THE EVANGELICAL REACTION of the Eighteenth Century. By JULIA WEDGWOOD. Crown 8vo. 8s. 6d.

Whewell.—WILLIAM WHEWELL, D.D., late Master of Trinity College, Cambridge. An Account of his Writings, with Selections from his Literary and Scientific Correspondence. By I. TODHUNTER, M.A., F.R.S. Two Vols. 8vo. 25s.

White.—THE NATURAL HISTORY AND ANTIQUITIES OF SELBORNE. By GILBERT WHITE. Edited, with Memoir and Notes, by FRANK BUCKLAND, A Chapter on Antiquities by LORD SELBORNE, Map, &c., and numerous Illustrations by P. H. DELAMOTTE. Royal 8vo. Cloth, extra gilt. Cheaper Issue. 21s.

Also a Large Paper Edition, containing, in addition to the above, upwards of Thirty Woodburytype Illustrations from Drawings by Prof. DELAMOTTE. Two Vols. 4to. Half morocco, elegant. 4l. 4s.

"*Mr. Delamotte's charming illustrations are a worthy decoration of so dainty a book. They bring Selborne before us, and really help us to understand why White's love for his native place never grew cold.*"—TIMES.

Wilson.—A MEMOIR OF GEORGE WILSON, M.D., F.R.S.E., Regius Professor of Technology in the University of Edinburgh. By his SISTER. New Edition. Crown 8vo. 6s.

Wilson (Daniel, LL.D.)—Works by DANIEL WILSON, LL.D., Professor of History and English Literature in University College, Toronto :—

PREHISTORIC ANNALS OF SCOTLAND. New Edition, with numerous Illustrations. Two Vols. demy 8vo. 36s.

"*One of the most interesting, learned, and elegant works we have seen for a long time.*"—WESTMINSTER REVIEW.

PREHISTORIC MAN : Researches into the Origin of Civilization in the Old and New World. New Edition, revised and enlarged throughout, with numerous Illustrations and two Coloured Plates. Two Vols. 8vo. 36s.

Wilson.—*continued.*

"*A valuable work pleasantly written and well worthy of attention both by students and general readers.*"—ACADEMY.

> CHATTERTON: A Biographical Study. By DANIEL WILSON, LL.D., Professor of History and English Literature in University College, Toronto. Crown 8vo. 6s. 6d.

Yonge (Charlotte M.)—Works by CHARLOTTE M. YONGE, Author of "The Heir of Redclyffe," &c., &c. :—

> A PARALLEL HISTORY OF FRANCE AND ENGLAND: consisting of Outlines and Dates. Oblong 4to. 3s. 6d.
>
> CAMEOS FROM ENGLISH HISTORY. From Rollo to Edward II. Extra fcap. 8vo. Third Edition. 5s.
>
>> SECOND SERIES, THE WARS IN FRANCE. Extra fcap. 8vo. Third Edition. 5s.
>>
>> THIRD SERIES, THE WARS OF THE ROSES. Extra fcap. 8vo. 5s.
>>
>> FOURTH SERIES. Reformation Times. Extra fcap. 8vo. 5s.

"*Instead of dry details,*" says the NONCONFORMIST, "*we have living pictures, faithful, vivid, and striking.*"

> HISTORY OF FRANCE. Maps. 18mo. 3s. 6d.
> [*Historical Course for Schools.*

POLITICS, POLITICAL AND SOCIAL ECONOMY, LAW, AND KINDRED SUBJECTS.

Anglo-Saxon Law.—ESSAYS IN. Contents: Law Courts—Land and Family Laws and Legal Procedure generally. With Select cases. Medium 8vo. 18s.

Arnold.—THE ROMAN SYSTEM OF PROVINCIAL ADMINISTRATION TO THE ACCESSION OF CONSTANTINE THE GREAT. Being the Arnold Prize Essay for 1879. By W. T. Arnold, B.A. Crown 8vo. 6s.

Ball.—THE STUDENT'S GUIDE TO THE BAR. By WALTER W. BALL, M.A., of the Inner Temple, Barrister-at-Law. Crown 8vo. 2s. 6d.
"*The student will here find a clear statement of the several steps by which the degree of barrister is obtained, and also useful advice about the advantages of a prolonged course of 'reading in Chambers.'*"—ACADEMY.

Bernard.—FOUR LECTURES ON SUBJECTS CONNECTED WITH DIPLOMACY. By MONTAGUE BERNARD, M.A., Chichele Professor of International Law and Diplomacy, Oxford. 8vo. 9s.
"*Singularly interesting lectures, so able, clear, and attractive.*"—SPECTATOR.

Bright (John, M.P.)—Works by the Right Hon. JOHN BRIGHT, M.P.
SPEECHES ON QUESTIONS OF PUBLIC POLICY. Edited by Professor THOROLD ROGERS. Author's Popular Edition. Globe 8vo. 3s. 6d.
"*Mr. Bright's speeches will always deserve to be studied, as an apprenticeship to popular and parliamentary oratory; they will form materials for the history of our time, and many brilliant passages, perhaps some entire speeches, will really become a part of the living literature of England.*"—DAILY NEWS.

LIBRARY EDITION. Two Vols. 8vo. With Portrait. 25s.

PUBLIC ADDRESSES. Edited by J. THOROLD ROGERS. 8vo. 14s.

Bucknill.—HABITUAL DRUNKENNESS AND INSANE DRUNKARDS. By J. C. BUCKNILL, M.D., F.R.S., late Lord Chancellor's Visitor of Lunatics. Crown 8vo. 2s. 6d.

Cairnes.—Works by J. E. CAIRNES, M.A., Emeritus Professor of Political Economy in University College, London.
ESSAYS IN POLITICAL ECONOMY, THEORETICAL and APPLIED. By J. E. CAIRNES, M.A., Professor of Political Economy in University College, London. 8vo. 10s. 6d.
POLITICAL ESSAYS. 8vo. 10s. 6d.
SOME LEADING PRINCIPLES OF POLITICAL ECONOMY NEWLY EXPOUNDED. 8vo. 14s.
CONTENTS :—*Part I. Value. Part II. Labour and Capital. Part III. International Trade.*
"*A work which is perhaps the most valuable contribution to the science made since the publication, a quarter of a century since, of Mr. Mill's 'Principles of Political Economy.'*"—DAILY NEWS.
THE CHARACTER AND LOGICAL METHOD OF POLITICAL ECONOMY. New Edition, enlarged. 8vo. 7s. 6d.
"*These lectures are admirably fitted to correct the slipshod generalizations which pass current as the science of Political Economy.*"—TIMES.

Cobden (Richard).—SPEECHES ON QUESTIONS OF PUBLIC POLICY. By RICHARD COBDEN. Edited by the Right Hon. John Bright, M.P., and J. E. Thorold Rogers. Popular Edition. 8vo. 3s. 6d.

Fawcett.—Works by HENRY FAWCETT, M.A., M.P., Fellow of Trinity Hall, and Professor of Political Economy in the University of Cambridge :—
THE ECONOMIC POSITION OF THE BRITISH LABOURER. Extra fcap. 8vo. 5s.
MANUAL OF POLITICAL ECONOMY. Fifth Edition, with New Chapters on the Depreciation of Silver, etc. Crown 8vo. 12s.
The DAILY NEWS *says:* "*It forms one of the best introductions to the principles of the science, and to its practical applications in the problems of modern, and especially of English, government and society.*"
PAUPERISM : ITS CAUSES AND REMEDIES. Crown 8vo. 5s. 6d.
The ATHENÆUM *calls the work* "*a repertory of interesting and well digested information.*"
SPEECHES ON SOME CURRENT POLITICAL QUESTIONS. 8vo. 10s. 6d.
"*They will help to educate, not perhaps, parties, but the educators of parties.*"—DAILY NEWS.

Fawcett.—*continued.*

FREE TRADE AND PROTECTION: an Inquiry into the Causes which have retarded the general adoption of Free Trade since its introduction into England. Third Edition. 8vo. 7s. 6d.

"*No greater service can be rendered to the cause of Free Trade than a clear explanation of the principles on which Free Trade rests. Professor Fawcett has done this in the volume before us with all his habitual clearness of thought and expression.*"—ECONOMIST.

INDIAN FINANCE. Three Essays, with Introduction and Appendix. 8vo. 7s. 6d.

ESSAYS ON POLITICAL AND SOCIAL SUBJECTS. By PROFESSOR FAWCETT, M.P., and MILLICENT GARRETT FAWCETT. 8vo. 10s. 6d.

"*They will all repay the perusal of the thinking reader.*"—DAILY NEWS.

Fawcett (Mrs.)—Works by MILLICENT GARRETT FAWCETT.

POLITICAL ECONOMY FOR BEGINNERS. WITH QUESTIONS. New Edition. 18mo. 2s. 6d.

The DAILY NEWS *calls it "clear, compact, and comprehensive;" and the* SPECTATOR *says, "Mrs. Fawcett's treatise is perfectly suited to its purpose."*

TALES IN POLITICAL ECONOMY. Crown 8vo. 3s.

"*The idea is a good one, and it is quite wonderful what a mass of economic teaching the author manages to compress into a small space... The true doctrines of International Trade, Currency, and the ratio between Production and Population, are set before us and illustrated in a masterly manner.*"—ATHENÆUM.

Goschen.—REPORTS AND SPEECHES ON LOCAL TAXATION. By GEORGE J. GOSCHEN, M.P. Royal 8vo. 5s.

"*The volume contains a vast mass of information of the highest value.*" —ATHENÆUM.

Guide to the Unprotected, in Every Day Matters Relating to Property and Income. By a BANKER'S DAUGHTER. Fourth Edition, Revised. Extra fcap. 8vo. 3s. 6d.

"*Many an unprotected female will bless the head which planned and the hand which compiled this admirable little manual. . . . This book was very much wanted, and it could not have been better done.*"— MORNING STAR.

Hamilton.—MONEY AND VALUE: an Inquiry into the Means and Ends of Economic Production, with an Appendix on the Depreciation of Silver and Indian Currency. By ROWLAND HAMILTON. 8vo. 12s.

"*The subject is here dealt with in a luminous style, and by presenting it from a new point of view in connection with the nature and functions of money, a genuine service has been rendered to commercial science.*"— BRITISH QUARTERLY REVIEW.

Harwood.—DISESTABLISHMENT : a Defence of the Principle of a National Church. By GEORGE HARWOOD, M.A. 8vo. 12s.

Hill.—OUR COMMON LAND: and other Short Essays. By OCTAVIA HILL. Extra fcap. 8vo. 3s. 6d.
CONTENTS:—*Our Common Land. District Visiting. A More Excellent Way of Charity. A Word on Good Citizenship. Open Spaces. Effectual Charity. The Future of our Commons.*

Historicus.—LETTERS ON SOME QUESTIONS OF INTERNATIONAL LAW. Reprinted from the *Times*, with considerable Additions. 8vo. 7s. 6d. Also, ADDITIONAL LETTERS. 8vo. 2s. 6d.

Holland.—THE TREATY RELATIONS OF RUSSIA AND TURKEY FROM 1774 TO 1853. A Lecture delivered at Oxford, April 1877. By T. E. HOLLAND, D.C.L., Professor of International Law and Diplomacy, Oxford. Crown 8vo. 2s.

Hughes (Thos.)—THE OLD CHURCH: WHAT SHALL WE DO WITH IT? By THOMAS HUGHES, Q.C. Crown 8vo. 6s.

Jevons.—Works by W. STANLEY JEVONS, M.A., F.R.S., Professor of Political Economy in University College, London. (For other Works by the same Author, *see* EDUCATIONAL and PHILOSOPHICAL CATALOGUES.)

THE THEORY OF POLITICAL ECONOMY. Second Edition, revised, with new Preface and Appendices. 8vo. 10s. 6d.
"*Professor Jevons has done invaluable service by courageously claiming political economy to be strictly a branch of Applied Mathematics.*"—WESTMINSTER REVIEW.

PRIMER OF POLITICAL ECONOMY. 18mo. 1s.

Laveleye. — PRIMITIVE PROPERTY. By EMILE DE LAVELEYE. Translated by G. R. L. MARRIOTT, LL.B., with an Introduction by T. E. CLIFFE LESLIE, LL.B. 8vo. 12s.
"*It is almost impossible to over-estimate the value of the well-digested knowledge which it contains; it is one of the most learned books that have been contributed to the historical department of the literature of economic science.*"—ATHENÆUM.

Leading Cases done into English. By an APPRENTICE OF LINCOLN'S INN. Third Edition. Crown 8vo. 2s. 6d.

"*Here is a rare treat for the lovers of quaint conceits, who in reading this charming little book will find enjoyment in the varied metre and graphic language in which the several tales are told, no less than in the accurate and pithy rendering of some of our most familiar 'Leading Cases.'*"—SATURDAY REVIEW.

Lubbock.—ADDRESSES, POLITICAL AND EDUCATIONAL. By Sir JOHN LUBBOCK, Bart., M.P., &c., &c. 8vo. 8s. 6d.

The ten speeches given are (1) on the Imperial Policy of Great Britain, (2) on the Bank Act of 1844, (3) on the Present System of Public School Education, 1876, (4) on the Present System of Elementary Education, (5) on the Income Tax, (6) on the National Debt, (7) on the Declaration of Paris, (8) on Marine Insurances, (9) on the Preservation of Ancient Monuments, and (10) on Egypt.

Macdonell.—THE LAND QUESTION, WITH SPECIAL REFERENCE TO ENGLAND AND SCOTLAND. By JOHN MACDONELL, Barrister-at-Law. 8vo. 10s. 6d.

Marshall.—THE ECONOMICS OF INDUSTRY. By A. MARSHALL, M.A., Principal of University College, Bristol, and MARY PALEY MARSHALL, late Lecturer at Newnham Hall, Cambridge. Extra fcap. 8vo. 2s. 6d.

"*The book is of sterling value, and will be of great use to teachers and students of political economy.*"—ATHENÆUM.

Martin.—THE STATESMAN'S YEAR-BOOK: A Statistical and Historical Annual of the States of the Civilized World, for the year 1880. By FREDERICK MARTIN. Seventeenth Annual Publication. Revised after Official Returns. Crown 8vo. 10s. 6d.

The Statesman's Year-Book is the only work in the English language which furnishes a clear and concise account of the actual condition of all the States of Europe, the civilised countries of America, Asia, and Africa, and the British Colonies and Dependencies in all parts of the world. The new issue of the work has been revised and corrected, on the basis of official reports received direct from the heads of the leading Governments of the world, in reply to letters sent to them by the Editor. Through the valuable assistance thus given, it has been possible to collect an amount of information, political, statistical, and commercial, of the latest date, and of unimpeachable trustworthiness, such as no publication of the same kind has ever been able to furnish. "As indispensable as Bradshaw."—TIMES.

Monahan.—THE METHOD OF LAW: an Essay on the Statement and Arrangement of the Legal Standard of Conduct. By J. H. MONAHAN, Q.C. Crown 8vo. 6s.

"*Will be found valuable by careful law studen's who have felt the importance of gaining clear ideas regarding the relations between the parts of the complex organism they have to study.*"—BRITISH QUARTERLY REVIEW.

Paterson.—THE LIBERTY OF THE SUBJECT AND THE LAWS OF ENGLAND RELATING TO THE SECURITY OF THE PERSON. Commentaries on. By JAMES PATERSON, M.A., Barrister at Law, sometime Commissioner for English and Irish Fisheries, etc. Cheaper issue. Two Vols. Crown 8vo. 21s.

"*Two or three hours' dipping into these volumes, not to say reading them through, will give legislators and stump orators a knowledge of the liberty of a citizen of their country, in its principles, its fulness, and its modification, such as they probably in nine cases out of ten never had before.*" —SCOTSMAN.

Phillimore.—PRIVATE LAW AMONG THE ROMANS, from the Pandects. By JOHN GEORGE PHILLIMORE, Q.C. 8vo. 16s.

Practical Politics.—ISSUED BY THE NATIONAL LIBERAL FEDERATION.
I. THE TENANT FARMER: Land Laws and Landlords. By JAMES HOWARD. 8vo. 1s.
II. FOREIGN POLICY. By M. E. GRANT DUFF, M.P. 8vo. 1s.
III. FREEDOM OF LAND. By G. SHAW LEFEVRE, M.P. 8vo. 2s. 6d.

Rogers.—COBDEN AND POLITICAL OPINION. By J. E. THOROLD ROGERS. 8vo. 10s. 6d.

Stephen (C. E.)—THE SERVICE OF THE POOR; Being an Inquiry into the Reasons for and against the Establishment of Religious Sisterhoods for Charitable Purposes. By CAROLINE EMILIA STEPHEN. Crown 8vo. 6s. 6d.

Stephen.—Works by Sir JAMES F. STEPHEN, K.C.S.I., Q.C.
A DIGEST OF THE LAW OF EVIDENCE. Third Edition with New Preface. Crown 8vo. 6s.
A DIGEST OF THE CRIMINAL LAW. (Crimes and Punishments.) 8vo. 16s.

Stephen.—*continued.*

"*We feel sure that any person of ordinary intelligence who had never looked into a law-book in his life might, by a few days' careful study of this volume, obtain a more accurate understanding of the criminal law, a more perfect conception of its different bearings, a more thorough and intelligent insight into its snares and pitfalls, than an ordinary practitioner can boast of after years of study of the ordinary text-books and practical experience of the Courts unassisted by any competent guide.*"—SATURDAY REVIEW.

A GENERAL VIEW OF THE CRIMINAL LAW OF ENG-LAND. Two Vols. Crown 8vo. [*New edition in the press.*

Stubbs.—VILLAGE POLITICS. Addresses and Sermons on the Labour Question. By C. W. STUBBS, M.A., Vicar of Granborough, Bucks. Extra fcap. 8vo. 3s. 6d.

Thornton.—Works by W. T. THORNTON, C.B., Secretary for Public Works in the India Office :—

ON LABOUR: Its Wrongful Claims and Rightful Dues; Its Actual Present and Possible Future. Second Edition, revised, 8vo. 14s.

A PLEA FOR PEASANT PROPRIETORS: With the Outlines of a Plan for their Establishment in Ireland. New Edition, revised. Crown 8vo. 7s. 6d.

INDIAN PUBLIC WORKS AND COGNATE INDIAN TOPICS. With Map of Indian Railways. Crown 8vo. 8s. 6d.

Walker.—Works by F. A. WALKER, M.A., Ph.D., Professor of Political Economy and History, Yale College :—

THE WAGES QUESTION. A Treatise on Wages and the Wages Class. 8vo. 14s.

MONEY. 8vo. 16s.

"*It is painstaking, laborious, and states the question in a clear and very intelligible form. . . . The volume possesses a great value as a sort of encyclopædia of knowledge on the subject.*"—ECONOMIST.

MONEY IN ITS RELATIONS TO TRADE AND INDUSTRY. Crown 8vo. 7s. 6d.

Wilson.—RECIPROCITY, BI-METALLISM, AND LAND-TENURE REFORM. By A. J. WILSON, Author of "The Resources of Modern Countries." 8vo. 7s. 6d.

Work about the Five Dials. With an Introductory Note by THOMAS CARLYLE. Crown 8vo. 6s.

"*A book which abounds with wise and practical suggestions.*"—PALL MALL GAZETTE.

WORKS CONNECTED WITH THE SCIENCE OR THE HISTORY OF LANGUAGE.

Abbott.—A SHAKESPERIAN GRAMMAR: An Attempt to illustrate some of the Differences between Elizabethan and Modern English. By the Rev. E. A. ABBOTT, D.D., Head Master of the City of London School. New and Enlarged Edition. Extra fcap. 8vo. 6s.

"*Valuable not only as an aid to the critical study of Shakespeare, but as tending to familiarize the reader with Elizabethan English in general.*"—ATHENÆUM.

Breymann.—A FRENCH GRAMMAR BASED ON PHILOLOGICAL PRINCIPLES. By HERMANN BREYMANN, Ph.D., Professor of Philology in the University of Munich late Lecturer on French Language and Literature at Owens College, Manchester. Extra fcap. 8vo. 4s. 6d.

Ellis.—PRACTICAL HINTS ON THE QUANTITATIVE PRONUNCIATION OF LATIN, FOR THE USE OF CLASSICAL TEACHERS AND LINGUISTS. By A. J. ELLIS, B.A., F.R.S., &c. Extra fcap. 8vo. 4s. 6d.

Fleay.—A SHAKESPEARE MANUAL. By the Rev. F. G. FLEAY, M.A., Head Master of Skipton Grammar School. Extra fcap. 8vo. 4s. 6d.

Goodwin.—Works by W. W. GOODWIN, Professor of Greek Literature in Harvard University.

SYNTAX OF THE GREEK MOODS AND TENSES. New Edition. Crown 8vo. 6s. 6d.

AN ELEMENTARY GREEK GRAMMAR. Crown 8vo. 6s.

"*It is the best Greek Grammar of its size in the English language.*"—ATHENÆUM.

Hadley.—ESSAYS PHILOLOGICAL AND CRITICAL. Selected from the Papers of JAMES HADLEY, LL.D., Professor of Greek in Yale College, &c. 8vo. 16s.

Hales.—LONGER ENGLISH POEMS. With Notes, Philological and Explanatory, and an Introduction on the Teaching of English. Chiefly for use in Schools. Edited by J. W. HALES, M.A., Professor of English Literature at King's College, London, &c. &c. Fifth Edition. Extra fcap. 8vo. 4s. 6d.

WORKS ON LANGUAGE. 39

Helfenstein (James).—A COMPARATIVE GRAMMAR OF THE TEUTONIC LANGUAGES: Being at the same time a Historical Grammar of the English Language, and comprising Gothic, Anglo-Saxon, Early English, Modern English, Icelandic (Old Norse), Danish, Swedish, Old High German, Middle High German, Modern German, Old Saxon, Old Frisian, and Dutch. By JAMES HELFENSTEIN, Ph.D. 8vo. 18s.

Masson (Gustave).—A COMPENDIOUS DICTIONARY OF THE FRENCH LANGUAGE (French-English and English-French). Followed by a List of the Principal Diverging Derivations, and preceded by Chronological and Historical Tables. By GUSTAVE MASSON, Assistant-Master and Librarian, Harrow School. Fourth Edition. Crown 8vo. Half-bound. 6s.

"*A book which any student, whatever may be the degree of his advancement in the language, would do well to have on the table close at hand while he is reading.*"—SATURDAY REVIEW.

Mayor.—A BIBLIOGRAPHICAL CLUE TO LATIN LITERATURE. Edited after Dr. E. HUBNER. With large Additions by JOHN E. B. MAYOR, M.A., Professor of Latin in the University of Cambridge. Crown 8vo. 6s. 6d.

"*An extremely useful volume that should be in the hands of all scholars.*"—ATHENÆUM.

Morris.—Works by the Rev. RICHARD MORRIS, LL.D., Member of the Council of the Philol. Soc., Lecturer on English Language and Literature in King's College School. Editor of "Specimens of Early English," etc., etc. :—

HISTORICAL OUTLINES OF ENGLISH ACCIDENCE, comprising Chapters on the History and Development of the Language, and on Word-formation. Sixth Edition. Fcap. 8vo. 6s.

ELEMENTARY LESSONS IN HISTORICAL ENGLISH GRAMMAR, containing Accidence and Word-formation. Third Edition. 18mo. 2s. 6d.

Oliphant.—THE OLD AND MIDDLE ENGLISH. By T. L. KINGTON OLIPHANT, M.A., of Balliol College, Oxford. A New Edition, revised and greatly enlarged, of "The Sources of Standard English." Extra fcap. 8vo. 9s.

"*Mr. Oliphant's book is to our mind, one of the ablest and most scholarly contributions to our standard English we have seen for many years.*"—SCHOOL BOARD CHRONICLE. "*The book comes nearer to a history of the English language than anything we have seen since such a history could be written, without confusion and contradictions.*"—SATURDAY REVIEW.

Peile (John, M.A.)—AN INTRODUCTION TO GREEK AND LATIN ETYMOLOGY. By JOHN PEILE, M.A., Fellow and Tutor of Christ's College, Cambridge. Third and revised Edition. Crown 8vo. 10s. 6d.

"*The book may be accepted as a very valuable contribution to the science of language.*"—SATURDAY REVIEW.

Philology.—THE JOURNAL OF SACRED AND CLASSICAL PHILOLOGY. Four Vols. 8vo. 12s. 6d. each.

THE JOURNAL OF PHILOLOGY. New Series. Edited by JOHN E. B. MAYOR, M.A., and W. ALDIS WRIGHT, M.A. 4s. 6d. (Half-yearly.)

Roby (H. J.)—A GRAMMAR OF THE LATIN LANGUAGE, FROM PLAUTUS TO SUETONIUS. By HENRY JOHN ROBY, M.A., late Fellow of St. John's College, Cambridge. In Two Parts. Second Edition. Part I. containing :—Book I. Sounds. Book II. Inflexions. Book III. Word Formation. Appendices. Crown 8vo. 8s. 6d. Part II.—Syntax, Prepositions, &c. Crown 8vo. 10s. 6d.

"*The book is marked by the clear and practical insight of a master in his art. It is a book which would do honour to any country.*"—ATHENÆUM. "*Brings before the student in a methodical form the best results of modern philology bearing on the Latin language.*"—SCOTSMAN.

Schmidt.—THE RYTHMIC AND METRIC OF THE CLASSICAL LANGUAGES. To which are added, the Lyric Parts of the "Medea" of Euripides and the "Antigone" of Sophocles; with Rhythmical Scheme and Commentary. By Dr. J. H. SCHMIDT. Translated from the German by J. W. WHITE, D.D. 8vo. 10s. 6d.

Taylor.—Works by the Rev. ISAAC TAYLOR, M.A.:—

ETRUSCAN RESEARCHES. With Woodcuts. 8vo. 14s.

The TIMES says:—"*The learning and industry displayed in this volume deserve the most cordial recognition. The ultimate verdict of science we shall not attempt to anticipate; but we can safely say this, that it is a learned book which the unlearned can enjoy, and that in the descriptions of the tomb-builders, as well as in the marvellous coincidences and unexpected analogies brought together by the author, readers of every grade may take delight as well as philosophers and scholars.*"

WORDS AND PLACES; or, Etymological Illustrations of History, Ethnology, and Geography. By the Rev. ISAAC TAYLOR. Third Edition, revised and compressed. With Maps. Globe 8vo. 6s.

GREEKS AND GOTHS: a Study on the Runes. 8vo. 9s.

Trench.—Works by R. CHENEVIX TRENCH, D.D., Archbishop of Dublin. (For other Works by the same Author, see THEOLOGICAL CATALOGUE.)

SYNONYMS OF THE NEW TESTAMENT. Eighth Edition, enlarged. 8vo, cloth. 12s.

"*He is,*" *the* ATHENÆUM *says, "a guide in this department of knowledge to whom his readers may entrust themselves with confidence.*"

ON THE STUDY OF WORDS. Lectures Addressed (originally) to the Pupils at the Diocesan Training School, Winchester. Seventeenth Edition, enlarged. Fcap. 8vo. 5s.

ENGLISH PAST AND PRESENT. Tenth Edition, revised and improved. Fcap. 8vo. 5s.

A SELECT GLOSSARY OF ENGLISH WORDS USED FORMERLY IN SENSES DIFFERENT FROM THEIR PRESENT. Fifth Edition, enlarged. Fcap. 8vo. 5s.

Vincent and Dickson.—A HANDBOOK TO MODERN GREEK. By EDGAR VINCENT and T. G. DICKSON. Extra fcap. 8vo. 5s.

Whitney.—A COMPENDIOUS GERMAN GRAMMAR. By W. D. WHITNEY, Prófessor of Sanskrit and Instructor in Modern Languages in Yale College. Crown 8vo. 6s.

"*After careful examination we are inclined to pronounce it the best grammar of modern language we have ever seen.*"—SCOTSMAN.

Whitney and Edgren.—A COMPENDIOUS GERMAN AND ENGLISH DICTIONARY, with Notation of Correspondences and Brief Etymologies. By Professor W. D. WHITNEY, assisted by A. H. EDGREN. Crown 8vo. 7s. 6d.

The GERMAN-ENGLISH Part may be had separately. Price 5s.

Yonge.—HISTORY OF CHRISTIAN NAMES. By CHARLOTTE M. YONGE, Author of "The Heir of Redclyffe." Cheaper Edition. Two Vols. Crown 8vo. 12s.

Now publishing, in crown 8vo, price 2s. 6d. each.

ENGLISH MEN OF LETTERS.
Edited by JOHN MORLEY.

A Series of Short Books to tell people what is best worth knowing to the Life, Character, and Works of some of the great English Writers.

ENGLISH MEN OF LETTERS.—JOHNSON. By LESLIE STEPHEN.
"The new series opens well with Mr. Leslie Stephen's sketch of Dr. Johnson. It could hardly have been done better, and it will convey to the readers for whom it is intended a juster estimate of Johnson than either of the two essays of Lord Macaulay."—*Pall Mall Gazette*

ENGLISH MEN OF LETTERS.—SCOTT. By R. H. HUTTON.
"The tone of the volume is excellect throughout."—*Athenæum*.
"We could not wish for a more suggestive introduction to Scott and his poems and novels."—*Examiner*.

ENGLISH MEN OF LETTERS.—GIBBON. By J. C. MORISON.
"As a clear, thoughtful, and attractive record of the life and works of the greatest among the world's historians, it deserves the highest praise."—*Examiner*.

ENGLISH MEN OF LETTERS.—SHELLEY. By J. A. SYMONDS.
"The lovers of this great poet are to be congratulated on having at their command so fresh, clear, and intelligent a presentment of the subject, written by a man of adequate and wide culture."—*Athenæum*.

ENGLISH MEN OF LETTERS.—HUME. By Professor HUXLEY.
"It may fairly be said that no one now living could have expounded Hume with more sympathy or with equal perspicuity."—*Athenæum*.

ENGLISH MEN OF LETTERS. — GOLDSMITH. By WILLIAM BLACK.
"Mr. Black brings a fine sympathy and taste to bear in his criticism of Goldsmith's writings, as well as in his sketch of the incidents of his life."—*Athenæum*.

ENGLISH MEN OF LETTERS.—DEFOE. By W. MINTO.
"Mr. Minto's book is careful and accurate in all that is stated, and faithful in all that it suggests. It will repay reading more than once."—*Athenæum*.

ENGLISH MEN OF LETTERS—*Continued.*

ENGLISH MEN OF LETTERS.—BURNS. By Principal SHAIRP, Professor of Poetry in the University of Oxford.

"It is impossible to desire fairer criticism than Principal Shairp's on Burns's poetry. .... None of the series has given a truer estimate either of character or of genius than this little volume. . . . and all who read it will be thoroughly grateful to the author for this monument to the genius of Scotland's greatest poet."—*Spectator.*

ENGLISH MEN OF LETTERS.—SPENSER. By the Very Rev. the DEAN OF ST. PAUL'S.

"Dr. Church is master of his subject, and writes always with good taste."—*Academy.*

ENGLISH MEN OF LETTERS.—THACKERAY. By ANTHONY TROLLOPE.

"Mr. Trollope's sketch is exceedingly adapted to fulfil the purpose of the series in which it appears."—*Athenæum.*

ENGLISH MEN OF LETTERS.—BURKE. By JOHN MORLEY.

"Perhaps the best criticism yet published on the life and character of Burke is contained in Mr. Morley's compendious biography. His style is vigorous and polished, and both his political and personal judgment and his literary criticisms are just, generous, subtle, and in a high degree interesting."—*Saturday Review.*

ENGLISH MEN OF LETTERS.—MILTON. By MARK PATTISON. Crown 8vo. 2s. 6d.

"The writer knows the times and the man, and of both he has written with singular force and discrimination."—*Spectator.*

ENGLISH MEN OF LETTERS.—HAWTHORNE. By HENRY JAMES. Crown 8vo. 2s. 6d.

"Probably no one living could have done so good a book on Hawthorne as he has done."—*Saturday Review.*

ENGLISH MEN OF LETTERS.—SOUTHEY. By Professor DOWDEN. Crown 8vo. 2s. 6d.

ENGLISH MEN OF LETTERS.—BUNYAN. By J. A. FROUDE. Crown 8vo. 2s. 6d.

CHAUCER. By Professor WARD.
COWPER. By GOLDWIN SMITH. } *In preparation.*
WORDSWORTH. By F. W. H. MYERS.

Others in preparation.

MACMILLAN AND CO., LONDON.

www.ingramcontent.com/pod-product-compliance
Lightning Source LLC
Chambersburg PA
CBHW030006240426
43672CB00007B/842